SHE WHO DARES

SHE WHO DARES

TEN TRAILBLAZING SOCIETY WOMEN

LYNDSY SPENCE

For Lola, Harriet, Mariga, and Henrietta

First published 2019

The History Press
The Mill, Brimscombe Port
Stroud, Gloucestershire, GL5 2QG
www.thehistorypress.co.uk

British Library Cataloguing in Publication Data.
A catalogue record for this book is available from the British Library.

ISBN 978 0 7509 8897 1

Typesetting and origination by The History Press
Printed and bound in Great Britain by TJ International Ltd

CONTENTS

ACKNOWLEDGEMENTS

I am grateful to the following individuals: Patrick Guinness for granting me permission to quote from Mariga Guinness's letters and diaries, to reproduce his photographs, and for answering my questions; Marina Guinness for sharing her amusing anecdote of Mariga; Lord Gowrie for his telephone interview; Josephine Batterham of the Derek Hill Foundation for permitting me to view Mariga's letters to Derek Hill; Lord and Lady Massereene for their permission to quote from Jean Massereene's letters; Julia Shirley for her generosity in sharing information on Mariga and for interviewing her mother, Rose Bryson, on my behalf; Isabel Boyle and Doris Morrow for their memories of Mariga during her years in Glenarm; Kathy Crozier and Claire Mann for a most enjoyable day at Castletown House and Conolly Folly; Aidan O'Boyle for his knowledge of Irish architecture and for assisting with source material; Benjamin Treuhaft for an enjoyable afternoon discussing Sydney Redesdale; John Hayden Hasley for his memories of Sylvia Ashley; Libby Cameron for answering my questions about Enid Lindeman; William Cross for sharing his collection of rare books; Andrew Budgell for his helpful editorial comments; Mark Spence and Yasmin Morgan for their many excursions in search of Mariga and co.; Stephen Kennedy for accompanying me on research trips to Dublin

Castle, Mountjoy Square and Glasnevin Cemetery; my family for encouraging my (hare-brained) projects.

I am especially grateful to Lord Gowrie for his permission to reproduce Derek Hill's portrait of Mariga Guinness, to the Bryson and Huxley families for making available their personal photographs of Mariga Guinness, and to Len Kinley and John Young for permission to use their archived photographs of the Massereene family.

I thank the following archivists for their help in accessing files and assisting with copyright permissions: Andrew Glew, the Tate Archive; Richard Ward, the Parliamentary Archives; Oliver House, the Bodleian Library University of Oxford; Georgia Satchel, the Mull Museum; Lesley Park, the Cumbria Archive Centre; Morx Arai, Huntington Library; Philip Magennis, Antrim Castle Gardens; Rebecca Geddess, Public Records Office Northern Ireland.

AUTHOR'S NOTE

The original title of this book, *These Great Ladies*, was inspired by Evelyn Waugh's appraisal of his society friends. For, in October 1931, the stage adaptation of his bestselling novel *Vile Bodies* opened at the Arts Club Theatre and caused a socialite's revolt. Many thought his satirical portrait, drawn from high society, struck too close to home. Lady Irene Curzon considered him a 'silly little creature'[1] and Lady Dorothy Lygon called him a 'snobbish cad'[2]. Emerald Cunard, formerly Maud Burke of New York, bought tickets but did not like the location of her seats and complained of having to take Prince George to the eighteenth row. 'Old trout,' snapped Waugh, 'she's only an American anyway.'[3] Doris Castlerosse, a wily, wilful courtesan known in lower echelons as Jessie Doris Delevingne, refused to pay for her ticket. Their behaviour prompted Waugh to remark, 'Oh dear, these great ladies.'[4]

Without harbouring Waugh's venomous bite, I consider the ten women who feature in this book to be great ladies. They were true individuals and held a unique place in society between the world wars and thereafter. Many have fallen into obscurity but their stories deserve to be told.

1

PRINCESS, PRESERVATIONIST:
MARIGA GUINNESS

The extremities of Mariga's life, the abandonment she felt from both parents and the memories of a lonely childhood, inspired in her a resilience against the modern world. She was born Princess Hermione Marie-Gabrielle von Urach in London on 21 September 1932, to Rosemary (*née* Blackadder), of Scots and Norwegian descent, and Prince Albrecht von Urach, a descendant of the German House of Württemberg – the same family as Mary of Teck, the Consort of King George V. 'She is much more German than my Great-Aunt Elisabeth, Queen Mother of the Belgians,' Mariga said of her cousin, Queen Mary. Related to every royal house in Europe, Mariga's pedigree was older than the House of Windsor: her grandfather, Prince Wilhem of Urach was briefly King Mindaugas II of Lithuania; her great-grandmother, Princess Florestine, was the daughter of Florestan I, Prince of Monaco; and amongst her reigning aunts and uncles was Elisabeth 'Sissi', the Empress of Austria. Years later, Mariga attended a dinner party and a guest spoke of Sissi and her alleged affair with King Ludwig. Mariga replied, 'They were just cousins.' The guest challenged her response, claiming that neither he nor Mariga could be certain. 'I have it on good authority,' she told him. She did not confide that Sissi and Ludwig were amongst her regal ancestors. But, then again, her upbringing was a world away from her noble birthright.

The fate of Mariga's paternal family was significantly altered after the Monégasque Revolution of 1910, followed by a constitution in 1911 which Albert I, Prince of Monaco, suspended during the First World War, for her father had once stood to inherit the principality from his cousin and Albert's heir, Prince Louis II, had no legitimate children. However after the First World War, France wanted a pro-French monarch to inherit the Monegasque throne, and so Louis adopted his illegitimate daughter, Charlotte, and she became his successor. In 1930 an American newspaper[1] reported that Albrecht had gone to Paris to persuade the French Foreign Office of his right as the legitimate heir of Louis, but he was unsuccessful. The visit was not entirely hopeless, for he met Rosemary at the German Embassy in Paris, and despite being two years her junior and engaged to a Spanish aristocrat, he proposed marriage and she accepted. A royal title did not equal wealth, and the couple had to work for a living. Albrecht painted, and his first exhibition was financed by his mother and was a commercial failure, for it coincided with the Great Depression. Rosemary was a journalist and cartoonist: she created a children's cartoon in *The Sketch*, designed advertisements for Shell, and in 1925 became the editor of the short-lived *Parade* magazine. She also contributed to the *Saturday Review*, the *Evening Standard*, and was engaged by the Manchester *Daily Express* to interview interesting people such as Feodor Chaliapin, whose answers consisted of sex and violence, and so could not be printed.

After Mariga was born, Rosemary and Albrecht continued their nomadic existence. She was not expected to live, owing to an infection she caught at birth, and having recovered two months later she considered November her real birthday. 'We don't show the baby to strangers,'[2] Rosemary told her sister, Erica, when she asked to see Mariga. It was a curious response, but Rosemary was prone to such eccentricities. It should also be noted that Erica disliked Rosemary.[3]

During those early years the family lived in Venice, in a flat rented from Anna Mahler, as Albrecht hoped to establish himself as an artist; he counted Pablo Picasso as a close friend, and he sketched a portrait of Adolf Hitler, but it was declined because Hitler thought the staring eyes made him look mad.

In 1934 Rosemary left Mariga with Albrecht and sailed to America, to visit her brother, Ian, and his family in Hollywood. Ian's stepdaughter, Willis, who later changed her name to Lili St Cyr and became a burlesque star, was fascinated by Rosemary's dyed blonde hair and purple eyes, and how she had swapped an ordinary life for a royal title and world travel. 'Go away, little girls, go away,' Rosemary said to her nieces, as she was not interested in the curious children whose framed photographs she turned to face the wall. It was rumoured that she had gone to Hollywood to pursue a career as a film actress, for she had attended the Royal Academy of Dramatic Art and played the part of 'an extra nun'[4] in Max Reinhardt's play, *The Miracle*, and had worked for J.B. Fagan at the Oxford Playhouse and appeared in his play *And So to Bed* but could not remember her lines and was fired from the production. She loved Hollywood and in an article for *Vogue* she wrote of 'a land fit for goddesses and the lovelies of the cinema to live in'. The studios, however, were dismissed as 'hell … stuffy heat, everyone working like the devil'.[5]

At the end of her stay Rosemary wrote to Albrecht and told him that artists were sought by Walt Disney Studios to work on their animated films, an idea then in its infancy. He declined her suggestion to settle in Hollywood, as during that period he had taken an interest in photojournalism and by chance had captured the first unpublicised meeting between Hitler and Mussolini. It led to a career as a journalist in Japan, covering the Chinese-Japanese war, and working as a foreign correspondent for several German newspapers.

Mariga's next home was in Kamakura, Japan, and it was there that her love of buildings began. Years later when a friend spoke of their talent for buying and selling houses for a profit, Mariga said that a 'house is for always'. To her, a house had a soul and to neglect it was on par with neglecting a human being, or worse: the latter could speak up for themselves. The architectural style of a building was not only aesthetically pleasing to Mariga's young eyes, but it offered a sense of stability in what had become an unhappy home life blighted by Rosemary's moods and, then, her deep depression. 'I adored Maman, though sometimes I was terrified by her unreasonable temper,'[6] Mariga wrote to her father.

Having been accustomed to travelling and meeting people along the way, this new solitary existence did not bode well for Rosemary.

Her husband was in China, reporting on the war, the Japanese did not mix with foreigners, and the staff at the German Embassy were aloof, regardless of her status as a princess. This, along with being thrown from her horse and suffering a concussion for a third time, added to a breakdown in Rosemary's mental health.

Although Mariga feared the pendulum of Rosemary's moods she loved her mother, and was taught by her to look at things as an artist would. In Japan it was decided by Rosemary that Mariga would have an informal education, perhaps a response to her academic career at Girton, which she attended on a scholarship to read English and Modern Languages. She was awarded a second class degree in the former and a third class in the latter. Whilst at university Rosemary met Arthur Quiller-Couch and became his mistress. 'He rather spoilt her,' her sister said. 'Her head was a bit turned – she never bothered to work at all.'[7] After her studies she travelled around Europe with a puppet show. Before leaving Girton, Rosemary got into trouble with the police and was fined 10s for riding her bicycle along a dark road without a lamp, and when questioned, she said, 'I am very sorry; I was only going very slowly.'[8] Thus, Mariga's lessons consisted of drawing, literature, music, dancing, foreign languages, and sightseeing, and her father's friend, Richard Sorge, a Soviet spy, taught her to play chess.

In 1938 Mariga's childhood was forever changed, for in recent months Rosemary had been troubled by the reality of another world war, as she had lost her favourite cousin, Lt Ian Wilson, in the First World War,[9] and she became obsessed with the idea that Emperor Hirohito was being misled by his generals. Acting on her concerns, Rosemary and Mariga went to Tokyo so she could warn the emperor in person, and as she entered his palace she was arrested by armed guards and injected with morphine. Mariga, who had held her mother's hand as they walked to the private apartments, was frightened by the scene and was carried away screaming and placed at the German Embassy. 'She always finds some logical explanation for doing these things,'[10] Albrecht wrote in the aftermath of Rosemary's behaviour. He also believed she would be cured by 'normal European surroundings'[11] and booked her passage on the *Scharnhorst* bound for Southampton, where she was met by an elderly friend, Hermione 'Mymee' Ramsden,[12] a granddaughter of the Duke of Somerset and an early Suffragette.

A short time later Albrecht also arranged for Mariga to sail on a Japanese liner, chaperoned by the daughter of the British military attaché in Japan, who did not find Mariga difficult to care for although she missed her parents.[13] Rosemary and Mariga accompanied Mymee to Norway, to her 10-acre wood, Slidre, overlooking the Jotunheim mountains. It had several wooden huts, executed in a traditional Norwegian style with elaborate carvings. Her stay there did little to restore Rosemary's mental health, as she became depressed and left for Berlin, to meet Hitler – as with Emperor Hirohito, she had perhaps wanted to warn him of a war. However, the meeting never materialised, and in despair she checked into the Adlon Hotel and slit her wrists using a glass inkstand. 'Of course it is awful for the child,' Albrecht wrote to Mymee. It was decided that Mariga would live with Mymee at her Surrey home, Marley House, and Rosemary went to Chirnside to stay with her mother.

Some time after their separation, Mariga was brought to visit Rosemary, during which relatives heard the child shrieking. When they entered the room Rosemary jumped through a window, and two days later was found by the police. At the end of this bewildering period, which lasted from January to April 1938, Rosemary agreed to be assessed by Dr Bill Harrowes, the medical superintendent of New Saughton Hall (also known as Mavisbank House), an asylum south of Edinburgh, who noted she had 'a well defined and well recognised variety of mental illnesses',[14] and was diagnosed with schizophrenia. Although Harrowes intended for her hospital stay to be as short as possible, he refused to let her be with Mariga, as 'such an experience may deleteriously affect the whole of the child's future.'[15]

After New Saughton Hall, Rosemary was committed to Craig House, where she lay 'in bed for years, refusing to speak'.[16] During this period Mariga became Mymee's responsibility, for Albrecht was in Germany working for the foreign office and liaising with the Italian press.[17] It was an eccentric childhood, living at Marley House in Surrey and spending her summers at Slidre, where an Aubusson carpet was laid out on the lawn and hot water came from an enormous tea urn from the Girl Guides in London. An old fashioned Fabian, Mymee believed that art and literature were the birthright of everyone. She was also a devoted spiritualist and was renowned for her experimental studies of parapsychology alongside her friend, Clarissa Miles, who had published their research on telepathy in the *Journal of the Society for Psychical Research*. It contributed to Mariga's unorthodox education, and Mymee would go through a succession of sixteen governesses to educate her, one being an exiled Ethiopian princess. On an outing to a park in Norway, Mariga, who liked to tease her governesses, pointed to the nude statues and said, 'Look at that one, don't you think it looks wonderfully naturalistic?' She was also enrolled in a boarding school at Malvern, Scotland, which she hated, so she left to resume her lessons at home.

Later, when Mariga was of age, Mymee sent her to the Monkey Club, on Pont Street, a finishing school for upper-class young women, where she learned domestic arts, typing, and how to behave in society. Its name was derived from the motto drummed into the students: 'Hear no evil, see no evil'.[18] This establishment played a part in connecting Mariga to her paternal family,[19] for during the winter term she boarded at More House, a Catholic hostel, and met her cousin Prince Rupert Löwenstein, who, in the future, would introduce her to the man she would marry.

In the summer of 1939 Mariga and Mymee went to Norway and almost became stranded when war was declared in September. Mymee thought it too dangerous to attempt a sea crossing to England, but on the eve of the German invasion they crossed the border to Sweden and from there flew to Brighton. The remainder of the war was spent at Marley House and for a period in 1944 they lived at Ardverikie, Mymee's family estate in Scotland – a protective measure against Operation Steinbock, the Luftwaffe's strategic bombing of southern England. Mariga hoped that, after the war, she would be reunited with her parents and they would return to Germany, to the family seat, Schloss Lichtenstein, in the Swabian Alps. She was almost correct in her estimation, for Albrecht had considered sending her to his youngest sister, Mechtilde,[20] who had three young children and lived with her husband, Prince Friedrich Karl Hohenlohe-Waldenburg-Schillingsfurst, at Schloss Waldenburg in southern Germany. It was not to be – Mariga continued to live with Mymee, Rosemary remained at the asylum, and Albrecht accepted a post in Rome as a foreign correspondent between the German and Italian press. Toward the end of the war he was appointed press attaché at the German Embassy in Berne. In 1943, he was falsely accused by Swiss spies of being a senior Nazi,[21] and in 1945 he was interned for helping to smuggle capital out of Switzerland to America.[22]

In 1945 the war ended and Mariga's dream of reuniting with her family remained unfulfilled. Rosemary had been given a lobotomy in December 1943, which at first had successful results: she was able to draw and play the piano, and according to Mymee was 'almost her old self except that she will not discuss plans for the future. I am afraid that she feels that there is nothing for her to look forward to.'[23] She also retained her independent mind, despite her treatment and surroundings, for a month later she wrote to Mymee, 'I adore your pleasant schemes to count me against the Germans but you can't. I love them and was always happy there and with my German.'[24] Perhaps she wished for Mariga to have control over her destiny, for in a letter to Mymee she addressed the question of her being brought up English and not German 'if she wants it … I am sure when she is sixteen she will be proud of the truth'.[25] Albrecht also remained absent, as in 1946 he was charged by German authorities for having created Nazi propaganda* and for membership of the Nazi Party, which he had subscribed to in 1934 to pursue a career as a journalist. He apologised and there was no further action: a lucky escape, for his superiors were tried during the Nuremberg Trials. It marked a transitional period, as Mariga was now old enough to realise that she had no place in her parents' lives, and when her maternal grandmother died in 1946 she felt she 'no longer belonged to anyone'. Mariga later wrote in a letter to Albrecht that she spent 'a miserable summer at the [Norwegian] hut in tears, but of course that didn't help'. She was also surprised when Mymee – whom she treated as a parent – was unsympathetic toward her grief. 'I think I nearly went mad – I seriously thought of throwing myself into a deep bit of the lake at Ardverikie but of course when it came to the point, I hadn't enough courage – the water looked so horribly wild.'

At the age of 16 Mariga was sent by Mymee on an architectural tour of Paris and Touraine, accompanied by a friend named Eva. The sight

---

*   The Reich Press Law of 1933 stated that newspapers must promote the Nazi cause. Although there was no law to force editors and journalists to subscribe to the Nazi Party, Joseph Goebbels, Minster of Propaganda, ousted those who did not.

of postwar Paris underwhelmed her, its buildings still in ruins after the Nazi Occupation. 'Paris … that sparkling city of beauty and romance … with its *Vogue* models and its Quartier Latin, who would have thought its houses would be so dusty and drab?'[26] At the end of the tour, and on her way to join Mymee in Norway, she stopped in Hamburg for a brief reunion with Albrecht. 'Suddenly I saw him. I knew him at once. That big head – its hair grey now, that bristly moustache, bad teeth, tall figure and long arms … But I didn't shout MAFFEN, I didn't burst with hysterical tears,'[27] she wrote in her diary. Albrecht, on his part, remained unmoved and he offered Mariga his hand to shake.

During their visit together, before the train whistle sounded and it was time to leave, they spoke of politics and liqueurs, and he gave her a magazine. Mariga imagined missing the train and staying with her father in Germany, but she sensed he would not know what to do with her. It was not the reunion she had dreamt of, since their last meeting in 1938, and after boarding the train she trembled with shock and 'longed to cry'[28] at the hopelessness of her father returning to her, or to her mother.

It was some time after their encounter that Mariga learned of her parents' divorce and of Albrecht's marriage, to Ute Waldschmidt, a woman eleven years her senior, with whom he had two children. 'When I heard about your new marriage in such a horrible, indirect way, you, my God of perfection, were tumbled forever I thought into dust,'[29] she wrote to her father. She believed that he would come back to her after the war, and would have landed 'some rich type-writing job, and that Maman would remain cured by money, pretty clothes and you'.[30] With Rosemary on her mind, she also wrote to Albrecht, 'You must understand that I cannot forget the bolts and bars at Craig House.'[31]

A year later Mariga went on a tour of Italy and stopped in Germany en route to England, to meet her stepmother and half siblings. It was a painful visit, for it reminded Mariga that she and her mother had been left behind by Albrecht, and she failed to understand the predicament he was in following Rosemary's breakdown. She knew she behaved badly, and wrote to her father: 'I have awful manners – all my governesses said so, but I never realise the gaffes till it's too late to do anything but apologise.'[32] She also said she could not love her stepmother, whom she called 'Momi', whilst Rosemary was still alive.

Throughout the years friends spoke of the barriers Mariga put up when interacting with a person; she loathed hugs and kisses, and shaking hands. Some explained this peculiarity as shyness, others thought she tried hard to overcome it. And yet she appears to have not been self-conscious when it came to decorum. An example of such was when she came to the breakfast room wearing only a bath towel, and as she passed through, Lady Rosse said, 'There goes a true aristocrat.' In the 1960s, Cecil Beaton described in his diary an encounter with Mariga, calling her 'the *malocchio*' (the evil eye), 'mad, frightening and horrible ... like some mad female impersonator creating alarming ambiance wherever she wandered'.[33] Beaton's appraisal might have been a response to her 'wandering eyeball'[34] when she had a drink or two.

In 1951 Mariga was faced with an uncertain future, as Mymee had died at the age of 83 and from the £16,000 she inherited she rationed her living expenses at £1 per day. For the first time in years she went to visit Rosemary at the asylum and found her in a distressing state, unable to recognise her and claiming her daughter was 5 years old. The medical reason for Rosemary's mental decline[35] remains unknown. Presumably she had fallen victim to her restrictive environment: 'I have nowhere (except the loan of two hooks in another lady's wardrobe, kept constantly locked, and under my bed, the mattress) in which to keep anything.'[36] She had lost her freedom – twice she had attempted to escape from Craig House[37] – her husband, and her child. Mariga continued to visit Rosemary once a year until the late 1960s: sometimes Rosemary recognised her and sometimes she did not.[38]

During this rootless existence she invented the name Mariga from her birth-name Marie-Gabrielle, for until 1950 she had been called Gabrielle. She also left for Germany, and passing through the French countryside she spied an old house for sale and went on a tour. She asked the estate agent if it had a ghost, and he said no. 'In that case I will certainly not buy it,' Mariga replied. When she reached Waldenburg she was reunited with Albrecht and his family, who lived in a log cabin on the estate and grew vegetables, as the castle had been occupied by the SS in 1945 and after the war the US Air Force destroyed both the castle and the town. They were indebted to the local butcher, who continued to supply meat without payment, and Albrecht wondered how he could afford to pay the bill. But Mariga did not grumble, for the circumstances of her early childhood inspired in her a philosophy to 'never complain, never explain'. To make ends meet and to earn pin money she exercised horses at a Waldenburg riding school, and modelled for fashion magazines in Stuttgart, where she attended classes at the Art Academy, as Albrecht had done years before. She also disguised herself as a reporter, having learned that Gary Cooper would be visiting the Mercedes Benz factory in Stuttgart (where Albrecht worked as chief press attaché), and she 'asked him every question that came into her head'.

Whilst living in Germany Mariga had fallen in love with her distant cousin, Prince Moritz von Hessen. Though, as fate would have it, the romance ended badly. Prince Moritz's mother, Princess Mafalda of Savoy, the daughter of King Emmanuel III of Italy, was the wife of Prince Phillip of Hesse, a member of the Nazi Party. Despite Prince Phillip acting as an intermediary between Nazi Germany and Fascist Italy, Hitler and Joseph Goebbels wrongly accused Princess Mafalda of working against the German war effort. Hitler called her the 'blackest carrion in the Italian royal house', and Goebbels echoed the sentiment when he, too, referred to her as 'the worst bitch in the entire Italian royal house'. As a consequence, Princess Mafalda was imprisoned at Buchenwald concentration camp, where the filthy conditions caused her arm to become infected. As a result the guards ordered it to be amputated, and she bled to death. The Nazis' treatment of Prince Moritz's mother, combined with Mariga's father's previous membership to the Nazi Party, conspired against the couple's happiness and they were forbidden to marry. Heartbroken, Mariga said she would marry the first man who asked her.

Returning to England Mariga was persuaded by her cousin, Prince Rupert Löwenstein, to move to Oxford. She boarded at the home of Mr and Mrs Ruddock: he was the head porter of Magdalene College, and enrolled at an extramural school, 'to learn something or other'.[39] It was in the Ruddock household that she met Rupert's friend, Desmond Guinness, and fulfilled her declaration of marrying the first man who asked her. A scion of the brewing family and the second son of Lord Moyne and Lady Mosley (*née* Diana Mitford), Desmond was considered 'the last of the individualists';[40] he wore leopard-skin trousers, though only on 'very informal occasions', and his rooms at Christ Church were decorated with Blackamoor statues and Gobelin tapestries. Together and apart, Mariga and Desmond each possessed star quality, and they made a striking couple: his bright blue eyes, referred to as 'Mitford eyes', the genetic trait of his mother's family, and her 'devastating smile'. Perhaps in one another they recognised the strain their respective parents had placed on them, for although they did not share their political views many did not forget and could not forgive those who had ties to Nazi Germany. Desmond's mother, Lady Mosley, was the wife of Sir Oswald Mosley (for whom she had left Desmond's father, Bryan Guinness) and had befriended Hitler in the mid-1930s, for which she had been imprisoned at Holloway and then placed under house arrest until the end of the war. There was also the stigma surrounding mental illness, particularly for the relatives who were often silenced by shame and secrecy. It was believed that madness, as it was then called, ran in the family. Mariga thought it to be true, and at a social gathering, she announced, 'I am related to the Wittelsbachs and a little bit mad.'

Mariga and Desmond were married on 3 July 1954, under Anglican Rites in Christ Church Cathedral, despite her being a Catholic. Amongst the aristocrats and European princelings was a stranger named Paddy O'Reilly, an elderly dustman from Dublin, who had received an invitation by mistake. Becoming something of a celebrity, the Irish press and television cameras documented O'Reilly's journey from Dublin to Oxford for the wedding. Convention never held much esteem for Mariga, and she walked down the aisle wearing one shoe, as she had misplaced the other. Some said that a curious journalist had stolen it. A few days after the marriage had taken place, Mariga's aunt, Erica, revealed the facts of Rosemary's condition to the Guinnesses, and she claimed to have asked the head doctor at the asylum if it was hereditary, as Mariga's father-in-law had wanted to know. 'If it had been my son,' the head doctor said, 'I would have moved heaven and earth not to let that marriage take place.' Desmond took a week to decide whether to remain married to Mariga, and was advised that Rosemary's mental illness was not hereditary.[41] The newly-weds honeymooned in Norway, and settled in a cottage outside Cirencester to study agriculture at the Royal College, as they both had ambitions to own a farm.

In 1955 Mariga and Desmond moved to Ireland to farm and from 1956–57 they rented Carton House in County Kildare, the family seat of the Dukes of Leinster, surrounded by 1,100 acres of parklands. On the estate was a shell cottage, created for the 1st Duchess of Leinster. Neighbouring Carton was Castletown House, the two estates divided by Conolly Folly, both of which had fallen into disrepair and would inspire[42] the couple to revive the Irish Georgian Society, its objective being to 'fight for the preservation of what is left of Georgian architecture in Ireland'.[43] In many ways Ireland offered Mariga a sense of belonging and a place to begin anew after a lonely childhood. 'Ireland is heaven, everyone is so dotty and delicious and no one dreams of taking anything seriously; except, perhaps, the Horse Show,' she said. She had visited, several years before, as the guest of Mark Bence-Jones, and stepped off the aeroplane wearing a tulle ballgown, having come from a party in London. Enchanted by the countryside, ancient ruins, and Georgian architecture hearkening back to when Ireland had a royal family and a dynastic past, Mariga said, 'I can't think how you can ever leave Ireland.' It was a prophetic statement, for, as it turned out, she never did. Her children were born there: Patrick in 1956, and Marina in 1957. In a letter to Derek Hill, Mariga wrote of 'a gloomy midwife person [sitting] about crossly, saying how unlike Cliveden [her last job] it all is'.[44]

Having lived at Carton House for three years, Mariga and Desmond bought Leixlip Castle, a twelfth-century castle, built by Adam Fitz Hereford, an Anglo-Norman follower of Strongbow. Then in a dilapidated state, its restoration was driven by Mariga's sense of practicality and artistic eye, inspiring within her a lifelong interest in Irish art and furniture, then considered redundant in a republic that no longer bowed to an Ascendancy. In 1958, the year they bought Leixlip, the Irish Georgian Society was officially founded by Mariga and Desmond – a revival in every sense, with a coterie of youthful members, though Desmond dismissed any notion they were part of the *jeunesse dorée*. 'We were interested in architecture, engravers and silversmiths,'[45] he said. It brought a new awareness to young people and convinced those who viewed the Georgian mansions and landmarks as a sign of English repression of their importance as a piece of history and a symbol of Irish craftsmanship.

Mariga moved into Leixlip, whilst Desmond was on a Guinness brewery course in London. She brought 400 books, a cat, and a rifle. After the grandeur of Carton, many wondered if they could be happy, perhaps a feeling inspired by the condition of the castle prior to its renovation. The baths were outside, being used as water troughs, and the electrical wiring was so unsafe the electricity board refused to reconnect the power. In those early days guests had to sleep on mattresses on the floor and the front door was never locked but was secured by propping a stick against the top step. 'Do hope mattresses are dry,'[46] Mariga wrote to Derek Hill, ahead of his visit to Leixlip. In another letter, she added, 'And again apologise for revolting rabbit lunch and dreggs of vinegary wine, oh dear.'[47]

Later when Leixlip was renovated and brought to life with antique furniture and art, interior decorators came to respect Mariga's design aesthetic. 'Amateurs, dealers and decorators all learned from Mariga much more than they would care to admit,'[48] said John Cornforth, the architectural editor of *Country Life*. Her eye for colour, particularly her bringing the soft greens of the Irish countryside into a large room by painting it in a bold hue, set her apart from the interior decorators who worked with the utilitarian lines of mid-century furniture. According to Cornforth, the drawing-room was tomato red, the dining room yellow, the entrance hall dark green. 'One must never forget that every room has a soul,' Mariga said. Modern touches in an historic house were frowned upon, and friends recalled Mariga spying a comfortable, tightly sprung sofa, and announcing, 'Look at *that!*' In a way, her respect for the past dictated how she lived her life, and in her later years, when she periodically lived away from Leixlip, the size of her Egyptian bed, with its high green canopy and carved sphinxes, dictated her lodgings. Adhering to authenticity, Mariga used wildflowers to decorate a room, as it was historically accurate and keeping within Leixlip's medieval origins; there would be foxgloves and bunches of laurel, arranged with paper flowers.[49] She also collected books and shells, and across her untidy desk she placed a military sword on top of the papers.[50]

Life had become an art form and an extension of her surroundings, and it was conveyed in how she looked and dressed. Now with a platform as chatelaine of Leixlip and a leader of their set, she began to dress in what became her signature style: black tights, patent shoes with buckles on the front, her long hair piled on top of her head, and her collection of eighteenth-century costumes were often worn for dramatic effect. In her later years, she appeared as a Tolstoy heroine: long skirts, ruffled blouses, and cardigans with holes in the elbows. On one occasion she wore a dress made of tinfoil, and on another she fashioned a bracelet from a lavatory chain. 'She never lost her sense of theatre,' said Lord Gowrie.[51]

The late 1950s and mid-1960s were to become the golden age of Mariga's life as a hostess, and she and Desmond entertained aristocrats, foreign royals, celebrities, local tradesmen,[52] and various colourful individuals they had befriended along the way. The parties thrown in the winter of 1958 set the tone, and continued until four o'clock in the morning. When Desmond became tired he wound up an antique Gothic organ which played 'God Save the King', signalling it was time to go home. In the early 1960s Princess Margaret and Lord Snowdon (who, when he was simply Antony Armstrong-Jones, had photographed Mariga in Venice) came to Ireland and were put up by Mariga and Desmond. Naturally, given the status of southern Ireland as a republic and the embittered feelings toward British royals, not everyone curtsied. Mariga herself failed to do so, explaining that she was the senior princess (with her lineage she was), but a friend told her that she was wrong: dispossessed royalty always curtsy. Princess Margaret's lady-in-waiting appeared flustered and remarked that it was a difficult scenario, for the princess did not know who would curtsy and who would not. Although some might have viewed it as breaching protocol, Mariga did not care about social hierarchies and believed life could be bearable if people were polite to one another.[53]

As both hostess and guest, Mariga was described as possessing a superficial vagueness. However eccentricity often prevailed, evident when she was driving along a country road on her way to a party, and crashed into the side of an unmarked police car. She wound down her window and asked the policemen, 'Are you the Pirates of Penzance?'[54] As it turned out, they were – they had sung in the Gilbert and Sullivan production at Leixlip the year before. The policemen overlooked Mariga's error and drove her to the party. Arriving late, she knocked on the door and was shown into the dining room, followed by the policemen. In her arms she carried what looked like wisps of hay, but they were, in her words, 'herbs for the cook'. This sentiment was a reminder of her practical side. She was a good cook and used herbs from the school of Elizabeth David and *Le Cordon Bleu*. It was haphazard, done by eye and nose, often delicious, but sometimes guests were better off with the cheese and biscuits. Dinners were candlelit, so often guests could not see what they were eating.[55]

The only thing she disliked were guests smoking upstairs at Leixlip, for it was 'very wooden, and the fire engines vague … I really mind this'.[56] She was rarely offended, though took exception when a guest, who claimed to be a socialist, accused her of being high-handed with the locals. Responding to the individual she asked what he was doing in her 'capitalist house', and why, as a socialist, he did not help the butler with the washing up. 'Socialists are always prepared to watch as you slave away,' Mariga said. 'The only people who ever offer to help are the English generals.' She then declared herself 'a REAL socialist … I believe that nobody has the same mind, so we must pool what everyone is good at'.[57]

This was particularly true of the Irish Georgian Society, a movement that was firmly rooted in Mariga and Desmond's identities. Their first restoration project was the Conolly Folly, an eighteenth-century monument commissioned by Katherine Conolly, wife of William Conolly, the richest man in Ireland, to provide employment for farmers during the famine of 1740–41. The building itself, with its eight arches and stone etchings of pineapples and eagles, had no significant merit, as it was neither a religious monument nor was it habitable, except for its philanthropic origins. Weather-beaten and with its coping stones dislodged by weeds and the elements, its obelisk pillar, standing 140ft-tall, had been left to fall into rack and ruin. With the government taking little interest in once privately-owned, dilapidated buildings, the Irish Georgian Society acquired the folly in 1960 and with the help of public donations they bore the responsibility of restoring it. Successful in their quest, it became the symbol of the Society.

Another restoration project which Mariga and Desmond were passionate about was Castletown House, a Palladian country house built in 1722 for William Conolly by the Italian architect, Alessandro Galilei. In 1965 Castletown and its contents were sold to Major Wilson, a property developer who intended to build 200 houses on the 100-acre estate, though as the big house remained vacant it was targeted by vandals who stripped lead from its roof and smashed the windows.

A campaign was headed by Mariga and Desmond, and in 1967 he bought the house and its land for £93,000, for which it was said that they 'had to remortgage [their] grandchildren's fortune'[58]. Critics also dismissed their fund-raising efforts and referred to the Irish Georgian Society as 'a consortium of belted earls'.[59] Mariga, however, was quick to challenge such opinions, and emphasised that they had approximately 5,000 members, with 2,000 subscribing from America. She also led members of the Irish Georgian Society and student volunteers in the restoration of the house – they polished brass balustrades, steamed original wallpaper, painted ceilings, and cleared brambles from the overgrown grounds. Original furniture was bought at auction houses, with Mariga and Desmond rarely missing a good sale both at home and abroad, and money was donated by rich benefactors. After its restoration, Castletown House became the headquarters of the Society, and Mariga gave Jacqueline Kennedy a guided tour when the former First Lady of the United States visited Ireland in 1967.

During the first decade of the Irish Georgian Society, Mariga and Desmond were an unstoppable force, each exploiting their strengths for the good of their preservation work. Mariga was credited with charming the public, or as friends recalled, she 'chatted up' parliamentary ministers, foreign visitors, rich sponsors, and those who were curious or, rather, suspicious of her. Desmond was tasked with writing books on the topics of Irish architecture, art and furniture, and with giving lectures in America, where his visits often lasted for months at a time. On a lecturing tour of St Louis, Missouri, Desmond was accompanied by Eoin 'Pope' Mahoney, a genealogist, though he was mistaken for a gynaecologist.[61] At another lecture, the topic being that of bodysnatching, Mariga was amused when members of the Society were inspired to bequeath their bodies to hospitals. 'Yet another branch of the society's activities,'[62] she wrote to Derek Hill.

There were tours led by Mariga to India and Russia, and trips over the Irish border for Georgian-themed cricket matches played against the Northern Ireland National Trust. Mariga wrote of a cricket match, hosted at Castle Ward, the family seat of Lord and Lady Bangor, 'The Northerners all wildly drunk, to show that they could, only to find most of our team were juvenile teetotallers.'[63] She thought Castle Ward was 'rather dry rotted' but her mischievous sense of humour was piqued by Charles Stewart Parnell's bed, loaned from a museum and exhibited for tourists. 'Of course we would never have had him in the house,'[64] said Lady Bangor.

For years to come Mariga and Desmond, armed with the Irish Georgian Society, fought those who planned to demolish Irish architecture. Amongst the historical properties they saved were Roundwood, Co. Laois; Damer House, Co. Tipperary; Doneraile Court, Co. Cork; and Tailors' Hall and St Catherine's Church, Dublin. Many campaigns were successful, some were not, but they seldom gave up without a fight. One such project was Mountjoy Square, which, owing to its symmetry (each side measured 140m in length), was the only true Georgian square in Dublin. Aside from its architectural importance, it was also of literary and political significance: James Joyce, Sean O'Casey and W.B. Yeats had resided there, and much of the 1916 Easter Rising was plotted at various addresses on the square. From 1966 until 1975 Mariga and Desmond led a campaign to halt Matt Gallagher, owner of Leinster Estates, from demolishing the south side of the square, particularly three original houses that were built in 1792. It was a promising beginning when a legal battle ruled in favour of the Irish Georgian Society and ordered Gallagher to provide support for the walls of number 50, to prevent further damage. Knowing that only a serious offer could 'sway the stony heart'[65] of Kevin Boland, Minister for Local Government, Mariga bought number 50 for £550 and moved in, despite it being surrounded by two Georgian properties which had been demolished to ground level. It was a reminder of their perilous structure: one house collapsed on two girls, resulting in their deaths, and the other killed an elderly woman. Arguing that restoration was the solution to such problems, Mariga borrowed £68,000 from 'a rather nervous bank'[66] to buy twenty houses from Gallagher, in an attempt not only to save them from demolition but to establish a charitable trust called Mountjoy Estates. However the plan failed and so she encouraged friends to buy houses, as she thought it the only tactic to fend off Gallagher, who wanted to replace them with modern office blocks, thus spoiling the architectural landscape of north Dublin.

During that period a Mrs O'Donnell bequeathed her house to the Irish Georgian Society, and Mariga went to meet her body at Shannon airport. 'So confusing,' she wrote, 'as all the Roses of Tralee seemed to be arriving at the same time.'[67] Despite her efforts the Irish Georgian Society did not acquire Mountjoy Square, though Gallagher failed to build his proposed office blocks, and in recent years the houses were rebuilt in an imitation Georgian style.

The late 1960s were a transitional period for Mariga, marked by the death of her father in 1969. His last words to her were: *'Tu es … enfin tu as.'*★ Reflecting on her loss, she said, 'I never expected my father to die.'[68] Her marriage to Desmond had come to an end, though Mariga believed he would come back to her in old age and that she would always have Leixlip. Over the years he had had several girlfriends and she was pursued by the writer John Hedworth Jolliffe, 'but perhaps she had wound him up more than was wise. Flirting can be taken up wrong'.[69] There was a serious relationship with Hugh O'Neill (later the 3rd Baron Rathcavan), whom Mariga referred to as 'Mr O'Neill', and who rented a small house close to Leixlip whilst working for the *Irish Times*. They went to London in 1970 and bought two Georgian houses on Elder Street, in the East End, and knocked them into one. In 1973 Hugh hit a wild boar whilst driving at night in a Belgian forest, and broke every bone in his body. Mariga flew to Belgium and brought him to the King Edward VII Hospital in London, where she livened up his hospital room with delicacies and champagne, with a telephone for business deals and a constant stream of friends.[70] Their arrangement was regarded as bohemian, as she was still married to Desmond, and Hugh's grandfather mirrored society's views at the time and disapproved of him living in sin. The affair lasted for several years

★ 'You are … finally you have.'

before coming to an end, perhaps because Hugh wanted to marry Mariga and have children of his own, and she did not think divorce was a priority.

Mariga would live in London on and off for years, in between her travels and settling in various places. Later there was a flat on Bolton Street, given to her by her father-in-law, when the affair with Hugh O'Neill was over and she had left Elder Street. It marked another restless period in her life, reflected in her 'knock-about' clothing and what she called, *'Les apparence extérieures de la pauvreté'** – a protective measure against being mugged. There were moments of eccentricity, however, when she gave dinner parties in her flat, often for fifteen or twenty people. On one occasion everyone got drunk and many were sitting on floor cushions, when a burglar crawled through the kitchen window. He passed the bathroom and saw her neighbour, Thea Porter, asleep in the bath, and was then confronted by a room full of people on the floor and Mariga standing with a carving knife. The burglar, thinking the woman in the bath had been murdered, fled the scene.[71] As time passed London became a lonely place, and Mariga missed the Irish countryside and the informality of socialising and entertaining. During a particular gathering friends found her in a reflective mood, and she said one should not speak of 'folk music' but say 'traditional music', and that one must never use the term 'gypsy' but 'traveller'. 'We are all travellers in life,' she remarked.

In 1975 Mariga moved to Glenarm, a village on the Antrim coastline in Northern Ireland. It must have been a difficult year, as Rosemary had died in the asylum, ending a phase of her life in which so much had gone unsaid.[72] Furthermore Mariga had come to Glenarm in an unsuccessful attempt to rekindle her relationship with Hugh, as it was close to his family seat, Cleggan Lodge, in the neighbouring village of Broughshane. She rented a former courthouse from her friend, the Earl of Antrim, whom she had known since her Oxford days. Despite the fractured politics at the time she was not put off by 'The Troubles', a period of conflict between nationalists and unionists, and calling on friends who lived in Belfast, she said, 'I want to see a riot!'[73] Perhaps as a sign of her good faith in people she asked Ian Paisley and Bernadette Devlin to

---

** 'The external appearance of poverty.'

tea,[74] as she hoped to broker an understanding between their differing loyalist and nationalist ideologies. The meeting never happened.

It was with this optimism that Mariga faced the conditions of her new home. Over the years it had had several tenants, such as the owners of the post office who lived upstairs, and it served as a canteen for American troops during the Second World War. When Mariga moved in, it was in the midst of a renovation and she later installed a fireplace from a Lutyens house in Yorkshire. She also discovered a skeleton in a cupboard and removed it to a cardboard box,[75] perhaps not wanting to attract the attention of archaeologists. Only a small side room on the top floor, which she inhabited, had electricity, and her Egyptian bed was propped up on bricks before the fire. Sacks of turf were piled in the hallway,[76] blocking most of the entry to the narrow staircase leading to her quarters. She accumulated the turf by organising a turf-cutting picnic on Sallagh Braes, in the Glens of Antrim, and dressed in a long skirt and with a parasol,[77] she watched the local turf cutters demonstrate how it was done. The Glenarm weather was changeable and far more ferocious than in Kildare, and the North Atlantic wind whipped through the draughty courthouse. The windows were encrusted with lime dust, sea-blown salt and ordinary dirt. There was no telephone, and everything was within walking distance on the narrow, sloping street. The post office was next door to the courthouse, a pub a few doors away, and around the corner was the barbican gate of Glenarm Castle, home to her friend the Earl of Antrim. There was a forest with a river running through it, a marina at the foot of the village, and a walkway to the hills of Antrim with views of the Mull of Kintyre.

Owing to the discomfort at the old courthouse and the inside of the kitchen range having fallen out, Mariga went to stay at the Agent's House, the former home of the Earl of Antrim's agent, but it was just as primitive. There were no watches, clocks or radios, and so she rarely knew what time it was. She had brought her Arabian stallion with her, a wedding present from her father-in-law, which she attempted to house upstairs at the courthouse. It was an impractical arrangement, due to the neighbours whose terraced houses adjoined the courthouse, complaining about the noise, and she was persuaded to remove the horse to a nearby glen.[78] Onlookers thought it an unusual sight, particularly when she tried to catch her horse with a red scarf, but it bolted and returned days later wearing the scarf.[79] However its grazing and general high jinks were disruptive and its fate was inevitable. Unable to telephone a vet to do the deed, she asked a police officer to shoot the horse. A friend was astonished to see its leg in a bucket of salt water,[80] but Mariga explained she was having the hoof made into an ornament as a memento.

As was a common theme in Mariga's life, her friends came to visit. Parties were ramshackle affairs, thrown in the kitchen, which was typical of her flair for entertaining under any circumstances. One guest was shown to a mattress in what had formerly been a holding cell but was serving as a guest room. After dinner, she explained to the ladies the location of the lavatory; however she advised the gentlemen to use the garden but 'kindly, not to pee on the petunias'. Another party, held during a snowstorm, saw Mariga entertain a group of Portuguese visitors, and she invited a few neighbours to dinner. It was a memorable evening for several reasons: Mariga spilled a tray of drinks around herself, decided she had had enough and sat down in a chair in front of the fire, slightly drunk, during which time there was a power cut, and an apple pie was served encased in a block of ice.[81] There were also picnics, often hosted at the side of the road which offered a view of the sea, and she invited locals to join her. But they were mostly held at Salmon Leap, her favourite waterfall, in the Glens of Antrim, where the wind caused the insides of the sandwiches to fly out and a block of cheese rolled down the steep hill.[82]

It was Mariga's eccentricity, and her kindness, which made the biggest impression on the locals. In the beginning they were suspicious of her background, vaguely aware that she was a German princess, and some wondered what she carried in her basket,[83] as she walked between the courthouse and the agent's house. The local youths, who loitered outside the courthouse, attempted to tease Mariga and her guests, but one evening during a party she appeared with a tray of sandwiches and invited them to join in the fun upstairs. This was typical of Mariga and her ability not only to sidestep tricky situations, but to form unlikely friendships. She also left the key to her car in the ignition, a sign of her good faith in mankind. As for her car, a battered Citroën Safari, it was as memorable as Mariga herself, and she was forever attempting to repair it whilst reading an *A-Z of Motoring* guidebook.[84] The car was also missing its back window, which she purposely removed so she could transport tree trunks from Glenarm forest to burn in her fire. As time passed her money ran out, and she complained that 'the worst part of being poor was that one could not buy books'. Her friends, the Pecks of Prehen House, gave her a valuable jewel to sell so she could buy a house with the money, but she gave it back.[85]

After five years of living in Glenarm, Mariga sensed it was time to move on. 'There is no purpose to my being here. Why, is somehow impossible to explain,' she said. 'Friends are at Leixlip and where but there can my children go? It is so impossible to guess what to do next.'[86] The courthouse had been sold to the local council and plans were underway to turn it into a recreational centre for elderly people, though Mariga suggested it would be better suited for holding musical recitals. Her friends spoke of campaigning for her tenancy to be extended, but she knew it was hopeless. Letters written by Mariga during that period spoke of her frustration, particularly her moving to Glenarm to be close to Hugh O'Neill, and after all she had given up she felt short-changed. Those friends, including her father-in-law, wanted her to divorce Desmond and move on with her life.[87]

Mariga returned to Leixlip in 1980, the decade marking the beginning of a bitter divorce battle between herself and Desmond. She did not want to leave her former marital home, nor did she want to forfeit her position in the Irish Georgian Society. By residing in the castle she wanted to prove a legal point, though she wrote to Derek Hill that 'DWG [Desmond Walter Guinness] seems unable to speak or write sensibly to lawyers or to myself. The bill will be horrific, for both of us'.[88] She was also locked out of Desmond's quarters and had to use the back door ('You know I am locked in at the others'), and 'not being Rapunzel' she had to climb in and out of the kitchen window, 'a feat too energetic for elderly people'.[89] When Desmond left for a lecturing tour of America she gave a picnic in the garden and proceeded to climb in and out of his kitchen window to take cutlery and plates. Many of her clothes were in London, at the home she had shared with Hugh, and she claimed he would not let her retrieve them. 'How can he fit into them though?'[90] she wrote to Hill, finding humour in the dire situation. As she had done in the old days, she gave guests impromptu tours of the castle, and during such an evening she opened the door of a historical bedchamber and discovered an unknown couple asleep. They were Desmond's guests. Suddenly it struck her that Leixlip was no longer her home and that she ought to leave. 'Sometimes I feel like a ghost,' she said.

Mariga and Desmond were divorced in 1981 and she received a settlement of £150,000. She leased Tullynisk House, a Georgian manor on the grounds of the Rosse Estate, at Birr, Co. Offaly, and spent £3,000 on renovations. Despite being inconvenienced by 'a swarm of rats',[91] she made the rooms warm and inviting, with turf fires and electric blankets, antique furniture, books, flowers, and shells. Costumes, too, were close at hand: military uniforms, footmen's liveries, antique dresses, baskets of shoes including her grandmother's wedding shoes in their original box, feather boas and plumed hats. Although she loved buildings and their contents, as she grew older she 'learnt that material possessions, however marvellous, do not really matter'.[92] She earned a small income writing a weekly column for a local magazine, offering tokens of advice such as the best place to buy knickers in Offaly. Writing came naturally to her, and throughout the years she dabbled with the idea of writing a book on famous picnics, which never materialised. She started a book on the history of the First World War but that, too, remained unfinished.

As Mariga had done so many times before, she began anew. 'She has suffered in her life but like a gallant oarsman in rough seas, clings on to those sturdy planks of pride, stoicism and love of friends,'[93] wrote Maureen Charleton. Friends thought that she was unhappy and drinking too much, but she was never aggressive although she became incoherent as the evening progressed.[94] In her youth she boasted of never suffering a hangover regardless of how much alcohol she drank. Perhaps in those early days nobody sensed she was unhappy: 'she was often drunk, but so was everybody else'.[95] Despite all that had happened she had not given up on life and was looking to the future. A new project consumed her attention and in Norway she planned to build an octagonal Gothic library, around an Aubusson carpet, to house Mymee's socialist books. Her enthusiasm for architecture and art remained, and with friends from the Irish Georgian Society she toured Russia. She also travelled alone to Budapest and Vienna, where, 'by following my own nose, such magic things appeared'.[96]

On 8 May 1989 Mariga died of a heart attack, at the age of 56, and was buried under Conolly Folly. On the weekend before her death she went on a Friends of the National Collection tour of North Wales, and appeared enthused by Mostyn Hall, a seventeenth-century house remodelled in a Jacobean style. She was, after all, in her natural habitat.

2

THE STUCCO VENUS:
ENID LINDEMAN

Amid the many accusations of gold digging, drug addiction and murder, Enid Maude Lindeman was certain of one thing: she was never going to be a wallflower. She was born in 1892 to Charles Lindeman and Florence (*née* Chapman) at their family home, Brinkburn, and raised with her five siblings at Bramhall, a gentleman's residence in Strathfield, an affluent suburb of Sydney. The Lindeman fortune was founded by her great-grandfather, Dr Henry Lindeman, an English surgeon who opened a medical practice in the lower Hunter Valley, outside Sydney, and in 1843 applied for a crown grant of land which he named Cawarra. There he founded his vineyard which became Lindeman Wines and was credited with launching the Australian wine industry, and after his death in 1881 Charles inherited the business. It was a nondescript childhood, though one of privilege, and when Enid was of age her parents sent her to boarding school, where she showed talent as an artist, but preferred the tomboy pursuits of riding, shooting and fishing.

At the age of 19 Enid met her future husband, Roderick Cameron, a 43-year-old shipping magnate from New York, whose international shipping line R.W. Cameron and Co. transported wool, kerosene, and farm equipment from the west coast of America to Australia and New Zealand. He proposed to Enid, and she accepted, but Florence Lindeman declined on her daughter's behalf, thinking she was too young to know her own mind. Years later Florence confessed to having been in love with Cameron herself. 'You wicked old woman,' Enid teased her mother. 'You know you were in love with him yourself. That's why you didn't want me to marry.' She harboured no bitter feelings toward Florence, and when she turned 21, she married Cameron in front of 230 guests at St Paul's Anglican Church, Burwood. Marriage had given Enid status, for although her name appeared sporadically in social columns, she was grouped with various young women from good families. Now she stood out, 'because the bride is a very pretty girl, and because she was marrying a millionaire'.[1]

After their honeymoon at Bowral, a town in the Southern Highlands of New South Wales, they lived at Cameron's 200 acre estate, Clifton Berley (also known as Clifton Burley), at Rosebank, in Staten Island. There was also a country house at Spitfire Lake in New York State, and the Cameron building, a sixteen-storey skyscraper in Manhattan, on the corner of 34th Street and Madison Avenue. Enid claimed when she emerged from the building, traffic came to a halt, 'to view this vision of perfection'. The statement validated the rumours that Enid was, what her acquaintances called, a mythomaniac. 'She'd invent stories about herself, and that could be dangerous,' a friend said. 'You don't know why those people lie, but they do.'[2] Whether the statement was true or not, Enid had married into an influential family with links to Scotland and Canada,[*] who were listed in the Social Register and the Four Hundred, an index of the best families in New York (coincidentally 400 was also the amount that could fit into Mrs Astor's ballroom). Seventeen months after their marriage, Cameron was diagnosed with incurable cancer and died a month later, at the German Hospital (known today as Lennox Hill Hospital), leaving Enid with a nine-month-old son, Rory, and an inheritance of several million dollars.

---

[*] Sir Roderick Cameron, of Scots heritage, was born in Glengarry County, Upper Canada. His father sat in the Upper Canadian House of Assembly. His Loyalist grandparents and father had immigrated to New York State, and returned to Canada after the American Civil War. He received a knighthood from the Canadian government in 1883.

All her life Enid was seldom without male company and following the death of Cameron she began an affair with Bernard Baruch, an American financier and presidential adviser to Woodrow Wilson and Franklin D. Roosevelt during the First and Second World Wars. He was twice her age and married, and known as 'the Lone Wolf of Wall Street': he advised her on financial matters. 'Can you imagine, after my beloved brother died, her very first lover was that dreadful Jew, Bernard Baruch?' remarked Enid's sister-in-law, Mrs Belmont Tiffany (*née* Anne Cameron), a doyenne of New York and South Carolina society, and twenty years her senior. 'Thank God she had enough sense not to marry him.'[3] As for marriage to Baruch, there was no question of him divorcing his wife, and Enid said it could never be, because 'he was not much good in bed and he was very mean'.[4]

In 1915 Enid and her baby son left for Paris, where she drove an ambulance for the war effort. The First World War marked an exciting time in Enid's life and she had several frivolous affairs, though one admirer, Edward Stanley, the 17th Earl of Derby, was Britain's Secretary of State for War and he resented the havoc she caused amongst the officers. One young man, so consumed by jealousy, had threatened to commit suicide if she did not remain faithful to him. This was not a new occurrence for Enid, as throughout the years five of her lovers would kill themselves: one blew himself up with sticks of dynamite, another threw himself under *Le Train Bleu* whilst she was on board, and another jumped overboard a ship into shark-infested waters when she had shown a marked affection for another man. Such was Enid's effect on the opposite sex, the wife of an admirer asked where she intended to be buried because her husband decided if he could not be with her in life, he wanted to be next to her in death. Enid could not answer her question; thus the woman responded, 'I don't intend to keep digging him up.' Thinking she needed a distraction, Lord Derby introduced Enid to Brigadier General Frederick Cavendish, known as 'Caviar', of the 9th Lancers, and the two married in July 1917. Her reason for marriage was simple: she needed someone to take care of her finances, for she was incapable of managing her money, and he needed a rich wife, for he had squandered his inheritance. Despite being penniless, Caviar was descended from the Anglo-Irish barons of Waterpark and was distantly related to the Dukes of Devonshire. He was renowned for his bravery on the battlefields – he had led cavalry charges during the Boer War, and had served in India. He was also handsome and a ten-goal polo player, and, for Enid, it made up for his lack of capital with only his army pay to keep him. After their marriage, Caviar returned to the Belgian Front and Enid continued to drive her ambulance.

After the war Enid and Caviar moved to Cairo, where he was given command of the 9th Lancers. It was 1919 and Egypt was a dangerous place: that year a revolution against British occupation provoked civil unrest and violent attacks on British military barracks. However Egypt appealed to Enid's flamboyance and cloistered amongst British ex-pats she seemed oblivious to the country's strife for independence, which was granted in 1922. There were picnics by the Nile, rides by moonlight in the Sahara desert, parties in sandstone villas surrounded by palm trees, and as a dare she slept with Caviar's entire regiment. By day she schooled Caviar's polo ponies, and by night she dressed as a man and played the piano or her Swanee whistle in the band of the officers' mess. In 1922 she began an affair with George Herbert, 5th Earl of Carnarvon, custodian of Highclere Castle and amateur Egyptologist, who employed Howard Carter to search for Tutankhamun's tomb in the Valley of the Kings. Upon its discovery, Lord Carnarvon gave Enid and Rory a private tour of the tomb, and they were amongst the first to see it. Carnarvon died a year later, from a mosquito bite that had become infected by a razor cut, though many believed it was the consequence of Tutankhamun's curse.

After several years of living in Egypt, Enid and Caviar moved to England, where he accepted the post of brigadier-general and commander of the 1st Calvary Brigade at Aldershot barracks in Hampshire. Although Enid later described her carefree years in Egypt as the happiest period of her life, she was growing restless with the military way of life, and her new home, nicknamed the White House, in Farnborough, was too provincial for her tastes. In 1925 she gave birth to a daughter, Patricia, and fifteen months later a son, Caryll, was born. Although Enid loved her children and was far more attentive than parents of her social rank, she wanted to pursue new and exciting things. She bought a black Buick and drove it herself, and as there were few women drivers in the 1920s she was proud of this achievement. There were trips to the Continent to play golf with the Prince of Wales on the links of Le Touquet, as it had become a fashionable sport for society women. The hobbies, masculine in their origins, were a contrast to Enid's striking looks, for by then her red hair had prematurely turned white, and dressed in a Chanel suit she wore her skirts shorter than was socially acceptable.

In 1931, whilst on holiday with the children and their nanny in Biarritz, she learned of Caviar's death from a cerebral haemorrhage. It had happened in their Paris flat and her absence was telling, for although they considered one another good company they preferred to lead separate lives. Enid was drawn to the stylish resorts on the Côte d'Azur and Caviar was happiest exercising his polo ponies in the English countryside. With a rich wife he could afford such luxuries and she did not begrudge him, for he had everything he wanted except her love. Soon after Caviar's death Enid became involved with Valentine Browne, Viscount Castlerosse, author of the famed gossip column the *Londoner's Log*, whom she had known during the war in Paris. As with Caviar he, too, possessed no money but he was the heir to the Earldom of Kenmare, and often on the receiving end of a generous loan (it was never repaid) from his employer, Lord Beaverbrook. He spoke of his desire to marry Enid, and she entertained the idea; however he was involved in a lengthy divorce suit from his wife, the courtesan Doris Delevingne. Instead she fell for Viscount Furness and it broke Castlerosse's heart when she broke the news on a golf course in Le Touquet.

Enid's third marriage was a bold move, for it was rumoured that Furness had murdered his first wife Daisy, who died aboard their yacht during a pleasure cruise of Monte Carlo; he buried her at sea. Some believed he would hang if the evidence was brought to light, but from a silken cord, as he was a Peer of the Realm. His second wife, from whom he was divorced, was Thelma Morgan Converse, a mistress of the Prince of Wales and the best friend of Wallis Simpson. 'I have seen many beautiful women. But from the moment Enid entered the room my heart stopped,' Furness said after that first sighting of Enid, at a casino in Le Touquet. Afterwards he pursued her with daily gifts of flowers and jewellery (which she kept in Kleenex boxes, as she thought it the last place a thief would look), and offered her his aeroplanes, yachts and chauffeur-driven Rolls-Royce cars. As he was one of the richest men in the world, Enid overlooked the horror stories and encouraged his fixation with her, though, true to form, she did not reciprocate his advances. It only served to inflame his interest and having learned from the travel agent, Thomas Cook, that she had booked a seat on the Golden Arrow from Paris to London he cancelled her ticket and sent his plane to fetch her. When she returned to her flat in Chelsea, she was given a letter from him and enclosed was a deed of sale; he had bought not only her flat but the entire building. Proud that she had received the aforementioned from Furness without making an effort, she said: 'A man is a predator, he enjoys the uncertainty of the chase. So never let him feel sure of his prey.' Perhaps a feeling of guilt or gratitude compelled her to acknowledge his gift, for she agreed to dine with him at the Savoy and on that evening their affair began.

After Enid's marriage to Furness in 1933 she discovered his true nature, for he was a man prone to cruelty and jealousy, and often the two intertwined. An inferiority complex drove his rages, as his father, Sir Christopher Furness, had worked as a stevedore on the docks of Hartlepool and eventually founded his own shipping company, Furness, Withy and Company. This complex was exerted through his lavish displays of wealth, most notably his hatred of travelling commercial class and therefore he owned a private railroad, two yachts, and an aeroplane piloted by Tom Campbell Black, who had taught Beryl Markham to fly. He also insisted that Enid accompany him to South Africa for several months, where, in a fleet of Rolls-Royce motorcars, they went on safaris. It was in Kenya that Enid met Idina Sackville-West and Alice de Janzé: the latter was embroiled in several scandals including the attempted murder of a lover in 1927 and, later, the 1941 murder of the Earl of Erroll, her friend Idina's husband. One visit, however, came to an abrupt end when Enid entered the drawing room and found a mass of naked bodies, and terrified Furness would find out she invented an excuse to leave. She knew he would blame her and she feared his temper, though she interpreted it as a sign of his love for her. 'There was nothing in the world he was not prepared to give me. Of all the men that loved me, and some were as rich as [Furness], he was the one who was prepared to lay the world at my feet,' she said.

However as much as Furness loved Enid he could not tolerate anyone or anything monopolising her attention. He despised her three children, and when Patricia called her stepfather 'daddy', he said, 'I am not your father, and do not address me as such.' The children were an unwelcome presence at his London mansion, Lees Place, and his country home, Burrough Court, near Melton Mowbray, but the latter was spacious enough for them to hide in a wing. In London they were sent to live at a flat on Curzon Street with their nanny, Miss Unger, whom Furness hated owing to her resemblance to Thelma, and he ordered Enid to 'get rid of that bitch, she looks just like the other bitch'.[5]

A father of three, Furness disliked his eldest son, Dick, and was heartbroken when his favourite child and only daughter, Averill, married Andrew Rattray, his white hunter in Kenya. His third-born child, a son named Tony from his marriage to Thelma, was called 'the bastard', as he believed him to be the son of the Prince of Wales. To compensate for Furness's jealousy toward her children, Enid signed her Cameron inheritance over to her eldest son, Rory. It was also done to protect the money from Furness, for she knew he resented financial independence in a woman and would force her to surrender it to him. All her life Enid remained devoted to her children, and friends admired this side of her character. 'Before anything else, Enid was a mother,' a friend said. 'Most of the things she did, marrying all those men, were for the children more than herself.'[6] It was during this period that Enid began to collect exotic animals. There was a hyrax which she fed from her own fork and taught to use the lavatory, and she invited her friends to take a peep, but only discreetly, as it was shy. She had various species of birds, including a parrot who could mimic her faux American voice and say, 'Phone, Pat,' whenever the telephone rang, so Patricia could answer it. She also owned a pet cheetah, who wore diamond Molyneux collars, and was taken for walks in Hyde Park. On one occasion guests were alarmed to find it dragging Enid across the drawing room, but she said, 'It happens all the time.'

Described by her daughter as 'the spirit of generosity', Enid often used Furness's money for a good cause. She had become distressed by the sight of ex-servicemen selling their paintings on the street, and would stop her chauffeur-driven car and talk to them. Learning of their unemployment and homelessness following the First World War she gave them money and found them homes. Sometimes she would visit them with her children, much to the disapproval of the chauffeur and nanny, whom she thought were the 'most tremendous snobs'. However, generosity often gave way to extravagance, and Enid's favourite pastime was gambling. This she did with great fervour at the race courses and casinos on the Continent, carrying with her a stash of pound notes for the occasion. She never showed any emotion if she won or lost, and her opponents were too distracted by her appearance to take notice of her reaction. 'My dear Enid! Could you not make a more discreet entrance? Next time perhaps you could just wear a basic little black dress and not throw us off our game?' exclaimed the Aga Khan when she entered the casino at Monte Carlo, wearing a clinging white dress, a three-strand diamond necklace, and the Furness tiara made from pink diamonds. Enid's clothing was an extension of her character; a sorceress, she wore low-cut gowns to distract men, and all the while she sat in silence, allowing them to dominate the conversation and pretending to be interested in what they had to say. It was also said that, when in Monte Carlo, residents at the Hotel de Paris stood on chairs to watch her pass through the lobby. Years later, when she attended the wedding of her friends Prince Rainier of Monaco and Grace Kelly, onlookers mistook her for a foreign royal and applauded as she left the cathedral.

As the 1930s drew to a close the marital problems between Enid and Furness intensified. No longer did she discreetly see other men and outsmart the detectives he had set upon her: she flaunted her affairs openly and did not deny them when he questioned her. In 1937 she began an affair with Hugh Grosvenor, the 2nd Duke of Westminster, known as Bendor, a rival of Furness's for he matched his wealth. As a reaction to Enid's infidelity, Furness refused to accompany her to the coronation of King George VI, but she remained unmoved by his threat and said she would go with 'somebody else', and that somebody else was Bendor. Furness retaliated by going overseas, a rare move for he rarely left Enid's side, for he was afraid she would cast her eyes elsewhere. She knew he missed her and was desperate to see her, and so she sailed with her children to America, to stay with her former sister-in-law, Mrs Belmont Tiffany. Furthermore she sent him a suicide letter, claiming she was going to shoot herself, and he rushed home and sent a search party to find her. Detectives located her at the London Clinic with a wound on her head, not from a gunshot but the result of a face-lifting operation. Furness was a shrewd character, and did not forgive Enid her stunt; he saw that she suffered the consequences. This, she confided in an interview in 1942:

I left my husband when his divorced wife, Thelma, returned to him. He turned my two children out of the house. There wasn't room for two of us, so I went to America for a year, where I was most unhappy. Then Lord Furness cabled me asking me to forgive him.[7]

In August 1939, days before Britain declared war on Germany, Enid and Furness left for the French Riviera to stay at his new villa, La Fiorentina, bought from Sir Edmund Davis, of Chilham Castle. They were unconcerned about the threat of war, a view shared by many of their contemporaries; Elsa Schiaparelli claimed she knew there would be no war 'just by instinct', and Diana Vreeland said it was 'all chemical and that Hitler only became a madman during a full moon'.[8] The children and their staff were sent to live a comfortable distance from Furness, at Clos, a large cottage which he had bought along with the villa. A young Belgian count and countess were also residing there, the latter a morphine addict whose supply of drugs had run out, and she was removed when Patricia found her crawling along the walls and looking in every corner, mumbling, '*Mon Dieu, Mon Dieu, c'est caché*' ('My God, My God, it's hidden').[9] It was an unhappy period for Enid, as Furness had become bed-bound by illness and remained in his room surrounded by day and night nurses; she rightly suspected that he was dying. News came that an evacuation ship would soon be leaving from Cannes, and she convinced him to sail home before it was too late.

On the day they left for Cannes only Patricia accompanied them, as Rory had enlisted in the war and Caryll had returned to school. Weakened by illness, Furness had to be carried to his Rolls-Royce, and in the backseat he drank from a hip flask, but his hands were shaking and he spilled a drop onto his shirt. A perfectionist, he refused to proceed until his valet was summoned to fetch a newly-ironed shirt and tie. When they reached Cannes, Enid and Furness dined with Patricia at the Carlton Hotel; it was the first time she had eaten with her stepfather, and his temper erupted when he spilled soup on himself. Enid placed a napkin on his shirt and attempted to feed him his soup and settle his rage by saying, 'Darling, don't get so upset. Once we are on board, it won't be so bad. At least we shall be amongst friends.' He told Enid to leave with her 'bloody friends' and to take 'that bloody little bitch'[10] with her. Then he demanded an injection of morphine, to which he was addicted. Enid had hoped to obtain a deportation order from Scotland Yard against Furness's drug-dealer, Dr Tikotz, a German doctor who travelled with him.[11] They never left for England, as Furness refused to travel on a 'cargo ship', and Enid stayed with him.

Their return to the Villa La Fiorentina marked a strange period for Enid, as Furness was diagnosed with cirrhosis of the liver and she was tasked with running the house, as the staff had resigned to join the war effort. It was a welcome distraction, for Furness was on his deathbed and suffering from violent hallucinations due to his consumption of morphine and lack of alcohol – he had always been a heavy drinker. Haunted by an invisible presence, said to be his daughter Averill who had died in 1936, he begged this entity not to 'throw her life away on a mere groom'. His death on 6 October 1940 left Enid in a perilous position, as she was trapped in the French Riviera due to his refusing to board the ship, the last one to leave Nazi-occupied France. Short of money, she pawned her jewellery and bought a few goats so she could turn their milk into butter and cheese. There was a detention camp close to the villa, and she would often see the prisoners. It was not long before Enid began helping them to escape, dressed in the gardener's clothes or any civilian attire she could find, and on one occasion the military police came to search the house but she had disguised a prisoner as her maid. The police soon grew suspicious of her activities, and Enid began to plot how she and Patricia could leave France, and owing to her connections in the British government she secured passage on a flying boat leaving from Lisbon. Knowing she would be searched along the way, she spent hours rolling Patricia's long hair into pin curls, inside which she hid money. They travelled on Enid's American passport from her first marriage, and caught a train across the border into Spain and then continued on to Portugal. In Lisbon they spent two weeks at a luxurious hotel whilst they awaited the flying boat to England, a dangerous crossing as they made the journey in total darkness to evade enemy gunfire.

In 1941, at the height of the Blitz, Enid and her daughter moved into Claridge's hotel, where she once again had staff at her disposal. She was also awaiting her share of the inheritance from Furness's will, which had been contested by Thelma, resulting in a lengthy court battle. The validity of the will came under scrutiny due to Furness altering it weeks before his death, in which he left Enid a fortune of £3.5 million along with several properties and his yacht, *Sister Anne*. Thelma believed she was entitled to the money and assets until her own son with Furness came of age. At this point, Furness's eldest son, Dick, had been listed as missing in action, and it was also rumoured that Thelma was plotting to marry her stepson to inherit the money, regardless. However, Dick was declared legally dead, and the case was once again pending. To earn money, Enid painted scenery for Pinewood Studios and worked as an interior designer.

As fate would have it, Enid discovered her old boyfriend, Viscount Castlerosse, had taken a suite at Claridge's, and now divorced from his wife, they resumed their affair. Over the years they had contemplated marriage to one another, but as Enid put it, 'My husband or his wife got in the way.' He had since succeeded his father to the Earldom of Kenmare but his friends continued to refer to him as Castlerosse, and Enid called him 'Val'. Although he never let his lack of money hinder his lifestyle he was at a loss since the declaration of war, for his gossip column had come to an end and his friend and benefactor Lord Beaverbrook was serving as Minister of Aircraft Production. In Enid he thought he was rekindling an old love affair from the last war, and in Castlerosse she thought she had found another protector. They moved into Lees Place, the London home she had inherited from Furness; however Castlerosse, who was severely overweight and suffering from ill-health, could not climb the stairs and soon returned to Claridge's. As with all the men in her life, he possessed a jealous streak and was bad tempered, though he was kind to Enid's children and became a father figure to Patricia. His former wife, Doris Delevingne, matched his temperament and the two were famous for their public scuffles (Noel Coward based his 1936 play *Private Lives* on the couple) in which they would bite and scratch one another. But Enid was not Doris, despite their similar treatment of men, and she chose to ignore his outbursts which she thought could be cured by 'building him up' and boosting his confidence.

The war years saw Enid live an unconventional life. She had taken a job at a munitions factory, which required her to use a welding iron. Although she was enthusiastic about this new vocation, she could not abide the early morning shifts and she transferred the equipment to her home. It was a familiar sight to see Enid sitting up in bed, wearing her flimsy nightgown and with goggles on her face, fusing pieces of metal together. During this period her London staff had left to assist in the war effort and she was without a lady's maid, so she appointed Walter, her footman, to the role. He relished his new appointment, and his duties included helping Enid dress and advising her on jewellery and hairstyles. It inflamed a rumour, which circulated through high society, that Enid, so spoiled by her servants, was helped in and out of her bath by two footmen. Her social life was confined to Lees Place, and evenings were spent with Patricia, watching the air raids from the balcony, counting the German bombers: whoever had the highest score won money. It became a haven for individuals with jobs in the Ministries, and on one occasion Sir Hugh Dowding, the Air Chief Marshal, was sitting at the dining table with his signet ring on a string. To those who questioned this, Enid explained that Sir Hugh was communicating with some of his pilots who had been killed in the war.

Unbeknownst to Enid, Castlerosse was corresponding with Doris, who was trapped in America and desperately trying to secure a passage home. He had promised to remarry her upon her return, and this spurred her on and eventually she obtained an air ticket with the help of Winston Churchill, who had painted her portrait several times. They met in London and, shrouded by the blackout, he took her to the Dorchester, but the light revealed her ravaged looks and he revoked his promise of a remarriage. A few weeks later Doris committed suicide and Castlerosse blamed himself. He began to pursue Enid, whom he assumed was a rich widow, for he was planning a golf club on his estate in Killarney, Co. Kerry, and needed her money for its completion. Although their circumstances differed, Enid was equally desperate and claimed Castlerosse had come into her life when she was 'down and out',[12] and he told her that if she promised to marry him he would transfer £3,000 into her bank account and sign Killarney over to her. She had once written in a letter to Lord Beaverbrook that it 'is a cruel world for a woman alone'[13] and in that vein she agreed to marry Castlerosse on his terms, but asked him to wait until her inheritance from Furness was settled as remarrying could jeopardise it. Ignoring her wishes, Castlerosse announced their engagement in *The Times*, and Enid felt rushed into the marriage. And, further appealing to Enid, he spoke of his elderly mother, Elizabeth the Dowager Countess of Kenmare, and how much of a disappointment he had been to her and that now she finally had reason to be proud. Devoted to her own mother, Enid agreed, though privately she had reservations.

Enid and Castlerosse were married in January 1941, several weeks after the death of Doris. Now the Countess of Kenmare, she followed her husband to neutral Ireland, where she established herself at Killarney. There, Castlerosse adhered to the traditions of his upbringing and attended mass every Sunday, insisting that Enid and her children go too, despite their not being Roman Catholic. Not in the least bit religious, Enid was amused to discover that his prayer book was a pornography book disguised with a biblical cover. Soon after their marriage she told Castlerosse that she was pregnant, and as she was often travelling between Killarney and London, and spending most of her time at Lees Place whilst he was laid aside with illness, he was convinced the child was not his. He flew into a rage and hurled chairs in her direction and called her a whore. 'I might be a whore,' Enid fought back, 'but it seems to me that I am the one paying for your servicing!'

Eight months after her marriage to Castlerosse, Enid found herself in the familiar state of widowhood. Doctors had warned Castlerosse that he would suffer a heart attack if he did not control his weight, and they advised him to abstain from sex. Enid disagreed, and said, 'It was one of the only pleasures left to him in life. So how could I ration him?'[14] As Castlerosse died without an heir, the question of the unborn child troubled his mother. Enid, who was 51 at the time, was accused of fabricating the pregnancy in order to hold onto the Kenmare estate until her Furness inheritance was settled. However, in letters to Lord Beaverbrook, she mentioned the baby, and although her conceiving a child was not impossible, it was considered scandalous given her age.

Her mother-in-law ordered her to have an abortion, stating that any child born to a woman of an 'advanced age' was bound to be an idiot; she had wanted her youngest and only surviving son, Gerald, to inherit the earldom. Enid listened to her argument and then agreed to abort the child, whom she said would have been a boy.

As the 1950s advanced, Enid devoted her herself to La Villa Fiorentina, the Riviera house Furness had bequeathed to her. She received her inheritance and was once again a wealthy widow, and she never remarried. Her son, Rory Cameron, a war hero and renowned decorator, took over the running of the villa and eventually transformed it into his residence, inviting Hollywood film stars and international aesthetes to stay. Although Enid enjoyed the privileges of her lifestyle, she had become content with her painting, sculpting, and animals. She still kept lovers, dotted around the Continent, and was often jetting off to the cottages she owned for such dalliances. As she grew older she had become more ethereal in appearance and behaviour, and, when around the villa, guests noticed she had no concept of time. She would appear as the guests were leaving, or in the afternoon she would be dressed for the casino in an evening gown and jewels. Arriving for dinner, usually late, guests would hear the clicking of her shoes on the marble floor and then the scuffle of her dogs, with her commanding, 'Be quiet! Be quiet!'

Having been gossiped about and associated with the unflattering rumour that she had killed all of her husbands, Enid would become embroiled in a dangerous scandal. In 1954 she and Donald Bloomingdale, a scion of the department store family, were in New York at the same time. It was an unremarkable coincidence, as Enid often visited her former sister-in-law, Mrs Belmont Tiffany, and Bloomingdale lived in New York and was close to Rory. On that particular visit Enid hosted a dinner party and Bloomingdale was invited, and having been introduced to Mrs Tiffany, she said, 'Bloomingdale, Bloomingdale. Oh! Pots and pans.' As the evening drew to a close, Enid retired to her room at the Sherry-Netherland hotel, where Bloomingdale kept a permanent suite. Over the course of the evening Bloomingdale, a drug addict, asked Enid for heroin and she gave it to him. It was said that the heroin was delivered in a lace handkerchief embroidered with a coronet and her initials, and another theory claimed it had been smuggled in a silver frame behind a photograph of Enid. Either way, the dose proved fatal and it killed him. The body was discovered by Bloomingdale's butler and he telephoned the family lawyer. Enid was put on an afternoon flight out of New York, assisted by her good friends, Norman and Rosita Winston. 'She was out of the country before any mention of Donald's death was ever made,'[15] said another friend, Bert Whitley. However her association with Bloomingdale's death was based on speculation. 'But everybody knew,'[16] remarked a friend from New York. At the Sherry-Netherland, Enid had borrowed Bloomingdale's typewriter to write a letter to Rory, and the following morning the news arrived that he was dead. 'How fast can you pack?' she asked her butler. She wanted to leave for London before the police arrived, as they had dined together the night before and she was the last person to have seen him alive. 'You know how the American police are,'[17] she said.

After the incident, Enid never discussed Donald Bloomingdale and for a long time she stayed away from New York. Her society friends had their theories, but they never asked her about it. Daisy Fellowes, with whom Enid shared a difficult friendship, was far more blatant. She was going to host a dinner party and invite twelve people. 'All murderers, very convenient,' she said. 'There are six men and six women. And Enid will have the place of honour, because she killed the most people of anyone coming.'[18] The remark was not unusual for Daisy, for she was never kind to Enid, describing her as 'an Australian with a vague pedigree'. Once, when they were conversing, Enid began with, 'People of our class . . . ' Daisy raised her hand and abruptly stopped her: 'Just a moment, Enid, your class or mine?'[19]

As much as Enid laughed off the rumours about herself, she confided that sometimes they hurt her. At a dinner party on Long Island her host pressed her for details on why she was known as Lady Killmore – a nickname bestowed on her by Somerset Maugham – 'But why do people say it?' he asked several times. Finally, Enid rose from the table and said she had endured enough, she was leaving. Predicting her reaction, earlier in the evening the host had sent her car back to Manhattan, but undeterred Enid walked to the highway and hitch-hiked home. In light of the Bloomingdale scandal, Enid's own drug-taking past was scrutinised. It had been said that she was a heroin addict, and that she was on the drug register. This was partly true: in the 1930s she had fallen from a horse and was prescribed morphine to ease a back injury and having become addicted she eventually entered a clinic to cure herself. She was addicted to Coca-Cola – its original recipe contained cocaine – drinking it the way most people consume water. If she was absent from a party or late to arrive, Daisy Fellowes would say: 'Probably busy with her needle.'[20]

In the evening of Enid's life she lived for part of the year with her daughter and animals at Ol Orion in Kenya, and the other part at Villa La Fiorentina with Rory. But Enid was not content to rest on her laurels and she did not see her age (she was approaching her seventh decade) as an obstacle. Her latest venture saw her buy Broadlands, a farm in Somerset West, South Africa, from where she busied herself with breeding racehorses. She hired her old friend, Beryl Markham, to train them. Together, they were convinced they would 'sweep the board'.[21] Their friendship was never easy, beginning in the 1930s during her marriage to Furness, and in those days Beryl was the lover of Furness's pilot, Tom Campbell Black, and a frequent visitor to Burrough Court. Beryl had kleptomaniac tendencies and, although short of money, she would always live in comparative luxury. Cameras and jewellery discarded in her presence would be sold, and Beryl would say, 'If you are stupid enough to leave it lying around then I would be stupid not to avail myself of it.'[22] Furthermore, Beryl possessed no morals when it came to other people's money. On one occasion she hired Sir Archibald McIndoe to perform plastic surgery on her nose, then she decided she would like a wardrobe on par with Enid's, and she sent both bills to Furness.

Enid's past experiences with Beryl should have been warning enough, but she would not listen to reason, nor would Beryl alter her ways. And so, despite thinking their business plan was a good one, Enid and Beryl's partnership was volatile at times. This was prompted by both women bringing their dogs to dinner, with Enid's two pugs and Beryl's two boxers fighting throughout. Beryl would say, 'Enid, I do wish you would control your dogs, darling.'[23] Enid would smile sweetly and raise her glass of Coca-Cola. In the mid-1960s their friendship was tested by several factors, notably Enid's refusal to allow Beryl to run the stables as she wished. Although only ten years older than Beryl, Enid exerted her authority, but she was often indecisive as to how the stables should be run. This frustrated Beryl, and she said, 'Enid was getting very old and difficult. She couldn't understand what I needed, and so I left.'[24] She felt the loss of Beryl greatly, and the running of the farm became increasingly difficult. Eventually Enid signed it over to her daughter, who transformed the grounds into a sanctuary for abused and endangered animals.

In 1973, Enid died at the age of 81. For the remaining years of her life an old back injury caused her great pain but she refused to take medication, fearing her old morphine addiction would return. She was determined to overcome weakness, but strong enough to recognise it. The motto for which she lived her life, springs to mind: 'Never be ill, never be afraid, and never be jealous.'

3

THE SERIAL BRIDE:
SYLVIA ASHLEY

Like many women who entered the exclusive sphere of the British aristocracy on merit alone, Sylvia Ashley's fabled life was built on a combination of myth and hard graft – in the early days, at least. She was born in Paddington, London, on April Fool's Day 1904, and christened Edith Louisa Sylvia Hawkes. Her father's exact profession was unknown, for newspaper notices listed various jobs including pub landlord, stableman, grocer, policeman, and footman. At the time of Sylvia's birth, a mere few months after the marriage of her parents, Arthur Hawkes and Edith Hyde, the family boarded at 112 Hall Place, Paddington.

Tall and slim with ash-blonde hair and high cheekbones, Sylvia was said to have had the manners of a duchess, 'and she built that character out of nothing'.[1] Her voice, however, 'wasn't up to the rest of her, it was tinny and cockney with ladylike overtones'.[2] As pretty as she was, friends and foes were quick to highlight her one imperfection: her teeth. From an American point of view, where a trip or several to the orthodontist was the norm, they were called 'the English teeth that all need doing'. Far from an aesthetic flaw, they were not crooked or discoloured, but had a large gap in the front. The French referred to it as *dents de la chance*, or 'lucky teeth'. But teeth did not hinder her, and she capitalised on her best assets: her fair colouring, her perfect figure, and her quick brain. David Niven referred to her as a 'glorious, willowy, lemon-meringue blonde lady', and his fellow actor, George Saunders, said, 'Nobody could say that [her] nose was a triumph of design. But her face and aura have produced enough brilliance to make a thousand chandeliers a fourth-rate illumination.'

At the age of 14 Sylvia left school and found work as a hairdresser's assistant, and she later helped in her father's pub, where her mother and younger sister, Vera, also worked. When she was 15 she worked as a dressmaker's mannequin and lingerie model, and posed for French postcards, which earned her more money. It is unclear which appointment came first, but she was soon given the nickname 'Silky' because the silk negligees she modelled looked good on her. The work was hard and the hours were long, but she had ambitions to marry a rich man and leave her old life behind. Thus, at twenty, she took a job as a chorus girl at the newly-opened Grafton Galleries, a nightclub in the basement of an art gallery in Mayfair, where it was said the nude paintings were covered to protect the patrons' modesty, or the artists' models in question. Advancing from chorus girl to hostess, she earned a fee for dancing with and entertaining the men. She also began an affair with Captain Gordon Halsey, the owner of the club and a rich entrepreneur who had made his fortune gambling at the casinos of Monte Carlo and Cannes. However a romance with Halsey proved a competitive market, for several of his employees were enjoying a dalliance with him, but she did not begrudge him or the women, for they were her friends. She was often involved with several men at once, and they paid tribute to her with gifts of jewels, furs, and expensive clothes. It made her a social outcast, for society women thought her common and a threat, the two criticisms which she used to her advantage, and at a Mayfair cocktail party she walked up to a countess and said, 'Do you know, I hardly recognise your husband with his clothes on.'

The siren call of the West End attracted Sylvia and she swapped nightclub performing for a part in the chorus line of C.B. Cochran's famed productions, similar to the Ziegfeld Follies on Broadway. She also secured a small part in *Midnight Follies* at the Hotel Metropole, followed by the George Gershwin musical, *Primrose*, directed by George Grossmith Jr. In their joint memoir, *Bring on the Girls!* P.G. Wodehouse and Guy Bolton recalled Sylvia's audition:

'Must I sing, Mr Grossmith?'

'Yes, Sylvia, you must. All of you have to sing if you want jobs as showgirls in *Primrose*. The Gershwin score demands it.'

'Oh, very well,' she replied petulantly, and going down to the floats she handed over a piece of music to the pianist in the pit. The piano struck a chord.

'God Save Our Gracious King/ Long Live Our Noble King/ God Save the King.'

A strict observer of protocol, George Grossmith Jr rose from his chair and stood at attention. His minions rose and stood at attention. Guy Bolton, on his way to announce his arrival, stood at attention. Thinking the anthem was finished, Grossmith Jr began to sit down, but Sylvia had memorised the lengthier version, and thus he remained standing and nobody dared to call a halt to her singing. They had wanted her to sing, had they not? Furthermore, Grossmith Jr was a traditional monarchist and Sylvia had been tipped off about this. It was not an impromptu performance, but one she had rehearsed ahead of the audition. Such behaviour was the norm for Sylvia and the recipients of her audition did not complain, notably Gershwin, with whom she had a brief affair.

Of all the rich and titled men who fell for Sylvia, and who in turn paid court to her, it was Anthony Ashley-Cooper, Lord Ashley, who took the bait. The son and heir of the 9th Earl of Shaftesbury, he had first set eyes on Sylvia at the Hotel Metropole, where she appeared in *Midnight Follies*. Although it was a small part in the chorus, Sylvia caused a sensation in a segment entitled 'Dancing Stars of London', in which she impersonated Joyce Barbour, a West End actress, and posed in her underwear. *The Sketch* published several photographs of Sylvia in this guise, ranging from her sitting at a dressing table, dressed in the infamous short slip, applying her lipstick; to training the show's Pekingese whilst in this state of undress. Following this unconventional introduction Lord Ashley attended the show every night and followed Sylvia as she changed chorus lines and productions, finally meeting her in person during a stint at the Strand Theatre in *The Whole Town's Talking*.

Their courtship became the gossip of London society, and Lord Ashley proposed almost immediately. Sylvia accepted, but the transition from showgirl to an aristocrat's wife – or 'The Earl and the Girl' as the press called the couple – was not without its problems. The Earl and Countess of Shaftesbury did not approve of their son's choice, and Lord Ashley's father dismissed the newspaper claims that a marriage was imminent. 'There'll be no marriage. There has been a misunderstanding,' he said, unable to accept that his potential in-laws had worked in service. Lord Ashley's sister, Lady Dorothea, also declared, 'Such an alliance is unthinkable.'[3] Fearing Lord Ashley would succumb to parental pressure and not wanting to return to her old life, Sylvia was determined to see the proposal through. On 3 February 1927, the two were married at St Paul's in Knightsbridge. Having refused to listen to his father's counsel, and with his own parents disbelieving the marriage would go ahead, Lord Ashley and Sylvia thought they had outsmarted their naysayers.

On the day of the wedding the Shaftesburys experienced a change of heart and left their country home in Salisbury on a 200-mile chase to London to stop the marriage. They arrived too late and, at midday, were faced with the reality that their son, who in the marriage register described himself as a 'bachelor and gentleman', had married Sylvia. Until that day Sylvia had never seen, let alone met, her mother-in-law. As the daughter of the Duke of Westminster and herself a Mistress of the Bedchamber to Queen Mary, it can be said that Lady Constance Shaftesbury, too, opposed the match. However, she said of her son's new bride, 'She is radiantly beautiful.'[4] The bride stunned onlookers with her short wedding gown of white satin which clung to her figure; shirking tradition, it was sleeveless and cut with a low neckline. Such was Sylvia's private doubt, the last stitch had only been completed the night before.

A reception for twenty-four people was held at the Hyde Park Hotel. 'I have nothing to say except that I am a very happy man,' Lord Ashley told waiting reporters as they boarded a train at Victoria Station. 'And don't forget to say,' added Sylvia, 'that I am a very happy girl.' The newly-weds left for a honeymoon in Biarritz and Cannes, and when Sylvia returned home she told reporters, 'Henceforth I belong to my husband. I do not intend to appear on the stage again.'

It took only weeks for Sylvia to realise that marriage to 'the good looking but dull' Lord Ashley had been a mistake. Casting a shadow over their new life together was his car accident two months later, resulting in him knocking over an elderly man who was walking along the road. He assisted the police in their investigation and was found not guilty, but eventually the victim died in hospital. The heavy mood continued, intensified by their living in the depths of the countryside, for Sylvia felt isolated from her friends and social life in London. They were also ill-matched in temperament: he was dim and she was witty, and he wanted to settle down to life on a Dorset farm. It was Sylvia who made the first move to end her marriage, for she packed her things and went to live at Lord Ashley's flat in Mayfair, and placed a notice in a London newspaper stating that she was reviving her acting career under her former name Sylvia Hawkes. But it appeared that either no producer was interested in casting her, or her enthusiasm for her old career had waned, as she received no offers. It can also be assumed Lord Ashley was cut off from certain family funds, for he became exasperated by Sylvia's spending and refused to pay her bills. Furthermore, he placed a notice in a newspaper claiming he would not be responsible for any credit she might accumulate:

> I, Lord Ashley of St Giles House, Dorset, hereby give notice that I do not hold myself responsible for any debts incurred by my wife after the date of this notice [25 July 1928], and that she has no authority to pledge my credit.

Although many believed Sylvia had married for money, the truth behind her committing to the relationship was far less fickle, for she believed Lord Ashley was in love with her. He was attracted to show girls and actresses, and before meeting Sylvia he had been involved with Rosie Dolly, of the Dolly Sisters, and after his marriage he continued to have numerous affairs. For a time Sylvia resented his treatment of her and was jealous of his infidelities, and after their initial separation she had a brief affair with Sir Henry 'Tim' Birkin, a millionaire racing-car driver, which presumably ended due to him being married. There was little point in continuing with their unhappy marriage, as Sylvia discovered she could not have children and Lord Ashley's title and family inheritance was dependent on an heir. Thus, in terms of securing the Shaftesbury bloodline, his parents had been right: she was an unsuitable wife for a future earl.

At the age of 26 Sylvia began an affair with Douglas Fairbanks, an ageing Hollywood star famous for his swashbuckling pictures and marriage to 'America's sweetheart', Mary Pickford, with whom he lived at Pickfair, an 18-acre estate in Beverly Hills. Dismissing Sylvia as an opportunist, many believed the affair was a ploy to revive her mediocre stage career, and Fairbanks, 'a chronic Anglophile', was accused of being attracted to 'anything resembling royalty'.[5] He was often accused of snobbery, and Sylvia, agreeing with this appraisal, joked he was 'a luggage snob', whilst she, 'like most English people, travelled with suitcases which looked as if they had been rescued from the rubbish'.[6] She was referred to as 'a commoner with an acquired title', '*that* Ashley woman' and 'Lady Ashtray'. Fairbanks's son, the actor Douglas Fairbanks Jr, known as Jayar, expressed his disapproval by investigating Sylvia's background, but his findings of her lowly origins and past love affairs had little effect on his father. Such criticisms failed to diminish the power Sylvia had over Fairbanks, for he thought her a swan in her gold lamé gowns which emphasised her svelte figure in comparison to Mary who rolled up a skirt rather than alter its hem and wore her hair unfashionably long to distract from her large head. For Sylvia the affair was also more than a flirtation and she encouraged Fairbanks to buy a house on Park Lane, where she could live as his mistress. In doing so, she gave up her London flat – she had since moved out of Lord Ashley's flat – to live with Fairbanks and was sued by her landlady, who claimed Sylvia had taken a twenty-one year lease on the property and had stopped paying rent without giving notice of her dissolving their agreement. After a court case played out in the pages of the gossip columns, Sylvia was ordered to pay £67 to her landlady, and Fairbanks settled the bill.

The British newspapers began to report on Sylvia and Fairbanks's involvement with one another, and they were photographed at nightclubs and at resorts on the French Riviera. She was thrilled, for he was considered the King of Hollywood; however he was reluctant for their affair to be known, for Mary remained oblivious to his philandering and perhaps he did not wish to end his marriage. However, the secret was revealed when a bracelet intended for Sylvia was mistakenly sent to Mary, and although hurt by Fairbanks's betrayal she thought her career and their reputation too high a price to gamble. Therefore Mary began to talk in code when corresponding with Fairbanks and she nicknamed Sylvia 'Rooney', the name of her mongrel dog, and whilst the telegrams were bitter in their tone they were careful of prying eyes. The habit of censoring their lives was familiar territory for Mary and Fairbanks and through their respective production companies (the Douglas Fairbanks Pictures Corporation and the Mary Pickford Company) they hired their own reporters to write favourable articles for the press.[7]

Sylvia's reputation was not afforded such courtesy and Lord Ashley petitioned for divorce, his evidence consisting of newspaper clippings and her indiscreet remarks. The most significant piece of evidence was Fairbanks's last picture, *The Private Life of Don Juan*, for during its production he rented North Mimms Park, in Hertfordshire, and Sylvia lived with him for the duration and followed him to Spain. They then went to the south of France and were photographed drinking and dining, and with Sylvia dressed in her signature flimsy gowns they danced until four o'clock in the morning. He was surprised to meet his colleagues from the Hollywood studios, and they were equally shocked by his hedonistic lifestyle and apparent unhappy frame of mind. Daryl Zanuck, head of Twentieth Century Fox, had reputedly urged him to go home to Mary, thinking it to his advantage if he abandoned Sylvia for the sake of his career. Surprisingly, Fairbanks returned to Hollywood for a discussion with Mary but it did little to restore their marriage, for she treated him coldly and refused to believe he had forsaken all others. Discouraged by her reaction, Fairbanks said to his niece, 'If Mary does not want me, I know someone who does.' The flippant remark instigated Mary's filing for divorce and Fairbanks returned to Europe, where Sylvia was waiting.

They resumed their travels and went to St Moritz, where they were photographed skiing, sledding and ice-skating – hardly the recreations of an unhappy man – and a shopping trip to Rome, then back to London and on to the Bahamas to collect the *Caroline*, a 160ft yacht with a crew of thirty-two. A crowd of onlookers gathered on the wharf and were greeted by Fairbanks with a smile, whereas Sylvia, perhaps uncertain of his fans and their loyalty to Mary, clung to his arm. They sailed to Miami, where she bought beach togs and evening clothes, and were joined by Benita Hume and Fred Astaire, as they made their way to Nassau and through the Panama Canal, heading for the South Seas and Tahiti, ending in Fiji. The latter part of their trip was cut short due to Fairbanks being summoned to Hollywood, and so he sailed to British Columbia and left Sylvia on Vancouver Island before heading south to California. During a meeting with his film studio, United Artists, he was given the news that *The Private Life of Don Juan* had performed badly at the box office. It was a blow to his confidence, for his finances had also suffered as a result of his lifestyle with Sylvia and the cost of the cruise was $100,000. The only remedy for his vulnerability was Sylvia, and in this current state of mind he telephoned and asked her to marry him.

The divorce hearing between Lord Ashley and Sylvia commenced in December 1935. She did not contest the evidence of adultery, which had been confirmed by Fairbanks's former secretary, Mr Edwards, who testified against the couple. Lord Ashley, who stood in the witness box for two minutes, claimed that he and Sylvia had lived together in 'comparative happiness' until she left him, and that he had 'only seen her once' since her return from America with Fairbanks. He explained that he had forbidden her to go, but she disobeyed him, and that he continued to give her an allowance. A *decree nisi* was granted to Lord Ashley on the grounds of Sylvia's adultery and Fairbanks was named as correspondent, with the judge ordering him to pay costs of £2,500. Mary had also obtained a divorce from Fairbanks and in her petition she cited mental cruelty, indifference and neglect.

Three months later, on 7 March 1936, Sylvia and Fairbanks married in a quiet ceremony at the mayor's office in the 8th arrondissement of Paris. Despite it being a day Sylvia had anticipated, she and Fairbanks had their first marital quarrel as they descended the steps, due to him not taking her arm. She chided him for his error and he took her hand, and said, 'Now dearie, please!' To sceptics their union appeared jinxed from the beginning when, on her way to the mayor's office, Sylvia's car hit a taxicab – thought to be a bad omen by locals. Furthermore, on the day of their wedding, Germany invaded the Rhineland, which pushed their nuptials to the back pages of the newspapers. However, one journalist marked the occasion with a poem:

Douglas Fairbanks, Junior's pa,
Looks for a new cine-ma
Having canned his Lady Mary
For that English Ashley Fairy

Sylvia and Fairbanks made their marital home in Hollywood, where many of his and Mary's friends were welcoming to her, although they whispered that it was Mary who was his great love. Their estimation was based on Mary's behaviour after her divorce from Fairbanks, as she began to drink heavily and had an affair with Charles 'Buddy' Rogers, an actor eleven years her junior, whom she married in 1937. For a brief period Gloria Swanson was a close friend to Sylvia, but the friendship ended after she, unbeknownst to both women, invited the two Mrs Fairbanks to a party. It had the desired response from the press, but Sylvia failed to see the comic side, as did Mary, and she never spoke to Swanson again. It was inevitable that Sylvia and Mary would encounter one another and during the war a press photograph captured them next to an aeroplane, with Norma Shearer in the middle. Perhaps it pleased Sylvia that Mary had to stand on the ramp to appear as tall as her. She was, after all, a natural publicist.

During this period Fairbanks retired from the screen and he and Sylvia travelled the world. As in the past their lifestyle drew criticism, particularly from Jayar who grew concerned when his father began to smoke and drink excessively, thinking that Sylvia had encouraged him to do so. Such feelings were not unfounded, for shortly after his marriage to Sylvia, Fairbanks had suffered from chest pains and was advised by his doctor to undergo an operation. He declined and instead went to Venice, where he and Sylvia rented the Palazzo Venier dei Leoni from her friend, Doris Delevingne. The operation, when it was finally performed, was too late to aid his health and he suffered a series of mini heart attacks. Doctors warned him to slow down, which halted their travelling. It was Sylvia who nursed him through his bouts of illness, though many believed it was done with an ulterior motive. Rumours began to circulate that she had forced him to alter his will in her favour, bequeathing to her a fortune of several million dollars and his properties. It did little to dispel the popular belief that she was a gold digger.

On 12 December 1939 Fairbanks, at the age of 56, died of a heart attack in his sleep. He had awoken the day before with pains in his wrists and a feeling of tension in his chest, and he had difficulty breathing. A doctor was summoned to the house and he was diagnosed with coronary thrombosis. Sensing his life was coming to an end, he asked his brother to deliver a message to Mary. 'Tell Mary, by the clock,' he said. It had meant love and faith, and during the happiest years of their marriage it was a turn of phrase they often used. 'He has passed from mortal sight quickly and spontaneously, as he did everything in life,' Mary said, in a press release. 'It is impossible to believe that his vibrant, gay spirit will ever perish.' Sylvia, however, claimed to be surprised by the turn of events, thinking his pain was the consequence of indigestion, and was ill-prepared for the finality of death. She called him the love of her life and channelled her grief into plans for a memorial service, marked by a prelude of having Fairbanks's body lie in state before a large window of their home, overlooking the Pacific Ocean, so thousands of fans could pay their respects. Then she commissioned William Cameron Menzies, the Hollywood set designer, to design a tomb so elaborate in its style that it took a year to complete. For the duration, Fairbanks's remains were held in a temporary tomb at Forest Lawn Memorial Park in the Hollywood Hills. There was a second memorial service to commemorate his final resting place in the Hollywood Forever cemetery and engraved on his marble sarcophagus was a quote from *Hamlet*: 'Good night sweet prince, and flights of angels sing thee to thy rest.'

The rumour that Sylvia had inherited Fairbanks's estate in its entirety was confirmed when Jayar challenged the will and was successful in stopping certain payments from his father's estate. She was forced to appeal to a Californian court, asking that certain funds be reinstated so she could live the lifestyle she had been accustomed to as Fairbanks's wife. The court complied, and she was given £600 – which would now amount to several thousand dollars – a month to live on. Two years later, Jayar filed a lawsuit with the Supreme Court against Sylvia due to their disagreeing over his father's belongings, particularly a tiger-skin rug, guns, two marble statues, and various artefacts which she did not wish to part with. According to the lawsuit, which had been reported in the press, Sylvia continued to receive the monthly allowance of £600 from her late husband's estate. This Jayar had also disputed, as the overall payments from her monthly allowance had amounted to £19,000, and she had inherited £50,000 in ready cash. The judge presiding over the case awarded Sylvia monthly payments of £400, which were to last until 12 October 1942, pending the final verdict, which was ultimately in her favour. 'Whichever way you look at it, the life of Sylvia Hawkes has been one surprise after the other,' wrote the *Sunday Pictorial* in their article, 'The Strange Things That Happened to Sylvia Hawkes'.

In 1941 Sylvia co-founded the British Distressed Areas Funds with her sister, Vera Bleck (the wife of film producer Basil Bleck), Constance Bennett and Virginia Fox Zanuck. From its headquarters in Los Angeles the charity used its funds to distribute food, clothing and medical assistance to war refugees. She travelled across America doing work for the war effort and whilst in Boston she met Edward Stanley, who had served with the Army and Royal Navy, and was the custodian of three baronies: Alderley, Sheffield, and Eddisbury. Their romance evolved at a rapid pace, with Stanley immediately proposing marriage and Sylvia accepting, despite being so unhappy in her first marriage to a British peer. As with her first two husbands she was accused of fortune-hunting but the truth was Lord Stanley was penniless and in 1938 he was forced to sell his family estate which resulted in many elderly tenants being evicted. His lack of money was the consequence of his drinking and gambling, and the large death duties from the baronies he inherited, as well as a divorce settlement he paid to his first wife. Therefore it was Sylvia who was the richer of the two, and with the eventual settlement from the Fairbanks estate she inherited £250,000 in cash, shares in United Artists which gave her a large income, and several properties. In love with Lord Stanley she was not alarmed when he asked for money and a car, and she offered him the choice of two she had 'on the stocks' – a Ford and a Rolls-Royce. He chose the latter and she paid its tax, insurance, and other charges. She also gave him $3,500 in cash and paid $6,500 into his bank account. They filed for a marriage licence at Boston's City Hall – he was on leave in the city – and were married in

January 1944 at the Plaza hotel, with Cole Porter giving her away. She cut the wedding cake with a sword, an extravagant display which, in hindsight, might have served as a warning for battle.

In the interval between Sylvia and Lord Stanley marrying and his going overseas they had spent little time in one another's company. In May, four months after they were married, Lord Stanley went to London and Sylvia joined him there in September, taking a suite at the Ritz hotel. It was not the reunion she had anticipated, for when they were together they fought and she realised she could not live with him, nor could she tolerate his cruelty toward her. Her husband, however, preferred her money over her temperament and tolerated the fighting as long as she paid his bills. Their final argument ended with him striking her, after which she walked out. They had been married for ten months and had lived together for two.

For four years a period of estrangement ensued, partly due to Sylvia living overseas in California and Lord Stanley remaining in London. She was named the guilty party in a divorce case, as he had filed for desertion and she did not contest the petition, though she asked for the money which she had paid into his account to be returned. He refused, stating it had been a domestic arrangement, given that her income was so large and he could only transfer a limited amount of his own money into an American account. His annual income from the Navy was £540 and his private allowance was £10,000 per annum – the latter a substantial sum in those days – but it scarcely covered his debts. The payments, Sylvia explained, were done to save him from embarrassment because 'he was always short of money'. The divorce was granted and the judge ordered Lord Stanley to pay £107 to Sylvia.

A year after the divorce was finalised, Sylvia became re-acquainted with Clark Gable, whom she had known during her marriage to Fairbanks and who was his successor as the 'King of Hollywood'. She insisted they were nothing more than friends, but he claimed they had been 'going around together for two or three years'. The gossip columnist Elsa Maxwell confirmed this when she took credit for 'getting them together', whilst Sylvia was still married to (but separated from) Lord Stanley, by suggesting they dance together at a party in New York. Perhaps in one another they attempted to replace their late spouses, for

Sylvia shared a similarity to Gable's late wife, Carole Lombard, and she continued to search for the unconditional love Fairbanks had given her. 'Her ravishing blonde beauty, her outspokenness, and her impeccable sense of humour, seemed to him to be out of same mould as Carole,' David Niven recalled in his memoirs. Within weeks he had proposed to her, a gesture which shocked his friends, and he spoke of his qualms should Sylvia say no. But she said yes, 'as fast as I knew how. I wouldn't give him any time to change his mind'.[8]

The following day Sylvia and Gable went to the Alisal Ranch in Santa Barbara, owned by friends of his, and stayed in separate cottages overnight. The next morning they drove 100 miles to San Luis Obispo, to obtain a marriage licence. The clerk at the marriage office had tipped off the press, and when they returned to the ranch a swarm of reporters was waiting for them. Regardless, they married in the parlour of the ranch in front of twenty-five guests dressed in their best jeans, boots and cowboy hats. It was something Sylvia was not accustomed to, but it should have served as a hint that marriage to Gable was venturing into the unknown, for during his marriage to Lombard the two enjoyed hunting, fishing, camping in the wilderness and cooking outside. 'I've had every kind of woman, now I have a siren,' said Gable. They left for a honeymoon in Honolulu, and upon arriving they received a telegram from his friend, Dolly O'Brien, who had written, 'Happy Leis.' Gable laughed but Sylvia did not, finding it so insulting that she stopped speaking to O'Brien. The excitement of marrying Sylvia mellowed and Gable quickly realised he had made a mistake. '[Gable] was a selfish man,' Niven said, 'Sylvia a selfish woman,' and neither was willing to compromise. It did not bode well for the newly-weds when, on the tenth anniversary of Fairbanks's death, Sylvia said, 'I know Doug is the only man I ever loved.'[9]

The couple moved into Encino, the ranch Gable had shared with Lombard, the décor unchanged since before her death. Sylvia thought it a harmless gesture to re-decorate Lombard's former bedroom and invited some friends from New York to come and stay in it. It was a difficult situation, for Gable was devoted to Lombard, and Sylvia, despite his earlier feelings for her, could not compete. Furthermore her new environment was not suited to her tastes, as she felt most at home at cocktail parties, aboard yachts, and holidaying in the French Riviera, but could not adapt to Gable's rugged lifestyle. Nor did she approve of his hunting, for she loved animals and had a Chihuahua named Minnie, often seen in Gable's arms. In the beginning she tried to please him, and swapped her fashionable clothing and jewels for plaid shirts, jeans and boots, and she begrudgingly went camping and partook in the pursuits he and Lombard had enjoyed. His friends scoffed at her efforts, and mockingly referred to her as 'Her Ladyship', and laughed at her taste in antiques and watercolours. When she asked Gable if she could build an extra dining room onto the ranch to store her furniture, he said, 'Sure, Ducky Doodle,' and gave her a withering look. The name, friends claimed, was far from a term of endearment.

Sylvia came to realise that Gable was a moody individual, on par with her former husband Lord Stanley, and she resented his changeable nature. He was also frugal, something Sylvia was not accustomed to, and when the press called her a kept woman she made her assets public. For the first time it was clear what she had inherited from Fairbanks: she owned around $6 million in property, there were two beach houses, the mansion in Santa Monica, and a 3,000-acre ranch; $750,000 worth of jewellery; $50,000 in profits invested from the films Fairbanks had bequeathed to her; and an inheritance of ready cash said to equate to $2 million. It prompted Gable to insist she pay her own way, as Lombard had done, and he demanded she sell her beach houses and evict her 'sponging relatives'. The latter she refused to do, for she had supported her mother for decades. However, it can be assumed she had distanced herself from her father, for on her marriage certificate to Lord Ashley she listed him as dead, though he was alive.

Money had served as an incentive when she was young and although she lived a lifestyle that afforded riches, she was not greedy. Years before, her friend Barbara Hutton told her that a woman from New Jersey had sent her a letter, explaining that she had seen Hutton in seventeen different fur coats and asked if she could send her an old one. 'I get these letters all the time,' Sylvia said. Hutton asked how she responded and Sylvia's reply was, 'I still remember what it's like to be poor.' Thus Sylvia was generous toward those who needed help. However Gable sensed she was being taken advantage of, and he resented the presence of her nephew, Timothy

Bleck, whom she looked upon as a son, for he was 'eating him out of house and home and always pestering him for money'.[10]

Their marital troubles continued and Sylvia left for England to settle her business interests. She returned to America with $100,000 worth of jewellery, which she told the gossip columnist Sheila Graham that she planned to auction. The information was printed and Sylvia was arrested by the FBI and fined $5,000 for contravening custom regulations. It was a legal technicality that did little to stir Sylvia, but Gable was mortified. He left for Mexico to film *Across the Wide Missouri* and was further humiliated when she followed and demanded a star dressing room, as it was unheard of for a star's spouse to demand such a privilege. It did little to endear her to Gable's co-stars and the production crew, for she had also transformed his log cabin into a mock English cottage with pink lace curtains, a wicker fence, and landscaped its exterior with turf, rose bushes, and trees planted in large pots. Furthermore she berated the casting director for using American actors made-up to resemble the Blackfoot tribe and asked why real Native Americans could not be cast in the parts and have subtitles on-screen for those who could not understand the Blackfoot dialogue. Gable, on his part, did his best to avoid her by sleeping outside.

Although Sylvia was deeply unhappy during the seventeen months they had been married, it was Gable who initiated a separation after realising she was 'not the girl he wants to be tied down to for the rest of his life'.[11] Sylvia claimed she was 'relaxing in the bath tub' when he burst into the room and delivered the news. The following day she left for the Bahamas to 'give him breathing space' and when she returned she discovered he had changed the locks. She retaliated by filing for divorce on the grounds of mental cruelty and hired Jerry Giesler, the most expensive celebrity lawyer in Hollywood, to defend her. In an attempt to withhold money from her and avoid adhering to Californian property laws, Gable suspended his contract with MGM and temporarily moved everything he owned to Nevada. However a judge ordered him to pay her 10 per cent of his earnings for the coming year and 7 per cent for the next four, the amount of which he refused to reveal. Later, Sylvia sent him a Christmas card with a simple message: 'THANKS A MILLION.'

Three years later Sylvia, at the age of 50, was pursued by Prince Dmitri Djordjadze, a Georgian nobleman living in exile in America and working as a hotel executive, race-car driver, and thoroughbred-horse racer. She had known him from her holidays on the Continent, having first met him at Le Mans and impressing him with her knowledge of cars and enthusiasm for racing. In those days there was no question of their marrying, for he was married to Audrey Emery, the former wife of Grand Duke Dmitri Palovich, a member of the Russian royal house of Romanov. They lived at Boone Hall, a historical plantation in South Carolina. Soon after Sylvia and Dmitri reunited at the St Regis, he divorced Audrey in 1952, and proposed marriage to Sylvia; she accepted. They married in 1954 and Sylvia was elevated to the rank of princess, which prompted her critics to wonder if she had acted out of self-interest. As sudden as the marriage was, Sylvia responded, 'It is essential for any wife to know her man. Marriage is only real when it is shared. If there is true love there is no problem.'

Despite Sylvia's optimism, from the beginning her marriage to Dmitri was plagued by rumours of a divorce. 'We have lots and lots in common,'[12] she said of her husband, though they appeared to lead separate lives, and in truth they shared little in common nor could they agree with one another. Their first serious quarrel was provoked by a business opportunity for Dmitri to manage a hotel in the Bahamas, but Sylvia 'put her foot down like a ton of bricks'.[13] She wanted no part of 'settling down all year round on some old island'. Leaving him in New York, she went to London to buy a house, and claimed she could not return to America for some time due to complications with her visa. It caused little concern for Dmitri, for in her absence he was pursuing a Texan oil venture and 'couldn't care less'.[14] London had been a ruse, for she was in Villefranche, and whilst there she learned of the *Sunday Express*'s planned serialisation of her life story. Its editor was an old boyfriend and she worried that certain aspects of her life which she hoped to conceal from the public would be revealed, particularly her first name, Edith, and her true birth year (she had begun to list it as 1907 rather than 1904). Although she sought legal action to prevent its publication, the serialisation went ahead, and, to quote an Australian newspaper who syndicated the article, it was 'entertaining'.

Whilst Sylvia was holidaying on the French Riviera, Dmitri was spending time in Palm Beach with his former wife, Audrey, and her son from her first marriage, Prince Paul Ilyinsky. Sylvia, too, was pursuing a new romance, and gossip columnists reported of an affair with Jacques Sarlie, an international financier and art collector who, at one time, owned twenty-nine Picasso paintings. The *Sunday Express* exposé, however, had affected her confidence and she became self-conscious about her age and worried that she was losing her looks. She once enjoyed being photographed by the press, but now she began to feud with them. 'I don't like being photographed in the morning,' she had snapped when they photographed her disembarking from the *Queen Elizabeth* in Southampton. The following morning's news reports were far from flattering, and a reporter noted that, although Sylvia was wearing a platinum mink, she had runs in her stockings. She also arranged for the sale of a 17-carat diamond ring at Sotheby's, and the press speculated which of her five husbands had given it to her. 'But all the boys contributed nicely as they made their way through her colourful biography,' a journalist wrote.

As the 1960s advanced and although still married in name only, Sylvia and Dmitri continued to live apart. She surrounded herself with her sister and her niece and nephew, and remained close to Timothy, whom she continued to view as a son. Thus it was a bitter blow when Timothy became paralysed from the neck down and suffered life-threatening injuries after a tree fell on his car. He received $1.5 million in damages and moved in with Sylvia, who cared for him until his death in 1969. After this she divided her time between an apartment in Los Angeles and a rented yacht in Monte Carlo. For many years London did not feature in her travelling itinerary, owing to the British law requiring that dogs had to be held in quarantine for six months. When her Chihuahua died she resumed her visits.

In the last years of Sylvia's life she no longer courted the press and had fallen into obscurity, though she continued to travel and to associate with the jet set of Monte Carlo. She died of cancer in 1977, at the age of 73. Since the age of 23 Sylvia had collected men, money and titles – not bad for a girl from the backstreets of Paddington, whose first ambition was to be an actress. She might not have advanced from the chorus but she ended her life a princess.

4

AN INGÉNUE'S PROGRESS:
JOAN WYNDHAM

Joan Wyndham's life was founded on eccentricity, beginning with the place of her birth, Clouds House, her father's family seat in Wiltshire. A made-to-order ancestral home, it was commissioned in 1885 by her great-grandfather, Percy Wyndham, and designed by Philip Webb, a scion of the Arts and Crafts movement, at a cost of £80,000. Its original concept was executed as a mark of revenge toward Percy's brother, who had evicted him after inheriting from their father the baronetcy of Leconfield. Resembling a piece of art, peacocks roamed the grounds and the interiors were decorated with William Morris carpets and the walls covered in shades of blue as a tribute to its namesake. It was no good appealing to his family, for Percy's mother, Mary, harboured peculiar thoughts and believed all matter of recreation was sinful – reading novels was forbidden, and dancing the waltz could send one straight to hell. Perhaps it inspired a sense of rebellion in Percy, for Clouds became a salon for The Souls, a group formed in the late 1800s as an antidote to the political conversations which dominated high society gatherings. Despite Percy's intellectual pursuits, he had a wicked temper and had once shot a gamekeeper in the foot for picking up the wrong pheasant. Regardless of the Wyndhams' individuality, they were never considered outcasts, partly due to their aristocratic bearing. In 1913 Joan's father,

Richard 'Dick' Wyndham inherited the house from his uncle, George Wyndham, who had died of a heart attack in a Paris brothel. The setting of his death remained a family secret, as did the rumour that he was the father of Anthony Eden. Lovers and illegitimate children lived alongside the family, and there was a servant child known as Odd Boy who did unpopular chores and was paid in humbugs. The unconventionality extended to Joan's parents, for her mother Iris had come to Clouds in 1920 and lived a platonic life with Dick, the result of a disastrous wedding night.

Joan was born on 11 October 1921, her arrival prompting Dick to mutter, 'Christ, it's a girl!'[1] There would be no heir for Clouds, and today it serves as a rehabilitation facility for recovering addicts. Iris knew she was an unsuitable wife and that they were incompatible, for the only marital advice her mother, Wendy, had given her was to apply scent and to never let Dick see her brush her teeth. They went their separate ways, with Iris remaining at Clouds and presiding over the servants, and Dick going to London where he was lauded as a champagne bohemian. He later died from a sniper's bullet whilst covering the Arab-Israeli war for the *Sunday Times*, after which Joan learned he had been one of Europe's great flagellists and was known as 'Whips Wyndham'. Iris, however, was considered an outsider and as such was never entirely accepted by English society. She had a Romanian mother, Wendy, who was brought up by a gypsy wet-nurse, and who greeted visitors with bread, salt and a five-gun salute. There was also the question of her paternity, for she considered herself a girl with two fathers: there was Wendy's husband, Andrew 'Pompous Percy' Bennett, whom she eventually divorced (he remarried a rich widow named Mrs Mustard), and her paramour, Lord French, the Viceroy of Ireland. It was believed Lord French was Iris's biological father, and Wendy lived with him at the Viceregal Lodge in Dublin, where the two created a fictitious life inspired by J.M. Barrie – Lord French was Peter Pan, Wendy was her namesake, and Iris was Little Michael (Darling).

It was a testament to Iris's naivety that she thought Dick would be happy to live a celibate life. She had also taken up with a local troop of Brownies, in the position of Brown Owl, and although she disliked her nickname B.O. she enjoyed playing leap-frog and writing plays for them to perform. None of this amused Dick, who spent his days painting and his nights with Irene, Marchioness of Queensberry, whom he invited to Clouds for Christmas. Their affair was discovered by Iris, who had gone to the drawing room to extinguish the candles on the tree and had found them kissing behind it. Joan remained sheltered in the nursery with her nanny for company, a severe woman who terrified Iris, and who put salt on Joan's tongue to stop her from crying and used spit to clean her face.

Divorce was inevitable, a move initiated by Dick who harboured false hopes of marrying Irene, though it was not to be, for she would never risk social disgrace. Instead he asked Rosa Lewis, proprietor of the Cavendish Hotel, to fix him up with 'a tart' so Iris could divorce him on the grounds of adultery, which she did in 1925.

In the years following Iris's divorce from Dick, she and Joan left Clouds and moved to a farm in Wendover, where they spent an idyllic period driving their pony cart through the village. They eventually moved to London and Iris bought a small house at Evelyn Gardens, off the Fulham Road, in Chelsea, and took in a lodger, Sidonie 'Sid' Houselander, an artist and sculptor, who also illustrated the Sacred Heart newsletter. Although they were at first suspicious of one another, having met when Iris hired Sid to paint Joan's nursery at Clouds, they later found common ground in their conversion to Catholicism: they were both fanatic. This was perhaps due to Sid's origins in spiritualism. She also wrote theological novels under her birth name of Caryll, and later her *non-de-plum* Sidionie, and amassed a following of readers who were devoted to her tales of ESP, prophetic dreams, and anecdotes of the bohemians she had known in her mother's boarding house. It was also rumoured that Sid and Iris were lovers, though Joan could never be certain, but she recalled the two women sitting in their Chinese cocktail pyjamas, sipping White Ladies, and listening to the gramophone. Years later Joan recalled a woman named Marilyn, a friend of Sid's who had briefly usurped her, for Iris had fallen in love and called her 'my darling little banana squirrel'.

Throughout Joan's early childhood Iris worried she had inherited Dick's traits, for she considered her child 'a little devil' whose bad habits were employed to hide her underlying goodness, which her mother thought her ashamed of. It was a strange observation, but one that inspired her to send Joan as a day pupil to the Convent of the Assumption at Kensington Square, and three years later, at the age of 10, she boarded at the Convent of the Holy Child Jesus in St Leonards-on-Sea. She learned little in those establishments, except that she had indecent thoughts. She developed a 'crack' (crush) on a sixth-former named Rosemary Dwyer and considered herself lucky if she could steal a strand of her blonde hair off the back of her tunic 'to be kept in my desk like some holy relic'. On laundry day she waited for opportunities to see Rosemary, and, 'If I was clever enough to spot Rosemary's clean underpants, I could thrust my hand in and not wash it for a week.'[2] It was therefore a shock to Joan when Rosemary took the veil and she called it 'one of the saddest days of my life'. Thinking she wanted to die she wrote to Iris, who advised her to stay away from 'dirty-minded people, bad influences and all sorts of filth in fact … But it won't affect your character really, provided you keep your soul polished up – then the dirt won't stick!'[3] However, Joan's grandmother, Wendy, had different ideas about childrearing and took her to a beauty parlour to have her thick eyebrows plucked and 'black muck' put on her lashes; afterwards they went for a meal of caviar and vodka, followed by an evening of gypsy music.

Several weeks later Joan was relieved to have fallen in love with a 'Real Live Man', for Mother Damien, a nun at her boarding school, had written to Iris of her 'romantic tendencies' with other girls. The man in question was John Gielgud, whom she had seen in *Hamlet* at the New Theatre. 'Oh dear! Those legs! Those knees!' she said of the knock-kneed Gielgud in his tights, but then he began his soliloquy and it made up for his shortcomings. 'Nothing seemed to matter but the beauty of his voice … I was an ardent fan,'[4] she later wrote. She sent him a letter and received a signed photo, on which she forged 'To Joan'. Then she realised he lived quite near, and she sometimes followed him home so she could kiss his doorknob. By chance, she discovered her friend's aunt had a friend in the cast and they got to meet Gielgud in his dressing room. She had sat through *Hamlet* numerous times, and when she came face-to-face with her idol she told him of a dream she had had, in which she saw him going into Selfridges to have a Turkish bath, wearing a green and white boater with a feather in it. The encounter inspired her to audition for the Royal Academy of Dramatic Art (RADA) and to pursue a theatrical career, which troubled Iris for she had spoken of sending her to the Monkey Club, on Pont Street.

Joan was horrified by the idea of a finishing school and instead spent the summer with her paternal step-grandmother and her aunt. The former was Violet (née Leverson), the daughter of Ada 'The Sphinx' Leverson, a writer who was a close friend of Oscar Wilde; the latter, Olivia Wyndham, was a drug-addicted society photographer known as Bunch, who lived in Harlem with her African-American girlfriend. Joan was fascinated with Bunch, who drank a lot and swore, and she became familiar with 'the famous word, the one beginning with b'.[5] It fuelled her own bad behaviour, for Joan, then 16, was also testing her ability to shock and she wrote in her diary, 'I wish I could have seen the head housemaid's face when she unpacked my case, and found a grubby suspender belt and my signed photo of John Gielgud – not to mention a paperback of Casanova's *Amours*.'[6]

The arrival of the Second World War marked an end to Joan attending RADA. The play she had been rehearsing was *Hedda Gabler*, much to Sid's horror – for it was to be spoken in German. Iris and Sid, old enough to recall the horrors of the last war, were pulverised by the news and went to their altar on the landing to light candles and pray to Our Lady of Peace. However Joan had a different view and sensed it would become the most exciting period of her life thus far. In recent years she had begun to keep a diary, and during the period of 1939–45 she '[scribbled] away in the air-raid shelter by the light of a hurricane lamp, and later hiding them under my mattress in case my mother should read them and die of shock'.[7] She volunteered three days a week at her local first-aid post at St Mark's College, working twelve-hour shifts, and whilst there she met Laura Cavendish, a former pupil of the Slade School of Fine Art, with whom she enjoyed 'a gentle lesbianism of the mind'.[8] There was also the Loaves and Fishes, a society founded by Iris and Sid to help lonely gentlefolk who had fallen on hard times – the helpers were called Sprats and the elderly people were referred to as Sea-horses. Their charitable work inflamed Sid and Iris's obsession with sin, with Sid consuming little food, thinking it wicked if she did, and Iris banning Joan from attending the theatre, as she thought it a bad influence. But Joan's theatre privileges were soon reinstated and she went to see *The Beggar's Opera* and liked it when Macheath said, 'Kiss me, you slut!'

The early days of the war had given Joan something of a social life, and she soon fell in with a group of artists and bohemians. Karl, a sculptor in his late thirties and former housemate of Ezra Pound, saw her wandering around the Fulham Road and thought she looked 'rather interesting', and his friend, Jack Squire, amused her by playing the piano and singing dirty songs. There was Gerthardt, 'a filthy German', whom she often heard playing the flute, but he preferred older women for they bought him dinner and he used her as a servant to run errands and mend his clothes. 'Well, dear, if you like that type there are plenty to be had,' Iris said. 'They swarm in art schools, prisons, doss-houses; they're laid out in rows in morgues.'[9] Despite her feelings for Gerhardt, when he made a pass at her she pushed him away. 'Little Red Riding Hood frightened of the Big Bad Wolf?' he said. 'Don't you like being kissed?'[10] Joan replied that she did not know; she had never been kissed. He then jumped off the bed, switched off the music, and told her to 'run home to mummy before Wolfie does anything naughty'.[11]

It was a strange and exciting time for Joan, as she began to make a life away from Iris and Sid. She enrolled at the Chelsea Polytechnic to study sculpting, as clay was cheaper than paint, and to her surprise Iris suggested she rent a studio on the condition she return home when the air-raid siren sounded. The studio was located above Madame Arcan's flat – she was an occultist and former mistress of Aleister Crowley – and it was decorated with furniture from jumble sales. During that period she began to visit the Artists' Café, where she met a penniless painter named Jo, who kissed her and then asked to use her studio. She could not decide if she loved Jo, but continued to let him use her studio and to kiss her, but he refused to go further because, as he told her, he did not sleep with virgins. Iris had warned her about men like her artist friends, and years before had told her the facts of life whilst driving around Hyde Park in her Austin Seven, furiously revving the engine to hide her embarrassment. Skipping the biological facts, Iris warned Joan to be careful with men in taxis, 'But you know when they're going to pounce – they give off this funny sort of smell!'[12] Despite this warning of lecherous men, Joan thought Jo to be considerate – 'if you say you're tired of striptease he'll do up your buttons again and be sorry',[13] – and he gave her cigarettes and lent her money when she had none. The fixation with Jo ended and she moved on to Leonard, a 23-year-old bohemian who learned that his wife was about to leave him when he discovered her and her lover's astrological charts. As with Jo, Leonard also kissed Joan and tried to corrupt her by telling her about sex, which reminded her of 'Mother Mary Damien giving a sex talk at school'. He also persuaded her to pose nude, which she likened to learning how to dive – 'when you take your dress off it's the first plunge'.[14] They went to the cinema and bumped into Leonard's wife and Joan slithered away, feeling like a fool; afterwards she met Jo and Gerhardt at the Artists' Café and they teased her for going around with a married man. 'In my present mood,' Joan wrote in her diary, 'I'd sit in the nude for every bloody artist in Chelsea and Fulham.'[15]

As the war advanced and the Germans invaded Calais, Joan declared that nothing could shock her any more. She thought of herself as an impostor in the world in which she was moving, and that she was not a real artist despite her group of friends and having rented a studio. The trouble was more than teenage angst, and Joan found herself in the midst of an identity crisis. In her diary she wrote, 'I see myself acting like a tart, and men hurting me and sponging on me, and trying to make love, and asking if they can pee in my sink.'[16] She decided that she and the other artists lived in a dream; it might have been desperate but it was not dull. When all seemed hopeless and she dug a pin into her hand to feel alive, a young man named Rupert knocked on the door of her studio and invited himself in, dismissing it as ramshackle and saying he preferred a butler and good cellar. He appeared feral, despite his upper-class background, and often knocked on the doors of artists and lived off their generosity, as his family money had run out and his mother and brother were living in tents in the drawing room, sitting on rubber mattresses and reading Leslie Charteris. After their exchange Joan learned he was living with her sculptress friend, Pru, who was aged around 30 and had been married to a Greek don. He pursued her in every field in Cambridge by making wolf noises, and, discovering that she had been unfaithful, he placed her in a lunatic asylum.

The news of the Nazi occupation of France brought Joan's London life to an abrupt end. She left with Iris and Sid to stay with a relation in the country but had decided if London was to be bombed she wanted to be there too. To her relief the house was overcrowded and before they returned home she stopped at her father's home, Tickerage Mill, at Blackboys in Sussex, as she had heard rumours he was in prison. His house was occupied by a party of writers, wearing odd clothes, and high on Benzedrine. They demanded to know who she was. 'You're not Dick's daughter,' one said, astonished, for they had thought Joan was a parachutist. She then learned that Dick was not in prison but recovering from a nervous breakdown at the London Clinic and they were expecting his mistress to arrive any day. The behaviour was typical of Dick, for he had taken no interest in Joan when she was a child and refused to pay maintenance, but despite his disregard Iris continued to love him, prompting jealousy from Sid. Joan left Tickerage Mill and went for a walk in the woods, where she was propositioned by young soldiers. They were caught by their sergeant, and after dismissing the boys he then made a pass at her.

Having returned to London, Joan realised she had outgrown her male friends. Gerhardt had left England; Jo enlisted in the war as a rear gunner. Leonard remained but she felt stifled by him and caught in the middle of his feud with Jo. To her surprise she found herself thinking of Rupert, and at that moment he knocked on her door and invited her to tea at Pru's house. She learned Pru had turned him out. 'Out of the house?' she then asked Pru, but Pru said no, only out of her bed, for her new boyfriend, a baron, had moved in. Then Rupert asked Joan if she would sleep with him, and she said she was uncertain. 'Would you rather I raped you in the proper he-man fashion, or will you tell me when you're ready?'[17] he asked. On another occasion, he said, 'You may look innocent enough but every now and then you talk like an old French whore.'[18] Joan wondered about Iris and Wendy, whose divan she and Rupert were laying on, and decided that she would approve. 'No wonder my mother is so sour and irritable, living with Sid and never having a man for sixteen years!'[19] she wrote of Iris in her diary. However Rupert was also involved with Squirrel, an upper-class woman from Knightsbridge, who was 28, dark, and beautiful. Joan considered her a rival as she made her feel 'all Kirbies and cardigan and size seven sandals'. It was then – feeling inferior to Squirrel – that Joan agreed to go to bed with him. Afterwards she said, 'If that's really all there is to it I'd rather have a good smoke or go to the pictures.'[20] But, in hindsight, she had achieved what she wanted: 'One night there was a really bad raid and the whole shelter was shaking, and I thought: ah well! The opposite of death is life so I might as well go and get myself devirginised!'[21] The studio was hit during an air raid, along with the building in which Leonard, Jo and Pru lived, and Rupert narrowly escaped death as he had gone down to the shelter to borrow money off a friend. They were given the news that Gerhardt had drowned, which nobody was surprised about because 'he was the sort of person one expected to find hanged'.[22] The Redcliffe Road was in ruins, everyone had been evacuated, and Joan sensed her life of debauchery had come to an end: 'In the good old days [Rupert] says there was so much love-making going on that the whole of Redcliffe Road used to shake steadily from nine in the evening till nine the next morning.'[23]

The excitement came to a halt when Joan thought she was pregnant. It had by now occurred to Iris that her 17-year-old daughter was promiscuous and she began to hint at Joan's predicament, saying 'how terrible it must be for a girl who had slipped up when she misses her curse for two months! Just think of the agony she must go through!'[24] Joan broke into a cold sweat and ran out of the house, to the bombed studio where she found a bottle of quinine pills left by Pru. The bottle instructed Joan to take one or more as directed, and so she took six. It made her violently ill and Iris diagnosed it as 'Siren Stomach', which she said was common during wartime. Joan told Rupert about the baby and he reacted badly, threatening to kill himself if it were true. Before he could follow through with his threat he was called up for the Royal Navy which further depressed Joan, and to cheer her up Madame Arcan gave her a book on black magic. The night before he left for Portsmouth she realised she was not pregnant and told him the news, but he reacted indifferently and said if all else had failed he would have had her kidnapped and 'forcibly aborted'. He had been saving money to buy something from Harry Bolitho, a backstreet abortionist, which he would have secretly mixed into her food. The news shocked her, but she did not mention her own experiment with the quinine, for she thought it a sin.

The pregnancy scare forced Joan to alter the course of her life and so she enlisted in the Women's Auxiliary Air Force (WAAF) and after passing her medical examination she went to the Galleries Lafayette and 'bought tarty underwear'. Before she left for her post in Leighton Buzzard, Bedfordshire, she discovered Rupert was on leave and was spending it with his mistress, and consumed once more by jealousy she agreed to his conditions to live as a *menage à trois*. The arrangement came to an end after she grabbed Rupert by the hair and hit him, and he retaliated by slapping her across the face and knocking her glasses off. They rolled around the floor, biting and hitting one another, and then he fell asleep. A few days later they bid one another goodbye and she left for Leighton Buzzard to begin her training for Special Duties. She lived in a hostel with a group of young women, ranging from debutantes to Marks and Spencer shopgirls. The Air Ministry Board gave each girl a test to see which social class they belonged to: they looked for dirty fingernails, holes in stockings, and attempted 'to find out if your mother was a char' by asking 'trick questions to see if you say "toilet" or "pardon"'.[25] Having passed her training, Joan was given the rank of officer and was posted to Stanmore, near London. This new post came as a shock in comparison with the drab conditions of the hostel, and she thought the mess resembled an old country house with its chintzy sofas and blazing log fires. 'Hello, Wyndham,' said a fellow officer upon her arrival, 'how about a gin and lime?'

The remainder of the war years were a hedonistic mixture of louche company and difficult scenarios. She fended off a drunken Dylan Thomas, who pestered her with kisses in the back of a taxi, and she had a relationship with a Czech artist, who took her to a former brothel for his planned seduction. There was also a neurotic Norwegian, who carved notches into her bedpost with a commando knife, and from whom she caught fleas. When the war was over she married Maurice Rowdon, the son of a dockworker, and turned up to her wedding 'all dolled-up like a tallyman's ink bottle'.[26] She had a daughter, named Clare, and they accompanied Rowdon to a teaching post in Baghdad. But Joan was soon restless, and the marriage ended when they returned to England. She had an affair with her Russian lodger, Shura Shivag, with whom she had a daughter, Camilla. They would marry years later. It was unconventional for its day, but Joan never cared for protocol.

Throughout the years she worked in a variety of jobs – writing for *Housewife* magazine, masquerading as a horoscope writer, working in a theatre, and as a publisher's reader. There were stints as a restaurant cook, and she opened an espresso bar in Oxford. In the 1960s she was a prominent figure in Swinging London, living in a five-storey house off the King's Road. Her coterie was an unusual mix of aristocrats, prostitutes, beatniks, and intellectuals.

Joan concluded her wartime diary with a wish for her future husband: 'He won't be a hypochondriac or a hedonist, or hate children or laugh at religion or think the lower-classes ought to be shot at sight; he'll have a heart and soul, and all the right feelings at the right time.'[27]

5

A DANGEROUS DEVOTION:
VENETIA STANLEY

History remembers Venetia Stanley as a temptress in the cabinet of Herbert Henry Asquith, known as Henry, Britain's wartime prime minister. In any era, especially one of political uncertainty and social upheaval, the friendship between the 25-year-old Venetia and the 60-year-old prime minister was a controversial subject. Described as tall, dark and handsome, Venetia had the self-assurance that came with her background as the youngest daughter of a rich baronet, though it was rumoured her biological father was George Howard, 9th Earl of Carlisle. At her family's seat, Alderley Park, she kept a menagerie of animals, including a pet monkey that slept on top of bookcases and pelmets and dropped on unsuspecting guests, and a bear cub who roamed around the estate and pounded on doors. Her father Edward Stanley, a Liberal politician, was the heir to three baronies (Alderley, Sheffield, and Eddisbury), and she was a distant cousin of the Mitford sisters who, two decades later, would run amok through high society. She was, with the exception of Henry's wife Margot, the only woman to know of his political secrets. The friendship, however, was disguised by Venetia's closeness to Henry's daughter, Violet, which many believed verged on lesbianism, as a common theme in their impassioned letters spoke of their longing to be together: 'I can think of nothing but you at every instant'; 'Don't stop loving me'; 'I do want you SO much'.[1]

Since meeting Violet during the debutante season of 1905, Venetia had been a significant presence within the Asquith household. Henry's marriage to Margot was platonic: 'Our relationship is absolutely unique,' she said. 'Every night however late I go and sit on his knee in my nightgown and we tell each other everything.'[2] Margot knew of Henry's interest in Venetia and dismissed it as a casual friendship inspired by 'her cleverness, enterprise, and good humour, as well as her talent for writing letters and genuine affection'.[3] In Margot's two volumes of memoirs she does not mention Venetia and she also concealed from early biographers Henry's fixation with her. Failing to recognise her father's obsession with Venetia, and only learning the truth years after their friendship had ended, Violet said, 'It cannot be true. Venetia is so plain!' In the beginning it was Violet who served to oust her stepmother from family life, and during Margot's long marriage she complained that she and Henry had spent only six weeks together. Thus Margot viewed Violet and Venetia as her enemies, and, renowned for her scathing wit, she thought her stepdaughter 'would have made a remarkable man'.[4]

From the beginning of Henry's premiership in 1908, Venetia was the recipient of his political authority, and as the most powerful man in Britain, with the exception of King George V, he reserved each Friday for a drive with her in his Napier motorcar. 'I shall always remember our mist and rain-blurred survey of the three counties,' he recalled after a particular drive. 'I purposely keep back, when we are together, so much more, I dare say, than you suspect.'[5] Having Venetia to himself did not prevent Henry from becoming jealous of other men, whom he viewed as usurpers, for behind the scenes at Downing Street two of his political secretaries were in love with the girls: Edwin Montagu with Venetia, and Maurice Bonham Carter with Violet. The moment Henry's fondness for Venetia turned to love happened on a Sunday morning in 1912, as they sat alone in the dining room, chatting and laughing, and 'in a single instant, without premonition on my part or any challenge on hers, the scales dropped from my eyes: the familiar features and smile and gestures and words assumed an absolutely new perspective; what had been completely hidden from me was in a flash half-revealed'.[6] On one occasion a footman was surprised to walk in on Henry playing musical chairs with Violet and Venetia. He was also known to correspond with Violet's friends and to think of them as companions, an arrangement which Margot called 'the little harem'. Contemporaries, however, did not think it entirely innocent and referred to him as 'a notorious groper'. Venetia's sister, Sylvia, was aware of Henry's behaviour toward young women and advised her to avoid being alone with him, and if so 'it was safest to sit either side of the fire … or to make sure there was a table between them'.[7]

Although Margot was frustrated by Venetia, she directed her feelings toward Clementine Hozier, for having, as she viewed it, stolen Winston Churchill from Violet. In her diary Margot had written of wanting to 'hit [Violet] with her fists', and thought Churchill 'a little treacherous gutter genius' and a bad influence on her stepdaughter, as he encouraged her to speak of politics. Regardless of Margot disliking Violet, she felt loyal toward her and thought Churchill's interest in Clementine an insult, for she lacked Violet's intelligence. Venetia was also privy to Violet's heartbreak and was with her at Slains Castle on the evening she learned of Churchill's engagement to Clementine. Violet responded by running away. Thinking her in danger, as she had been missing for several hours, Venetia alerted the others and for hours the servants and house guests, armed with fire torches, trekked the rocky coastline searching for her. Henry was convinced Violet had fallen from a cliff into the North Sea and wept to Margot, who prayed for her safe return. Churchill wondered if he ought to call off the engagement, but Venetia, unlike the others, retained the confidence of someone who was part of a ruse and knew Violet would be found alive.

Shortly after midnight fishermen discovered Violet lying on a patch of grass close to the castle, offering the excuse that she had slipped on the rocks and knocked herself unconscious. A doctor was summoned by Henry, who contradicted Violet's story that she had suffered a blow to the head, as an examination proved she was not injured. The press arrived at the castle, demanding to interview Violet and report on her thrilling near-death experience, which brought Margot to the conclusion that Violet, on the verge of a nervous breakdown, had staged the incident, and referred to it as, 'This unfortunate, foolish and most dangerous escapade.' The feud between Violet and Clementine placed Venetia and Margot on equal footing. Margot dismissed Clementine as having no brains and accused her of being 'mad',[8] undoubtedly a jibe at her moodiness, or 'emotional, electrical storms'.[9] Venetia, who was a cousin of Clementine's, said she was sane to the point of dreariness. Regardless of their mutual dislike of Clementine, their dynamic changed when Venetia realised Margot was emotionally unstable and she knew of the chinks in her armour. Far more significant to Venetia was the knowledge that Margot had been ordered by the doctor to 'close the bedroom door'[10] to Henry, as she had risked her life throughout five pregnancies in which only two children survived. Therefore Venetia's presence was not only a threat but a cruel reminder that Henry favoured a younger woman with her life ahead of her.

However there were striking similarities, not only in looks but in intellect, between Margot and Venetia which Henry must have found attractive. As with Venetia, Margot also came from a rich family, the Anglo-Scottish Tennants, and spent an eccentric childhood at The Glen, a country house designed in a Scottish baronial style. Her father, Sir Charles Tennant, was described as violent, his moods often deciphered by the young Margot and since childhood she knew how to pacify him; her mother, Emma (*née* Winsloe), was affectionate toward, but not proud of, her children and found them plain, especially Margot, whom she had hoped would be a beauty. A horse-riding accident obscured Margot's once-promising features and left her with a broken nose, which, when healed, gave her an aquiline profile. Lady Tennant instilled in Margot that the only difference between boys and girls was not their gender nor their social rank but circulation, for the men on her side of the family had cold feet. Margot could also relate to Venetia's devotion to Violet, for in her youth she and her sister, Laura, were inseparable. The two Tennant girls had entered society together and became members of a set known as The Souls, a pre-war group of intellectuals whose main objective was to form a salon where they could meet without arguing about politics. The Souls abhorred hedonistic pursuits, such as violence, alcoholism and adultery, and they regarded the arts as the most important thing in life. In 1885 Laura married Alfred Lyttleton and a year later died after giving birth to her only child, a son, who died at the age of 2. Margot never recovered from the death of her sister and closest friend, and as a result she began to suffer from chronic insomnia, which plagued her for the rest of her life. Venetia and Violet also moved at the centre of society, in the Coterie, a group of intellectuals who were the offspring of the Souls, but whose recreational habits were deemed unacceptable. Nicknamed the 'Corrupt Coterie', they drank and smoked in an age when it was frowned upon for a woman to do either, and they took morphine and cocaine, which were easily obtained from a chemist.

Whilst Margot and Violet wrongly thought Henry relied on their advice and valued their opinions, it was Venetia whom he came to trust; unlike Margot who was renowned for gossiping, she could keep a secret. She boosted his morale and encouraged his sobriety, for he was often drunk and on one occasion at the House of Commons he fell to the floor and had to be rescued by Winston Churchill, and was a steadying influence during the years of political unrest: Irish Home Rule, the Suffragette Movement, the rise of the Labour Party, and the First World War. His former appointment as Home Secretary in William Gladstone's government made him sympathetic to Ireland's attempt to pass a second Home Rule Bill in 1892, however as prime minister he failed to handle the 'Irish Question'. He considered the Suffragette Movement 'a rather pitiful exhibition of so-called masculinity'[11] and opposed the granting of the vote to women, as he wondered if their vote could improve the government, although he changed his mind after his premiership. During debates in the House of Commons and in meetings with his cabinet, Henry sent Venetia tokens of affection and state secrets on War Office notepaper. In his letters he spoke of a fretful king regarding the issue of Irish Home Rule; he wondered if he should create a new office for David Lloyd George; and he promised not to act until she had given him her response.

On the eve of Britain entering the First World War, Henry was on the verge of a nervous breakdown and it was rumoured he was suicidal. His dependence on Venetia was greater than before, and he was so desperate to receive and read her letters he once postponed a meeting with the king. By 1915 Venetia was receiving two to three letters a day from Henry and he grew moody if she failed to respond, thinking he had fallen out of favour with her. Venetia's letters to Henry were either lost or destroyed but his correspondence to her portrays a prime minister who would have rather been in her company than guiding his country through a world war. 'My fondness for Venetia has never interfered and never could with our relationship,'[12] he assured Margot, as she became convinced Venetia was 'teaching Henry to avoid telling [her] things'. The first political topic he had written to Venetia about was the economic budget: 'You might be able to come here to hear the budget: in any case after it, at tea time, in my room.'[13] His budget caused outrage in the House of Lords for its policy of increasing income tax to fund the war and he also received criticism for the munitions shortage on the Western Front, leading to the Liberals forming a coalition government with the Conservative Party. It was then decided by Henry to talk in code, so he could relay secret information about the war: 'I have got such a good metaphor about you, which I will tell you in confidence.'[14] He also forwarded to her a telegram from Lord Kitchener, as he wanted her to know what was happening across the Channel, before anyone else.[15]

During Henry's dependency on Venetia she was also being pursued by his private secretary, Edwin Montagu, who had been in love with her since 1911 and had, on various occasions, proposed marriage. Although Venetia rejected him he continued to accompany the trio on their holidays, and on one particular trip they went to Sicily. The couple played hide and seek in the garden with Edwin, whom Violet thought was 'the best person in the world to play it with' and she wrote in her diary that he was 'so frightened and so frightening'.[16] Around that time Henry and Violet visited Alderley Park, but the press failed to pin any significance to the visit, or to their friendship, and he was photographed with Venetia's pet penguin. The visit marked a turning point in their relationship, for Lady Stanley was growing unhappy with Henry's devotion to Venetia, and she encouraged Edwin's pursuit. It was everything Henry feared, for he did not want to share her with another man. 'Have you been cultivating new acquaintances or playing fast and loose with old ones?' he wrote to her. 'Step into the confessional and let me know the worst.'[17]

In the years that Venetia had known Edwin, she did not conceal her disinterest, or that she was stringing him along for her own vanity and amusement. It did not quell his infatuation, and in time she began to consider him as a potential husband. Her apparent change of heart occurred on her 26th birthday, marking a watershed moment in her life, for in those days it was a comparatively late age for a woman to marry. Reluctant to acknowledge her birthday, she wrote to Edwin that she hoped her future would be filled with 'permanent fun'. With Edwin's inheritance from his late father, Samuel Montagu, 1st Baron Swaythling, a merchant banker, he could offer Venetia all the 'fun' she desired. It would also grant her the freedom to continue her unconventional behaviour, and so, after years of refusing Edwin's proposals, she agreed to marry him. They both knew she was marrying for money, and she told Edwin she did not find him attractive nor did she love him, and that their marriage would be celibate. She also suggested they could have affairs with other people; however in the early days of their marriage his devotion prevented him from doing so. He agreed to her conditions, perhaps thinking their dynamic would change once they were married. Friends who knew Venetia realised she was marrying Edwin as a last resort, and sympathised with him. Henry's son, Raymond Asquith, wrote to Conrad Russell, 'I do not think he will be either a dull or a tyrannical husband, and I understand that the terms of alliance permit a wide licence to both parties to indulge such extra conjugal caprices.'[18]

'This breaks my heart,'[19] Henry wrote to Venetia, after learning the news of her engagement. She responded with only one word, which caused him further pain, and he implored her to write a lengthy letter. Although he thought a second letter from Venetia was 'most revealing and heart-rending'[20] he felt embittered by her suggestion they stop writing to one another, and declared it 'terrible … No hell can be as bad',[21] and he called their mutual silence 'cruel and unnatural'.[22] They resumed their correspondence after what Henry called the 'two most miserable days of my life'.[23] Violet was equally disturbed by the news, and in her diary she wrote that the thought of Venetia marrying Edwin 'filled [her] with horror'[24] and referred to his 'physical repulsiveness … the thought of any erotic amenities with him is enough to freeze one's blood'.[25] Furthermore Violet wrote to Edwin and accused him of blackmailing

Venetia into converting to Judaism, a move she predicted would ruin her reputation. Edwin resented Violet's words and forwarded her letter on to Venetia, who mistook the criticism as concern for the step she was taking and thought Violet ultimately approved. Surprisingly Venetia found an ally in Margot, who approved of the marriage and ordered Violet to refrain from teasing Venetia. However there was a motive, as Margot believed Venetia would be too busy devoting herself to marriage and Edwin's political career to give Henry a second thought. 'Your part to play,' Margot wrote to Edwin in 1915, 'is to persuade both Violet and Venetia that if they don't marry they will be miserable formidable egotists and amateurs.'[26]

Although Lady Stanley had thought Edwin a welcome distraction from Henry, she, along with her husband, was alarmed by Venetia agreeing to marry him and of her conversion to Judaism. Their reasons were entirely anti-Semitic, for they could not accept Edwin's religion, nor could they abide his late father, Samuel Montagu, whose proto-Zionist movement and funding of synagogues in England were part of a rivalry with Nathan Rothschild. However their backgrounds were similar, for both the Montagus and Stanleys were involved in the Liberal Party and had founded their fortunes in trade: Venetia's maternal grandfather, Lowthian Bell, was a self-made ironmaster from Newcastle-upon-Tyne, and Samuel was the son of a watchmaker from Liverpool. They also overlooked Samuel's philanthropy, particularly his offered reward of £100 for the identification and subsequent conviction of Jack the Ripper, and criticised the family's social mobility. The latter sentiment was hypocritical, for they knew Venetia's future marriage and conversion were motivated by self-interest, as Samuel's will stipulated that Edwin could only inherit his millions if he were to marry a bride of the Jewish faith. Still it was not enough to persuade her family, particularly her elderly father, and both her parents boycotted the wedding.

Henry also voiced his disapproval and sent a poem to Venetia, describing her as a 'Christian child' who had been 'too easily beguiled' by the 'silken tents of Shem'.[27] The silken tent was a reference to the nickname Venetia and Henry had given Edwin's lavish family home at 24 Queen Anne's Gate in London. There were anti-Semitic undertones, too, as Jews were said to have descended from Shem. His narrow outlook contradicted his views on social reform, for in 1908 he proposed the government introduce a state pension and his People's Budget of 1909 inspired the creation of the Welfare State. However, as with Henry's blatant anti-Semitism, he was also homophobic, and as Secretary of State in Gladstone's government he signed the arrest order for Oscar Wilde, who was imprisoned for committing sodomy and gross indecency. Nevertheless, Henry's opinions were largely accepted by the upper classes, and were echoed by the Stanleys, who held a similar disdain for Judaism. Marrying Edwin was one thing, but converting to his faith was another.

Prior to Venetia confirming her engagement to Edwin, Henry suspected something was afoot and that her attention, when responding to his letters, was being spent elsewhere. 'It is depressing to read how and with whom you are spending your time,'[28] he wrote. His letters, although desperate in his wanting Venetia to himself, adopted a bitter tone and he warned her not to fail him, for that would precipitate his complete collapse, not only emotionally but politically too. 'Will you still be the same in 1915?'[29] he had asked. It was therefore poignant that her letter, containing the details of her engagement, arrived on the day he received the worst press of his political career, which led to his resignation in December 1915. Feeling as though he had lost his element of stability, his thoughts turned to betrayal: not only had Venetia betrayed him, but Edwin had too. In a letter to Venetia's sister, Sylvia, Henry wrote, 'I don't believe there are two living people who each in their separable ways are more devoted to me than she and Montagu: it is the irony that they should deal a death-blow to me.'[30] Margot had also treated Edwin as a confidante, and years before she had expressed to him her opinion of Venetia: 'How I loathe girls who can't love but claim and collect like a cuckoo for their own vanity.'[31]

Before the wedding, while Venetia considered her conversion to Judaism, she accepted a voluntary nursing post at an army hospital in France. It removed her from London and the scandal of her impending marriage and the temptation of Henry. 'It seems ages since I felt the touch of your hand,'[32] Henry wrote to Venetia, frustrated by her lack of correspondence. The year before and during Venetia's voluntary post at the London Hospital, Henry did not bid his son goodbye before he left for the Front, but instead went to catch a glimpse of Venetia in her nurse's uniform.[33] During her time at the French hospital, in 1915, her letters to Edwin lacked any mention of the wounded and dying soldiers, or of her feelings for him. Instead she wrote to complain about the 'dreadful condition' of her hands, caused by the 'acids and disinfectants', and of the pimples and freckles that had developed on her face. The hospital, she told Edwin, was crowded and dirty, and 'the one real tragedy about the place', she explained, was the inability to have a hot bath. 'Isn't that dreadfully squalid?' As time passed she grew to enjoy nursing and the freedom the vocation gave her, as, far more importantly, she was removed from Edwin and his 'harassments of the engagement'.[34] She wrote to Edwin that she did not want to come home, as her 'desire for a new sensation is too strong'. Fearing she would change her mind, Edwin responded to ask of her conversion, and implored her to confirm a date for her departure from France. But Venetia remained vague and explained that her hospital work was 'too thrilling' to leave. In the end, Edwin told her the two rabbis he had engaged for the conversion were leaving for the Front in July, and he encouraged her to submit her application before the twelfth. She agreed, and returned to London on 10 July.

Venetia's homecoming was met with mixed feelings. Edwin was relieved, but Henry adopted a high-handed approach in his letters to her. He 'prayed with [his] whole soul' for her happiness and admitted it would have been out of character to be disloyal to her; however he asked her not to respond and not to 'wish me now to say more'. After Henry's parting words to Venetia, he wrote to Diana Cooper and offered her the 'vacancy' as his mistress, which she declined. Then he began a new friendship, albeit through letters, with Mrs Hilda Harrison, a war widow, whom he considered his new, if platonic, confidante. Venetia turned her attention to the conversion, which she had warned Edwin was a farce; she was going through the motions to save his inheritance and to restore his relationship with his mother, whom she met for the first time on her wedding day. When Edwin requested their future children be brought up Jewish, Venetia called him a hypocrite, for he did not practice his faith, and perhaps she reminded him of his prior promise, that their marriage would be platonic. 'Were I to be washed 1,000 times in the waters of

Jordan ... I should not feel I had changed my race or nationality,' she wrote to him. 'I go through the formula required because you want it for your mother's sake and because I think one is happier rich than poor.'[35] Further threatening Venetia's conversion was her inability to study the book that 'Old Joseph', the rabbi, had given her because she found it too boring. In the end, however, she memorised enough to pass the test, and was therefore received into the Jewish faith.

Two days before Venetia married Edwin, she visited Henry in person; it was to be their last meeting for several years. Afterwards he sent her a letter, thanking her for giving him 'unforgettable and undying memories'. On 26 July 1915 Venetia and Edwin were married in a traditional Jewish ceremony, and absent amongst their small gathering of family and close friends were Henry and Violet, who chose not to attend. He sent Venetia two silver boxes with a brief note: 'With all my love and more wishes than words can frame for your complete and unbroken happiness.'[36]

Although historians have questioned the seriousness of Venetia's affair with Henry, thinking it a harmless infatuation on his behalf, her marriage to Edwin has also been scrutinised. Some believed the marriage was never consummated and that Edwin, torn apart by self-hatred and hypochondriac tendencies, and sensing he would die young, was grateful for the little attention Venetia gave him. He appeared to have had a mistress, Pearl, with whom he had a child – 'Pearl has just given me a little daughter and we are very happy about it'.[37] Venetia was also conducting her own affairs, and a significant admirer was the press magnate Lord Beaverbrook, whom she trusted with her investments and who gave her financial advice. They travelled around Europe, often accompanied by Beaverbrook's close friend and employee, Viscount Castlerosse, and their mutual friend, Diana Cooper. Jean Norton replaced Venetia as Beaverbrook's chief mistress; however there were no ill feelings, for their friendship outlasted their affair. Henry, who followed Venetia's social activities from afar, thought it 'a rotten social gang ... who lead a futile, devastating life'.[38]

In 1923 Venetia gave birth to her first and only child, Judith Venetia Montagu. It was widely accepted that Judith was the daughter of William Ward, later the 3rd Earl of Dudley; however she was brought up as the child of Edwin and he settled a trust fund on her. A timely gesture, for in 1924 Edwin died at the age of 45: the cause of death was unknown but was believed to be blood poisoning. His death did not trouble Venetia and she settled into widowhood with a generous inheritance, which granted her the freedom to live as before, and to travel extensively around Europe. Although Judith was raised by nannies she was grateful to her mother for giving her a good education and independence, as Venetia valued those qualities above all else.

In the years following Edwin's death Venetia and Henry resumed their friendship, beginning when she wrote to him for the first time in a decade. The letter lacked their earlier intimacies, and she addressed him as My Dear Mr Asquith, a departure from her usual Darling, and spoke of how Edwin had admired him and 'what a real and lasting grief your political separation was'.[39] Regardless, there were glimpses of her devilish character which had attracted Henry all those years ago; 'Do you remember how we used to laugh at [Edwin]?'[40]

Henry came to see Venetia at Breccles Hall, her Tudor country house in Norfolk, and made the acquaintance of Judith. With tears in his eyes he looked at the child, and said, 'This, then is the child.' It was a bittersweet visit for he was in ill health and had suffered the loss of movement in one leg, and upon arriving at Breccles he could not exit the car without assistance. 'It was most good of you to take me in,' he wrote in his last letter to her, three months before his death on 15 February 1928.

Until Venetia's death from cancer on 3 August 1948, she refused to be bound by her gender and class, and continued to live with the freedom she had always known. She travelled the world in her own de Havilland Gipsy Moth aeroplane, piloted by Rupert Belleville, and although many found it indulgent she saw it as the 'simplest, cheapest, and most modern way of seeing the world'. Beaverbrook remained her ardent admirer long into their old age, and she always retained a fondness for him. But it was Henry Asquith who had captured her heart.

6

THE MACHIAVELLIAN QUEEN:
SYLVIA BROOKE

In 1946 Vyner and Sylvia Brooke, the last Rajah and Ranee of Sarawak, a kingdom of half a million subjects and unexploited riches in gold, silver, diamonds, antimony, quicksilver and coal,[1] stepped off a flying boat at the mouth of the Sarawak river and boarded their royal yacht, *Maimuna,* for the last part of the journey. Not since their coronation in 1917 had they witnessed such a spectacle of crowds waving handkerchiefs and flags. As Sylvia walked the customary four paces behind her husband, she wondered if he regretted signing his kingdom over to Britain as a crown colony. 'I would have given anything to save Vyner from being hurt as this was hurting him; but there was nothing I could do for him now,'[2] Sylvia wrote. She thought herself a victim of circumstance and not the menacing force behind the dissolution of three generations of rajahs. Rather than submit to the line of succession, as stipulated in the previous two rajahs' wills that only a male Brooke could inherit the throne, she wanted to alter it in favour of her eldest daughter, Leonora. Having failed in her quest, she convinced Vyner to sign over his kingdom: if her own flesh and blood could not inherit, then nobody would. She was, as the Colonial Office called her, 'a dangerous woman, full of Machiavellian schemes'.

The quest for power might have been an antidote to an unhappy childhood, for Sylvia claimed her parents did not love her. She was the youngest of four children, born on 25 February 1885, and dismissed by her mother, Nellie, as ugly; a feeling validated by the dog, who vomited after its first sight of her. Her two brothers, Oliver and Maurice, were prized higher than girls, and her sister, Dorothy, known as Doll, was also neglected and spent her lonely days sitting under a wigwam, pretending to be a squaw. Their father, Reggie Brett, 2nd Viscount Esher, loved Maurice, whom he called Mollie, in an incestuous way: 'I was the first human-being who kissed you at all, and quite certainly the first who kissed you passionately.'[3] The dynamic was intensified by Nellie's obsession with Reggie, whom she had married at 17, and her jealousy of Maurice. It was a strange childhood, spent at Orchard Lea near Windsor Forest, for the children were deprived of friends their own age, as their parents did not want their minds to be contaminated by others. Instead Maurice formed his own friendships with schoolboys from Eton, particularly a 15-year-old named Teddie Seymour, who stayed at Orchard Lea and toward whom Reggie was openly affectionate, stroking his hair until he fell asleep. The boy inspired rivalry and admiration, as Sylvia also loved Teddie and envied the attention Reggie gave to him. Like many influential individuals, Reggie's perversions went unchallenged, for he was a Liberal politician and royal courtier, who was close to Queen Victoria and her children, and he exploited his power without remorse.

The friendship between Reggie and his friends set the tone for visitors and staff, and what was deemed acceptable. When Sylvia was a child an older boy, perhaps a friend of Maurice's, undressed her so he could see what a naked girl looked like. 'I don't think much of THAT,' he said, as Sylvia stood shivering. At the age of 12 she was molested by her father's secretary, who had caught her unaware in a darkened room. The behaviour was not uncommon in their home, for her father's friend, Lewis 'Lou Lou' 1st Viscount Harcourt, had attempted to rape Doll in an empty building on the estate, but she managed to kick free. In 1922 Harcourt killed himself, after his sexual assault of Sylvia's young cousin, Edward James, was whispered about in society. Sylvia had conflicted feelings of her experiences, as she was raised to be subservient to the male sex and each morning was ordered to lace her brothers' boots.

However she could not forget those early encounters and before the age of 12 she had twice attempted suicide: first by eating rotten sardines, and then by burying her naked body in the snow. Having failed, she withdrew to her attic bedroom and spent her days reading horror books.

'There was so much love inside me,' Sylvia said, years later, 'and I had no one whom to lavish it [on].' She became fixated with the idea of marriage as she hoped it would carry her far from home and compensate for her parents' lack of attention. After coming out as a debutante in 1903 and partaking in the London season, Sylvia realised she was, in her words, a flop. Her parents wished to see her engaged, and so they held a luncheon at the Savoy and invited eligible bachelors, military men, and literary stars. For the occasion Sylvia bought a velvet jacket and a pair of false pin curls to frame her face, but they blew away and she could not afford to replace them. The disappointment of being an unsuccessful debutante was replaced by an ambition to become a novelist. She entered a competition in *Women and Home* magazine with a short story, 'Sweet William', and was surprised to win the first prize, a cheque for £20. After this feat J.M. Barrie and George Bernard Shaw took an interest in her writing and became her mentors, and in 1908 her collection of short stories, *Pan and the Little Green Gate*, was published by Hodder & Stoughton. A year later she published a second collection, *The Street With Seven Houses*, which was lauded as 'original and clever'.[4] Her fledgling literary career did little to impress her parents, and so she attached herself to Barrie, who encouraged her work. 'Select your man and ask him,' Shaw had once told her. So, acting on his advice, she proposed to Barrie, who declined her proposal and suggested they remain friends.

The rejection was made bearable by an invitation to join the Greyfriars orchestra, an all-female ensemble founded by Ranee Margaret Brooke, the wife and consort of the second White Rajah of Sarawak, to help find wives for her three sons. Sylvia played the drums, cymbals and triangle, though not very well. Reggie and Nellie were suspicious of Ranee Margaret, who had grown close to Doll, for they suspected she was a lesbian with an unhealthy interest in their two daughters. For years the ranee had lived apart from the rajah, their first separation prompted by the death of their three children from cholera, and with the line of succession uncertain she returned to Sarawak and produced three sons, who survived into adulthood. Their final separation occurred after her husband killed her pet doves and served them to her in a pie, and so she left for England and moved into Greyfriars, a country house in Ascot, and surrounded herself with artists, musicians and writers. When her eldest son, Charles Vyner Brooke, arrived in London from Sarawak she decided his shy nature would never attract a wife, and so she intervened. Of the ranee's nineteen girls he chose Sylvia, and, having watched her for weeks, asked if he could tune her drum. 'I wished then that my pin curls had not blown away. I wished too there were buttons in my sleeve cuffs instead of safety pins,'[5] she recalled, years later.

The Bretts thought little of Vyner, who went by his middle name to distinguish himself from his father, the rajah. His being the heir to the Kingdom of Sarawak, in north-western Borneo, did not impress Reggie and he thought Vyner was a social climber, which was partly true, for Ranee Margaret wanted her sons to marry rich women. It also played to Reggie's xenophobic views that the rajah's subjects were Malay, Chinese and the Dyak, a native tribe of Borneo who practised Ngayau – headhunting. The kingdom was in its infancy, having been established in 1841 by Vyner's great-uncle, James Brooke, an English explorer and diplomat who was given the land by the Sultan of Brunei as a reward for helping him suppress an uprising of the indigenous people. In 1868 Charles[*] inherited Sarawak and in 1901 Margaret asked King Edward VII to grant him the royal prefix of His Highness; he was later given a baronetcy, both of which Vyner stood to inherit. A philistine by nature, Charles resented Margaret's interference, though he did not reject the king's honours, and remained in Sarawak, where he 'wished to live and die in peace in my own narrow way of thinking'.[6]

During a hiatus in the orchestra Sylvia began to receive letters from Vyner, who wrote to say he had found her drumstick. Her parents were aghast and forced her to read the letters aloud, at the breakfast table, and she denied that he had any interest in her. However when a second letter arrived with the words 'I love you Sylvia, and always have done so and

---

★   Rajah Charles Brooke changed his surname from Johnson to Brooke after his elder brother, Brooke Johnson, who had been disinherited by James Brooke for insubordination.

always will', she was banished from Orchard Lea and sent to Roman Camp, the family's seventeenth-century house in Perthshire. The letters from Vyner continued to arrive and Sylvia hid them in her bloomers and smuggled her own to the post office. She was certain of one thing: Vyner wanted to marry her and was willing to wait until she came of age and could break from parental authority. Ranee Margaret thought otherwise, and when Vyner came to Greyfriars on leave she demanded he propose to Doll, for she liked her better. Vyner went to find Doll but lost his nerve and placed a necklace in her hand, a present from his mother, and departed. Far from a threat to Sylvia, Doll harboured a fear of men that lasted until the age of 40. Instead she became an ally to both Vyner and Sylvia, and helped in their disastrous attempt to elope, which ended when his motorcar broke down and he could not meet her at the Squirrel Inn. The opportunity was lost and Vyner sailed to Sarawak, leaving Sylvia in a limbo that lasted for five years.

For those five years Sylvia and Vyner corresponded, and he often signed his letters 'your always true friend'. When he returned to London in the summer of 1910 she lied and said she was in love with another man. The reason was unclear, except she could not understand why anyone would find her interesting; nor did she think herself worthy of love. For months the two did not write, until finally, in December, Vyner sent her a letter suggesting they meet. She showed it to Reggie, who declared him 'a nice fellow' and suggested she meet with him. So, Sylvia met him at the Prince's Restaurant in Piccadilly and was disappointed by his formality. This she attributed to his recent bout of illness, as a chill had turned into an abscess on his liver and, not expected to live, he had been given the last rites. However she was amused by his stories, particularly of being locked in a lavatory and therefore unable to attend a party with his mother and the Empress Eugenie of France. A week later Vyner proposed to Sylvia and she accepted, and their official engagement was the topic of press reports. She was now called a society beauty, even though she knew they were flattering her, for all her life she was convinced she was ugly. It was an exaggerated perception of herself, for although she was not classically beautiful, her diminutive height and dark colouring gave her an exotic air. George Bernard Shaw thought so, and he wrote to oppose the engagement, thinking Sylvia far better suited to an older man such as himself, despite him being almost thirty years her senior and unhappily married. The press, however, were far more fascinated by Maurice resigning from the Coldstream Guards to marry Zena Dare, a comedic actress, who retired from the stage at the height of her fame to marry him. Sylvia was disheartened, though not surprised, by her father's response, for he dismissed her marriage to Vyner as leaving the family and welcomed Zena as his daughter-in-law – 'thus began the second incest'.[7]

On a damp day in February Sylvia and Vyner were married. As she put on her wedding dress she felt as if her soul had left her body, and as she walked to the altar she imagined a Malay woman entering the church and claiming Vyner had fathered her child. 'These were not the terrors of Sylvia Brett, the twenty-four-year-old bride,' she wrote. 'They were those of the doubting, unhappy little girl … still intense, still afraid that happiness could never be hers.'[8] The reception at Orchard Lea did little to allay Sylvia's concerns, for Vyner's father, Rajah Charles, begrudgingly made the journey from Borneo to England, and wanted to leave soon after his arrival. Reggie showed the rajah the door, and it failed to engender affection between the two families, for the rajah disliked Sylvia and did not think Vyner a capable heir. He also mistrusted Reggie, who was by then private secretary to King George V, and sensed he wanted to commercially exploit Sarawak. As a consequence he wanted to disinherit Vyner in favour of Bertram, his younger and favourite son, whose wife, Gladys (*née* Milton Palmer), heiress to the Huntley and Palmers biscuit company, he approved of. However Gladys was not without eccentricity: she had met Bertram years before, having been recruited by Ranee Margaret to play the mandolin and triangle in the Greyfriars orchestra, and had odd habits such as sleeping on pillows filled with straw. Once she stepped off an aeroplane in the nude. As Sylvia left Orchard Lea she thought, 'In a few hours I shall be in bed with a man I hardly know, and I haven't the faintest idea what is going to happen to me.'[9] In her memoirs she compared Vyner's footsteps at her bedroom door to the sound of an executioner's drum. 'The following morning I hardly dared look at Vyner,' she wrote. 'He made one of his funny faces and said, "Well, that's that, now we go on to Rome."'[10]

Their honeymoon to Italy was not the romantic excursion Sylvia had thought it would be. They began in Genoa, where Vyner had lived as a young boy, and went on to Rome, the days consumed by sightseeing and following directions from his dated guidebook, the addresses long-since extinct. He also refused to adhere to schedules and to book tickets in advance, and so trains were left to chance and often did not arrive. Sylvia scarcely knew where they were going or what each day would entail. The only certainty was his joke book, which he read from and bored her with the details. They went south, to Sorrento and Capri, and headed north to Venice: the last stop a disappointment, for Sylvia had memorised the descriptions of gondolas in Vyner's guidebook and was disheartened to find they were replaced with motorboats. She then discovered she was pregnant and the couple returned to England, to a rented house at 8 Cadogan Gardens, to await the baby.

The birth of Sylvia and Vyner's first child, a daughter named Leonora, on 18 November 1911, was a disappointment for Rajah Charles and the people of Sarawak. He had prepared an elaborate ceremony with bell-ringers on standby, as he had anticipated a grandson and heir, and so the occasion passed unmarked. It was a ritual that he undertook twice more, with similar results, for Sylvia bore two more daughters: Elizabeth, in 1913, and Valerie, in 1915. The press nicknamed them, in the order of their birth, Princess Gold, Princess Pearl and Princess Baba, though Vyner was quick to note their title was not princess but *dayang*. However as the years progressed Sylvia craved publicity and was delighted with the attention her daughters attracted due to their love affairs and careers in show business. Many in society did not take the Brookes's royal status seriously and she was addressed as Mrs Vyner Brooke and lived in a cramped maisonette on Davis Street, London. Regardless, she once confided to Reggie that she wanted 'crowns plastered everywhere'. The statement repulsed Vyner, who preferred turkey farming at their gabled house at Stanton Harcourt, Oxfordshire.

A visit to Sarawak fulfilled Sylvia's longing for pomp and ceremony. Six months after the birth of Leonora, Sylvia accompanied Vyner on the lengthy sailing to Sarawak, their days filled by him telling her of his escapades with other women, particularly prostitutes. It was everything she had dreaded, and she compensated by telling herself it was Vyner's way of wanting her to understand his weakness. Rajah Charles, more disagreeable than before owing to a hunting accident in which he lost his eye and wore in its place a glass bead (bought for a discount), resented Sylvia's presence and thought it an unnecessary expense, and Ranee Margaret, with whom she stayed before sailing, thought Vyner weak-minded and under her influence. Their arrival by steamboat in Sarawak made up for the misgivings and as they sailed up the river they were greeted with a gun salute, fireworks and crowds waving handkerchiefs and a banner reading, 'Welcome and Long Life to Their Royal Highnesses'. As they stepped off the steamboat and onto dry land, Sylvia adhered to custom and followed four paces behind Vyner, as they approached a guard of honour carrying a Sarawak flag, and the band of the Sarawak Rangers played the national anthem. Although shy at first, as she could not speak the language nor was she confident with royal customs, she attracted attention due to her diminutive height, which the Malays thought far from regal. They were devoted to Ranee Margaret, and Sylvia knew she would be difficult to emulate. She did, however, inspire admiration at Astana, the royal palace formed of three white bungalows connected by passages, and the Malay women gathered at her feet and showered her with rice.

Still, there was an uneasy feeling surrounding their visit, for it was rumoured Rajah Charles wanted to alter the line of succession in favour of Bertram, for Gladys had given birth to a son, Anthony, which was marked by a twenty-one gun salute. It had been put in place, the rajah explained to Vyner, as a precautionary measure should Sylvia fail to provide a male heir. She thought it a personal attack and it set in stone her feelings toward Anthony, who was an innocent bystander in the rajah's plans for Sarawak. It also did not settle her qualms when, having borne three daughters and due to medical reasons, she was unable to have any more children. The Malay women placed their hands on her stomach and asked if she was with child. 'No,' Sylvia sadly replied, 'no babies any more.'

Sylvia's insecurities came back to her. Not only was she being usurped by Gladys and Bertram, who had since visited Sarawak, when Bertram was declared the heir presumptive to the throne, but the family's fortune was at the mercy of Rajah Charles, who often invested in ill-advised schemes which offered little to no return. There was £15,000 in a reserve fund, which Vyner had expected to inherit, but now this rested on Sylvia and their future children. A rumour began to circulate that the British government had placed a bid on Sarawak, which the rajah was tempted to accept, and so Sylvia and Vyner would lose their kingdom and their money. 'Our children will be left selling matches in the street,'[11] she wrote to Reggie. Those close to Sylvia grew tired of her leaping to conclusions, and Reggie had the last word when he called her 'a damnable extremist'. Her letter to Rajah Charles, which she admitted was rude and was later destroyed, stunned the old man, for he was accustomed to being a god-like figure in his family and his sister never addressed him by his first name. She also underestimated how ruthless her father-in-law could be: he was, after all, a man who had married Ranee Margaret even though he loved her mother instead. The conflict between Vyner and Bertram eased and a truce was formed; however, Vyner continued to resent his father. It paralleled with Sylvia and the mischief she caused in her own family, as she was now feuding with her brother, Oliver, and his new American wife, Antoinette, and wrote scathing letters emphasising her sister-in-law's social gaffes. This cattiness, as Reggie called it, contrasted with the meekness Sylvia had displayed in childhood, and it prompted Oliver to call her 'a female Iago'.

Tensions returned when Rajah Charles asked Vyner to come to Sarawak but he was ordered to leave Sylvia at home or risk losing his allowance. He obeyed his father and departed without Sylvia, which she resented while she remained at home with their children. They were now living at Wimbledon Common, and although she loved her daughters and found them beautiful and clever, she felt stifled by motherhood. Leonora's seriousness puzzled Sylvia and if she were to laugh, the child would slap her arm and order to her stop. Gone, too, was Vyner's silliness and he became a serious individual who loathed society gatherings and the extroverted character Sylvia often became, with her bohemian parties and Malay costume, which caught the attention of the press. After the birth of a third daughter their marriage became platonic, and she later wrote, 'Strange to say, Vyner, with all his desire for adventures with women, was not what I would call a great lover, nor even, as the saying goes, "good in bed". He made love just as he played golf – in a nervous unimaginative flurry.'[12] She claimed to be asexual, but challenging this statement was her affair, lasting from 1916 until 1920, with Barry Gifford, who had served Rajah Charles for almost five years before returning to England to enlist with the Royal Flying Corps. In Vyner's absence she had grown accustomed to being alone and went to Roman Camp to visit her family, and it was there she learned that Britain had declared war on Germany. Four months later Vyner arrived in England and attempted to enlist in the army as a private, but his age (he was over forty) and his past liver ailment prevented him from doing so. He joined an anti-aircraft battery stationed on top of the Cannon Street Hotel and later took a job at an aircraft factory in Shoreditch. As for Sylvia, she remained in Scotland and rented a house in Callander Street, turning it into a military extension hospital for the sick and wounded, which she ran with her sister-in-law, Zena. She was not a successful nurse, for the sight of blood made her faint, and she went to wash dishes in the pantry.

In 1916 Sylvia and Vyner's war work was interrupted by a request from Rajah Charles, asking them both to come to Sarawak. Although curious as to why her father-in-law had invited her, she was also hesitant to make the sailing, for she knew the dangers of German U-boats and feared being torpedoed. She was also worried Vyner would find her an unsuitable travelling partner, and so she invited Doll to liven things up, but Doll, who was living with Lady Ottoline Morrell, refused. Instead Doris Stocker, a chorus girl at the Gaiety Theatre, accompanied them, and Sylvia was pleased that her pretty looks and sense of humour lifted Vyner's spirits. In Sarawak the trio stayed at the Residency house, as there was no room at Astana, owing to the addition of Doris, and the 87-year-old rajah's mistress, Mrs Waller, the wife of his doctor. It was during this visit that Sylvia was offered an insight into the extent of Rajah Charles's behaviour, for during dinner parties he urinated over the veranda rail, in view of his guests, and Sylvia attempted to make light of it by saying, 'Listen, it's begun to rain.'

On 17 May 1917 Rajah Charles died at the age of 88 and Vyner ascended the throne of Sarawak with Sylvia as his consort. There was a memorial at Cirencester church, close to his estate, Chesterton House, during which the Sarawak national anthem was sung and, perhaps a foreboding sign, Sylvia did not stand, as she was feeling unwell and was later diagnosed with tuberculosis. She went to South Africa to recuperate and Vyner left for Sarawak with Bertram, whom he invited to assist with the administration of the kingdom. This invitation did little to lift her mood, for she continued to mistrust Bertram, and in this frame of mind she began a flirtation with a young officer, who let himself into her hotel room at the Mount Nelson and removed his coat and glass eye, and climbed into bed whereupon he fell asleep. There was also a young Air Force officer who called her a 'frigid flirt' and hurled her onto a cactus bush. 'I had been brought face to face with the evil side of my own character,'[13] she said. Finally she went to Sarawak for the coronation, and never before had seen the ritualistic customs of the people she and Vyner would govern over, nor did she understand the custom of young Malay boys dressed as women with crescent-moon eyebrows and scarlet lips to ward off evil spirits nor the malice of the Dyaks, who believed headhunting brought them luck. She was further perplexed when Vyner refused to take part in the coronation ceremony and when he was finally coaxed into his robes, Sylvia discovered they were infested with silverfish. As the years advanced he became bored by government affairs and ruling a kingdom, though, like his father, he was on intimate terms with his people and cared for their welfare. His new role meant long spells of loneliness for Sylvia, intensified by the Malay women and their inability to speak unless spoken to. Thus she socialised with Vyner's government officers, even though she realised they flattered her in the hope of a promotion.

Sylvia's accession to Ranee of Sarawak was everything she had wanted, and yet it instilled in her an insecurity she had not felt since childhood. She resented how her spending had to be accounted for, even though Sarawak's economy did not suffer due to the war, and Vyner gave the British government £30,000 toward its war effort. She returned to London without her husband and lived with Doll at their parents' home on Tinley Street, but the sisters' behaviour upset the housekeeper and she reported their immoral behaviour to the Bretts. Sylvia failed to understand what she had done, except allow her male friends to sleep on the floor and bring two prostitutes home so she could paint their portraits. Writing to their parents behind Sylvia's back, Doll thought her sister 'very bitter' and nervous, and risked 'going mad when her change of life came'. In this frame of mind Sylvia wrote a novel, *Toys*, which explored the theme of reincarnation and earned her unfavourable reviews. However her next books, *The Cauldron* and *Lost Property* were successful. She also wrote a three-act play, *Heels of Pleasure*, which opened at the Arts Club and closed due to bad reviews. After the war she was inspired to pursue a career as a film actress and she visited America with the intention of doing so, but failed to secure a screen test. Years later she went to Hollywood and sold the rights to a film treatment based on the white rajahs for £500; she also lectured under the title 'Queen of the Headhunters'. It was a move which validated society's feelings that Sylvia was vulgar, a view that was echoed in Sarawak, particularly when she took to the skies in an aeroplane called *The Flying Carpet*.

The next two decades saw Sylvia fixated with the line of succession, for although she knew her daughters could not inherit the throne, she harboured plans of having a future grandson succeed as rajah. As things stood, Bertram and his son, Anthony, were Vyner's heirs apparent, as Rajah Charles had wanted them to be. In retaliation Sylvia began to spread rumours that Vyner was planning to disinherit his brother and nephew in favour of his eldest daughter, Leonora, who had since married Kenneth MacKay, 2nd Earl of Inchcape, with whom she had a son, Simon. Such rumours reached the Colonial Office, who wrote to Vyner to remind him that any such plan must be presented to His Majesty's Government. Vyner responded that it was a rumour, despite knowing Sylvia was determined to place Leonora and Simon on the throne. By then she had no familial influences preventing her from acting foolishly, for Reggie had died in 1930, Ranee Margaret in 1936, and Nellie in 1940. When she failed to achieve her own way she suggested to Vyner they sell Sarawak to the British government and live comfortably on the money, for she wanted to divide her time between London and Hollywood, which she called her spiritual home. 'I was one of England's best ambassadors,' she said of her visits to America. 'There is a country for you, and a president!'[14] To strengthen her case she began to spread rumours about Anthony, claiming he had misspent government money, relied on astrology before making a decision, was an exhibitionist, and held delusions of grandeur that extended to placing a cardboard crown on his motorcar. Vyner entertained Sylvia's rumours and issued a proclamation which denounced Anthony as his successor, and Anthony retaliated by consulting a solicitor regarding the malicious gossip being spread about him. Eventually Vyner wrote to Anthony and apologised and invited him to return to Sarawak as a district officer, but Sylvia wrote to Bertram and reminded him that Leonora triumphed over his son in the popularity stakes.

The Second World War fuelled Sylvia's paranoia, as she became convinced there would be a Japanese occupation in Sarawak and therefore her money would stop. She began to eat little, though confessed to Doll she still needed her gin. To earn a living she turned to self-promotion and went to America to find sponsored work, though very little materialised except for writing articles and lending her name to an advertisement for Chateau Martin Winery and appearing on Ripley's *Believe it or Not* radio segment. She also dreamt up new schemes to earn money and overthrow Anthony, such as forming a constitution in Sarawak, giving its people self-governance in exchange for £200,000. The Brookes kept the money even though the plan faltered due to the Japanese occupation, a thing she feared. 'I am that paradox – a despotic ruler who has used his powers to give his people self government,'[15] Vyner told the press during a sojourn in Melbourne. Sylvia then decided liberation would be best for Sarawak and broached the idea with Vyner, who worried about the cost of restoring his kingdom after the occupation, and realised there was little incentive for him to do so. The Colonial Office thought Sylvia a dangerous woman – though, in time, they considered her proposal of handing Sarawak to the British government as a crown colony. Vyner worried he would have to pay back the £200,000 he had kept from the failed constitution. On 26 July 1946 Vyner abdicated and ceded Sarawak to the British government without agreement from the Dyaks, which led to a violent anti-cession movement, lasting for four years. He received £100,000 and an annual income of £30,000 to be shared amongst his dependents.

Sylvia was to discover that life for a deposed queen carried no privileges and Vyner wondered if he had been too hasty in relinquishing his power. Anthony moved to Singapore and sided with the anti-cession movement, calling his home Sarawak House, which irritated Sylvia, for Gladys moved there as well, and mother and son planned to restore Brooke rule. However he was prevented from entering Sarawak, which, to Sylvia, must have offered a small victory. She was also lonely, for she and Vyner occupied separate houses, and her children's love affairs and failed marriages carried them far from England. Elizabeth had married Harry Roy, a bandleader whom Sylvia loathed, as she thought his East End roots beneath her daughter, and Valerie had married Robert Gregory, an American wrestler. Both Elizabeth and Valerie divorced their husbands and remarried, and both attempted to break into Hollywood films with bit parts. Doll also relied on Sylvia for money, which she called her 'begging letters', for she abandoned London society for New Mexico, living with D.H. Lawrence and his wife, Frieda. By the late 1940s Sylvia and Vyner's money had run out and he appealed to the Colonial Office for a stipend, and in turn they agreed to the conditions of his 1911 marriage act which gave him £4,000 a year and Sylvia £3,000. She turned her hand to writing again and published two books, *The Darlingtons* and *Headwind House*, but both were commercial failures. In 1963 Vyner died and bequeathed £23,000 to Sylvia and their daughters, but she kept the lot and was challenged by Leonora, who spoke to the press about her mother's greed. It did little to stir Sylvia, as she was living in Barbados and painting pictures and selling them to tourists.

Until her death in 1971 at the age of 86, Sylvia exploited her position as the last Ranee of Sarawak. She spoke on television, published a bestselling biography, *Queen of the Headhunters*, and delighted in the knowledge she had overthrown Anthony, whose quest for restoring the throne had led to a nervous breakdown. Two decades before, she had watched the Coronation of Queen Elizabeth II on television, claiming it was the 'best way' to view it, though for a woman who loved attention she must have longed for her old life. 'I used to say to myself,' she wrote in her memoirs, 'I am still the Ranee of Sarawak, surely that must mean something.' In the end, she realised, it meant nothing.

7

THE BARONESS:
IRENE CURZON

In an age when women, like children, were to be seen and not heard, Irene Curzon was determined to be viewed as something more than a decorative figure. It was a forward-thinking stance, for her father, George Curzon,* expected women to be brilliant and beautiful, but never ambitious or opinionated. He looked to women as providers of comfort, but never overpowering in their thoughts or outranking him in their importance. Irene was not an exception to his rule, though to emphasise her high-born status she was carried on a pillow in the arms of her nurse.[1] She was born on 20 January 1896 at Balfour House, in London, and named Mary, after her mother, and Irene, for the goddess of peace and the season of spring. To avoid confusion with Mary the child was known as Irene, and to Curzon's horror his American wife pronounced it 'I-reene' rather than the English way of 'I-renée'.

Curzon and Mary were the king and queen of their social sphere, and her popularity was rivalled only by Consuelo Vanderbilt, the unhappy wife of the Duke of Marlborough. Their marriage in 1895

---

* In 1898 Curzon was created the 1st Baron Curzon of Kedleston, and in 1911 he was given the rank of a marquess, and in 1921 an earl. As the daughter of a marquess and then an earl, Irene could affix Lady before her name.

was a love match and a dynastic union, between a dollar princess – her father, Levi Leiter, said to be worth $20 million, owned the Chicago department store, Field and Leiter – and a rising political star in Lord Salisbury's government, serving as Under-Secretary of State for India and then Under-Secretary of State for Foreign Affairs. American newspapers praised Mary as one of the most beautiful young women ('her beauty was of the Oriental type'[2]) in the country, and she was nicknamed 'The Belle of Three Cities'[3] – Newport, New York, and Washington. 'Do you have sea-fish in America?' her father-in-law, Lord Scarsdale, asked her, and he wondered if she could make a mince pie or correctly serve tea. He thought her American origins were inferior, a view shared by many of the English aristocracy. Responding to his criticisms, Mary said, 'Why don't you ask me if there are any civilised or white people in America?'[4]

From the moment of her birth, Irene was determined to make her presence known. On Christmas Eve Mary feared she would miscarry the baby and a doctor was summoned from London to the Priory, their rented country house in Surrey. He gave her an injection to prevent it. A week later Mary was placed on a litter inside a horse-drawn Landau carriage and surrounded by white roses as she was taken to London, to await the birth of Irene. In years to come it was Mary's millions that Irene inherited but it was her father's gumption she mirrored; he was, after all, a man who in his tenure as Under-Secretary of State at the Foreign Office asked to be appointed the Viceroy of India. He had no official training for the post, nor did he hold a senior government position, but he believed he was the best candidate for the job, having visited India four times and being on friendly terms with the Amir of Afghanistan, who was then negotiating terms regarding the borderline between his kingdom and British India.

The first three years of Irene's life were spent in England, in a world of privilege. During dinner, powdered footmen in liveries stood behind chairs, during which ten courses were served, and in times of illness the pavement outside was covered in straw to muffle the noise of pedestrians, and a red carpet was put down if a ball was being held. In 1898 a second daughter was born, Cynthia Blanche, known as Cimmie, and Curzon was tasked with finding a wet nurse for the children. His preoccupation with the children's upbringing and overseeing of the hiring of servants, a responsibility that usually fell to women, was the result of his own childhood at the hands of an abusive nanny, who beat him and made him walk through the village wearing a cone hat with the words 'liar, sneak, and coward' written on it. Thus, for Irene and Cimmie, he engaged a nurse whom he thought scientific and practical in her approach to childrearing.

In December 1898 Irene sailed on the *Arabia* en route to Bombay to join her father in Calcutta, where he began his reign as Viceroy of India in January 1899. At their new home, Government House, there were 600 servants, and a further 400 at the viceregal lodges in Simla and Barrackpore. It was a golden age for the family, as India was the jewel in the British Imperial crown, and upon Curzon's departure for Calcutta, Queen Victoria had only one request: to treat the Indians well, but to preserve Britain's power. Every Thursday there were dinner parties held for 120 guests, a display of wealth that contrasted with the Indian famine of 1899–90, which claimed the lives of millions and encouraged militants to arm themselves against colonial rule. The administration reforms Curzon enforced were equally unpopular, namely within the education system and police service – the latter an attempt to stifle growing nationalism – and the costly restoration of the Taj Mahal under his Ancient Monuments Preservation Act of 1904. In 1905 he presided over the partition of Bengal, which proved an unsuccessful venture and resulted in his resignation.

Sheltered from the ebb and flow of Curzon's popularity, Irene and Cimmie's lives revolved around the nursery, where they were spoilt by the servants. A third child, Alexandra Naldera, was born in 1904 and named after her godmother, Queen Alexandra, but the servants nicknamed her 'Baba'. The children often left for London with their mother whilst Curzon remained in India, the lengthy voyage taking a month and sometimes longer depending on the weather. In London, they resided at their home at 1 Carlton House Terrace. They stayed for six months at a time, allowing Mary to resume her social life. Her place in the hierarchy had been established on Indian soil when she hosted the Coronation Durbar, in Delhi, to proclaim King Edward VII and Queen Alexandra as Emperor and Empress of India. It was the end of a golden age, for in 1906 Curzon and the children were dealt a bitter blow when Mary suffered a heart attack and died.

Following Mary's death, Irene and her sisters moved to Hackwood Park, a large eighteenth-century house, close to Basingstoke, surrounded by an ornamental woodland. A rarity in Edwardian Society was Curzon's attentiveness to his three motherless daughters, though far from affectionate he was fixated with their clothing, education, and health. Irene thought it controlling, and she resented his obsessive nature and the self-indulgent manner in which he publicly mourned Mary. It was an interesting observation, for Irene was also an emotional being and as her sisters aged she managed their lives and attempted to solve their problems. In the present time, however, she found it farcical, for Curzon barely tolerated Mary's mother and he resented his two sisters-in-law marrying into the English gentry. He had once forbidden Irene from going to New York with Nancy Astor to meet her maternal grandmother, who did not challenge his behaviour as she feared the children would be kept from her during her visits to England.[5]

As Irene grew older her father regarded her with a detached interest. He thought his daughters troublesome, a feeling that was mutual. Given that she was 10 years old when her mother died, perhaps Irene failed to understand Curzon's grief, for he considered Mary's death the worst experience of his life. If she had any sympathetic feelings for her father they were overshadowed by criticism, for she thought it hypocritical that he had affairs with married women when he claimed to abhor adultery and promiscuity in others. His feelings were mostly directed to the lower classes, and when he discovered a servant had spent the night with a footman he 'put the wretched little slut out in the street at a moment's notice'.[6] His mistress was Elinor Glyn who was married to Clayton Louis Glyn, and was a famed novelist whose book *Three Weeks* created a flurry of scandal when published in 1907. It was an arrangement that lasted for years and the two were socially accepted as a couple, with Curzon and Elinor living together with their respective children during the holidays. Surprisingly, given Irene's feelings for Curzon, she loved Elinor and thought of her as a stepmother.

Throughout Irene's childhood she was unaware that she was an heiress and that Mary had bequeathed to each of her daughters an annual income of £10,000. They were made wards of the court and once a year Curzon was summoned before a judge to justify his spending of their money, which he had access to until they turned 21. He explained it contributed to keeping a roof over their heads and to maintaining the lifestyle they had known when their mother was alive and during his years as the Viceroy of India. It drew criticism from his mother-in-law, as Mary had bequeathed to him an annuity of £4,000 and she resented his spending the family money when he treated her with disdain and only tolerated her visits to Hackwood.[7] But money was the last thing on Irene's mind and at the age of 12 she began her interest in hunting, and rode with the Tyne and the Garth packs. Her first accolade of the season was the fox's brush and at the end of the season she was given the mask, instilling in her a love of hunting and the thrill of the chase. There were also interesting guests coming to visit or to stay, and Hackwood was brought to life by Elisabeth, Queen of the Belgians, and her three young children who lodged there during the First World War. The arrival of the royal children began a rivalry, for Prince Charles gave Baba's dog a kick and Princess Marie José pulled its tail. In retaliation Cimmie threw a photograph of their cousin, Kaiser Wilhelm, on the floor and invited them to trample on 'this grandson of Queen Victoria'.[8]

In 1913, Irene came out as a debutante and Curzon marked the occasion by hosting a ball at Carlton House Terrace. The rooms were filled with flowers, and he hired three grand pianos and Casano's band of twenty musicians to provide the entertainment. Amongst the 400 guests were the Devonshires, Sutherlands, Rutlands, and Marlboroughs. King Edward and Queen Alexandra were absent from the ball, owing to the death of their brother-in-law, the Duke of Argyll, but that afternoon they had tea with Irene and Curzon. As with many debutantes who were launched on the eve of the First World War, Irene's suitors would be killed on the battlefields. This, combined with Curzon's determination to control not only her company but the guests who had been invited (all friends of his and thus older), hindered her chances of becoming engaged. Perhaps this boded well for Curzon, for whilst she remained under his roof he could spend her inheritance as he pleased. He had also decided to remarry, though not to Elinor Glyn, whom he abandoned after she became widowed and was therefore available to marry. Instead he proposed marriage to Grace Duggan, a rich American widow and mother of three children, who accepted his offer. Irene had also received a marriage proposal, her first, from Guy Benson, the son of a merchant banker, and she immediately agreed. As a sign of his affection he kissed her on the forehead and said, 'You are a brick, old thing!' This, she decided, was an unromantic gesture which did not live up to her expectations and she broke off the engagement. In a letter to Nancy Astor, Curzon wrote, 'Such a woman deserves the best and some day she may attain it.'[9]

With Curzon preoccupied with his new wife and ambition to have a son and heir, Irene took the opportunity to exert her independence. She began with a plan as to how to spend her inheritance, which Curzon objected to without providing an explanation. Thinking him unreasonable she explained she was not running away or trying to hurt him, she was merely planning for the future when her money would be her own. He accused her of neglecting him and of being an ungrateful daughter, and when this failed he locked himself in his bedroom and sobbed until worn out. It was a gesture she barely minded, for she was accustomed to his manipulation techniques and continued to build a life around hunting at Melton Mowbray and her social affairs in London. The latter was a distraction from life at Hackwood, where there was a tense atmosphere following Grace's several miscarriages and where Curzon's attention was focused on his stepchildren, and neglecting his own. Furthermore Curzon claimed his daughters had created a secret world to alienate him, and Irene blamed him and Grace for causing her 'untold misery' which forced her to seek happiness elsewhere.

The fulfilment Irene sought was found in voluntary work, a lifelong commitment which began in 1916 when she lectured and sang for the boys at the Broad Street Club, to whom she gave a billiard table. She became a patron of the YMCA in London and visited its establishment for British servicemen in France, where she set about improving the conditions by purchasing armchairs, tables, a gramophone and records.[10] As she was not yet in charge of her inheritance, she had to ask Curzon to send her £50 to buy the club their amenities, and she doubted he would for he lacked a charitable spirit. Her time in France offered her a life away from Curzon, and the responsibilities she felt toward Cimmie and Baba were transferred on to the recipients of her charity work. It was marred only by periods of hospitalisation, for she contracted the Spanish 'Flu, jaundice and internal inflammation.

In the New Year of 1917 Irene came of age and would soon inherit her Leiter trust fund. However, Curzon, a man of expensive tastes, wrote and suggested she pay a percentage of it into his bank account, for it would contribute toward the upkeep of his properties and therefore keep a roof over Cimmie and Baba's heads. But Irene did not agree with his proposal and consulted with the family's lawyers, Humbert and Taylor. They dismissed Curzon, for Irene had since moved out of Hackwood and was living with friends, and was therefore not benefiting from the homes he wished her to maintain. Her absence had encouraged Curzon to become more possessive than before, and he scoured the gossip columns for mentions of her name and was quick to react if she had been associated with a young man. Sensing this was a step too far, she wrote to her father and explained she wanted to 'relieve' him of 'all further responsibility' and asked that he surrender his control of her finances, and that she would pay her own taxes, and to make an arrangement with the bank for her share of maintaining Hackwood, which would give her the right to enter the house.

This marked a period of transition for Irene, for although she succeeded in retrieving her money from Curzon she knew her father was a resentful man and eventually he would sever ties with his eldest daughter. Curzon was losing control of his children, for Cimmie had recently become engaged to Oswald Mosley, a maverick politician then allied with the Conservative Party, a war hero, and the son of a penniless baronet. It worried Curzon, and with good reason too, for he sensed Mosley was attracted by Cimmie's fortune and would break her heart. In time his estimation proved correct, but Cimmie ignored her father's advice and married Mosley on 11 May 1920. Irene was ecstatic, Baba more so – at the age of 16 she was passionately in love with her new brother-in-law, and Mosley did little to discourage her. He also began a lengthy affair with Grace, and once seduced Irene after a day's hunting at Melton Mowbray, which she regretted, though Cimmie remained oblivious of their betrayal. She also missed her father, for whilst their relationship had never been easy, there was an element of control that she often used to her benefit when discouraging men whose interests she could not stifle. Ronald Storrs, the governor of Jerusalem and Judea, was such a man she hoped to forget, for whilst he was 40 years old, he overlooked their age difference and proposed to her several times. It was her political upbringing that had attracted him, as he believed she would make a good wife to a governor or ambassador, and could advance his career. Those were the vital elements that Curzon had looked for in a wife, and although Irene had been brought up to believe such things were attractive in a woman, she found Storrs a forceful character and refrained from giving him a direct answer. Writing to Curzon she asked for his advice and, owing to his embittered feelings, he refused to communicate directly with Irene, and instead used Baba as a channel to convey his messages. He said he thought Storrs had no social manners, and that she ought to refuse him. However it had taken several weeks for Curzon's letter to reach Irene and during that time she came to a decision: she thought Storrs was repulsive, and therefore declined his proposal.

The letter from Curzon, as detached as it was, inspired Irene to restore their relationship. Unfortunately, it was too late, for in the New Year of 1925 she received word that her father's bladder had haemorrhaged and, following an operation, he developed a congested right lung, and was not expected to live. She had been in bed with influenza and a temperature of 102, but she got up and motored to Carlton House Terrace. However, Curzon refused to see her and a footman turned her away. Shattered by the rejection, she went to the Carlton Hotel and remained in bed for two days. In her diary she did not mention his death, on 10 March 1925, and instead wrote that her beloved dog had been sent to the kennels. She was to suffer another blow when Curzon's will was read and Grace was the sole beneficiary of his homes and money, and Mary's jewellery. To his daughters he bequeathed Mary's clothes, which had been carefully stored since her death, and Irene inherited his barony of Ravensdale, which unlike his earldom, could be passed through his female descendants.

There were more similarities between Irene and Curzon than she cared to admit, for like her father she was overly emotional and promiscuous – the two qualities she detested in others. His death coincided with a difficult time, and she turned to God, as she did many times in her life, despite her actions being anything but pious.

At Melton Mowbray she fell in love with Gordon Leith, a handsome investment banker and a married man, but sensing their affair had gone too far she left England for a lengthy period of travel. She went to India, to visit Baba and her new husband, Edward Dudley 'Fruity' Metcalfe, and on to Los Angeles to stay with Elinor Glyn, who was working as a scriptwriter in Hollywood, and whilst there was introduced to the reigning stars of the day and had her teeth crowned and capped. The tangled lives of the stars distracted her from her problems with Leith and she found herself in the familiar role of confidante: Charlie Chaplin confided that his marriage to Lita Grey was coming to an end. Bea Lillie expressed her disappointment when John Gilbert jilted her, and Irene watched as Pola Negri wailed during Rudolph Valentino's funeral. A year later she returned to London and was met by Leith at Claridge's, where she had taken a suite. They did little to conceal their affair, though she must have felt conspicuous about his presence at the hotel, for she bought a house at 3 Deanery Street, off Park Lane, in Mayfair, with plenty of room for her servants and space for her dog, Winks, to run free. The commitment from Irene was too great and Leith returned to his wife, a beautiful woman nicknamed Cuckoo, despite having promised Irene they would marry.

After the affair with Leith came to an end, Irene fell for Bobby Digby, who left her for Jean Norton, the mistress of Lord Beaverbrook. He had treated her badly, and in her diary she wrote he 'made her cry and said [her] determined spirit broke any man'.[10] Hoping for a distraction, Irene threw herself into the hunting season but it was interrupted by a hard frost and an outbreak of foot and mouth disease. During her time away from the hunting fields she began an affair with Flash Kellett, which ended when his wife, Myrtle, a mistress of the Prince of Wales, demanded they stop seeing one another. She then reconciled with Leith and they went to Paris for a week before joining Cimmie and Mosley at their villa in Antibes, in the south of France. It was a disastrous holiday: Cimmie and Mosley argued for the duration. Irene confided in them her dilemma about Leith, and Mosley said he found her religious beliefs overbearing and thought her emotionally unstable. Aside from their drunken encounter after a long day's hunting, Mosley had never found Irene attractive.

A lonely Christmas spent without her family encouraged Irene to pursue another affair. She began a romance with Arthur Rubinstein, a classical pianist she had known for years, as during her debutante season he had professed his love for her and she had rebuffed him. However, Leith continued to dominate Irene's thoughts, and torn apart by her moral outlook and of her love for him, a friend advised her to seek counsel from Mosley. This she did, and Mosley approached Leith and asked if he intended to marry Irene. 'Afraid not, old boy,' was his answer. Baba delivered the news, and Irene vowed never to see him again. Deeply unhappy, she lost vast sums of money playing bridge and attended parties every evening, which ended with heavy drinking and louche behaviour. It conspired to make her feel foolish, and she focused her heartbreak on Rubinstein, with whom she decided she was 'half in love'. Surprisingly, given her support of Cimmie and all she had gone through with Mosley, she found a critic in her younger sister. Cimmie advised Irene to find a husband before it was too late, and in her present emotional state the words hurt her deeply. She came to realise that all the men she loved were unattainable to her, and that, unlike her sisters, the chance of motherhood was passing her by.

Regardless of Irene's unhappiness she remained devoted to Cimmie and supported her through her latest marital crisis. Mosley had begun an affair with Diana Guinness (*née* Mitford), the twenty-three-year-old wife of Bryan Guinness, of the Irish brewery family. Although mistresses were a common theme in his marriage to Cimmie, before Diana he had never been in love with them and they were never a threat. Irene was furious on Cimmie's behalf, as the recent birth of her third child had left her weakened and prone to illness. Perhaps Irene was jealous that Diana had the courage to pursue the man she desired, regardless of his wife. She had, after all, wanted Gordon Leith to leave his wife for her. However, Cimmie thought leaving Mosley too great a price to pay, for she was devoted to his political ideologies. He also encouraged Cimmie's political ambitions and was proud when she campaigned for him. In 1929 she was elected a Labour Member of Parliament for Stoke-on-Trent, which took a toll on her health and was believed to have caused a miscarriage. In 1926 Mosley, emboldened by Cimmie's support, had denounced the Conservative Party by 'crossing the floor' and standing for Labour, and then in 1931 he founded the New Party, which failed but set the foundation for his British Union of Fascists (BUF), which followed in 1932.

Irene attempted to oust Diana in Mosley's affections by taking an interest in the BUF, though she did not hold fascist views, and it was done out of loyalty to Cimmie. She was also alarmed by the news that Baba was also having an affair with Mosley, to which Cimmie remained oblivious. Whilst her sisters' marriages were in trouble, Irene's own life was in turmoil; she continued to see Arthur Rubinstein, despite his aloof treatment of her, and she was drinking too much. Then came the devastating blow to her pride, when Rubinstein announced he was marrying Nela Młynarska, a Polish ballerina half his age. Irene gave him a wedding present of green candlesticks from Fortnum and Mason, and doubted he would go through with the marriage, as she thought he enjoyed a life without commitment. This was true, for on the afternoon of his wedding he slept with Irene as an experiment to see if he felt trapped by marriage. Afterwards Rubinstein confessed to Nela, who dismissed Irene as 'biggish, handsome, and sort of manly'.

The realisation that Irene had been a pawn in Rubinstein's game and had been passed over yet again saw her turn to alcohol. Cimmie and Baba intervened and forced her to see Dr Ironside, a doctor who specialised in treating addiction. However she refused to enter a nursing home and instead went to the countryside, where she abstained from alcohol and succeeded in overcoming her addiction. She also fell in love. The latest man in her life was Miles Graham, a handsome divorcee with two children, who courted society women in an attempt to further his political career. He was also renowned for his womanising and for having a volatile temper, as he had once chased an acquaintance with a knife. When he proposed to Irene she accepted and the two spoke of having children of their own, an ambition of hers. Baba resented Irene's newfound happiness, as she depended on her sister to care for her children whilst she carried out her own love affairs. Reacting furiously to Baba's reaction, Irene wrote to Cimmie to say she did not want her youngest sister at the wedding. The letter was delivered to Cimmie, who was at the London Clinic convalescing from an appendectomy and she discarded it to her bedside table, where Baba read it. Within days

Cimmie would be dead from peritonitis, and Baba and Mosley presided at her bedside, with Irene banished to the waiting room whilst she took her last breath.

Following the death of Cimmie on 16 May 1933, Irene's first instinct was to blame Diana, for she had caused her sister untold misery. She also resented Baba and her long affair with Mosley, as each woman had taken him from Cimmie. Surprisingly, or not, Irene and Baba found common ground in their hatred of Diana, and they reunited for the sake of Cimmie's three children: Nicholas, Vivien, and Michael. Miles Graham remained on the scene, and his roving eye was caught by Baba: he suggested to Irene that she ought to imitate her sister's style. He also asked Baba to take charge of Irene's wedding trousseau, and they bought lingerie from Fortnum and Mason, and a wedding ring from Cartier. However during a walk in the woods Miles confessed he was in love with another woman, and Irene fled before saying another word.

Irene concealed her unhappiness by becoming a surrogate mother to the three Mosley children. The youngest, Micky, a baby when Cimmie died, thought of Irene as his natural mother and she showed him photographs of her sister so he would not forget her. She also played poker with the older children, who called her Aunt Ni, and asked their opinions of Diana, or Mrs Guinness, as they called her. 12-year-old Vivien held the same view as Irene, and she accused Diana of killing her mother, or at least contributing to her untimely death. Not only had Mosley shirked his parental responsibilities but Baba had also entrusted her three children to Irene, who resented how she was treated 'as a sort of governess' with 'no thanks, no love'.[11] She was also entangled in Baba and Mosley's affair, which prompted him to tell Diana that they could not see one another for some time, as he was mourning Cimmie. It was a difficult arrangement for Irene to accept, but for the sake of keeping Mosley away from Diana she encouraged Baba's pursuit of him. Eventually he returned to Diana, who had recently divorced Bryan Guinness, and fearing they would marry, Irene ordered Baba to accompany him on a motoring holiday to France. In his absence, Irene spoke to Mosley's mother, a formidable woman known as Ma, and was discouraged when she placed the onus on Diana and called her a 'determined minx'. Although Irene agreed with her sentiment, she knew Mosley was not without fault, and was surprised when Ma wept and said Cimmie had died to save his soul.

The love triangle between Mosley, Baba and Diana was influenced by something deeper than love, for he was simultaneously using the two women to further his British Union of Fascists. Baba served as a go-between for himself and Dino Grandi, Benito Mussolini's Italian Ambassador to England, and she became known as 'Baba Blackshirt', as Mosley's men wore black shirts as part of their paramilitary uniform. Diana also proved useful, for her younger sister was on friendly terms with Adolf Hitler and several high-ranking Nazis. This was of particular importance, for when Mosley's aristocratic benefactors abandoned the BUF, he used Diana to appeal to Hitler for financial support. In recent years, however, he had lost support from Irene, as she distanced herself when the party's manifesto moved away from restoring Britain's industry and solving the economic depression of the late 1920s and early '30s, to attacking Jews both verbally and physically. Her main objective was to care for Cimmie's children and to protect them from the influence of Mosley, for she feared he would corrupt their innocence. The children went to live with Irene. Mosley did not object, as whilst they were under 21 he controlled the trust funds they had inherited from Cimmie, and used the money to fund the BUF.

Once again Irene found solace in voluntary work, which became the mainstay of her life. She was the first woman to give a speech at the annual gala in commemoration of the Magna Carta at Runnymede, and she was the first Caucasian woman to attend the Emperor of Abyssinia's (now Ethiopia) coronation in 1930. However, the charitable causes she was most devoted to were the founding of youth clubs in the East End, the Highway Club, and the Boys and Girls Club. One night a week she travelled by tube train to the clubs, and once a year she took the children on holidays to the English seaside and across the Channel to France. She was also involved with the Shilling Theatre Company, which made plays accessible to the poor. Tickets cost 1s 3d, which covered the entertainment tax, and Irene subsidised the running of the company as well as the venues where the plays were performed. Another cause which she championed was women's rights, especially amongst the poor and sex workers of the East End, perhaps a reaction to her upbringing, as Curzon was president of the National League for Opposing Women's Suffrage. As a remedy to the women who had to work to support their families, Irene and Baba founded the Cynthia Mosley Day Nursery, in Lambeth. Of her charity work, the press wrote:

> No woman ever carried a title more justly, more nobly. She is first, last and always, a woman – sympathetic, divinely intuitive, intelligent, utterly charming. To meet her is to recognise one's superior in every degree of living. Her name would not be complete without a title before it. [12]

The happiness Irene found with the children and her charity work was overshadowed by difficulties in her private life. Her beloved dog, Winks, at the age of 15 had come to the end of his lifespan, and having treated him like a child, she was distraught. She wrote in her diary, 'My love lay with his paws and head dozing on my lap and he looked up at me and pressed his wet nose up against me and I kissed him goodbye.'[13] There was also a new admirer in her life, Nevile Henderson, who was head of the mission in Belgrade and soon-to-be British ambassador to Nazi Germany. Although he was kind and attentive and, more importantly, not married, Irene thought him slow and boring, and she attacked those qualities. The only remedy to such problems was a three-month cruise to the Americas, followed by the Far East. When she reached Colombo, a letter from Baba was waiting with the news that Mosley had invited Diana to stay at Savehay Farm, the home he had shared with Cimmie. She also received word that her Shilling Theatre Company had folded. And Nevile had written to say he had made up his mind and that she would not be a suitable wife. The letter from Nevile did little to stir Irene, and she felt relieved. However, the thought of the children staying under the same roof as Diana troubled her and she ended her cruise in Monte Carlo and returned to England. The homecoming was timely, as Irene worried about the children's future and the freedom with which Mosley spent their money. Consulting with her lawyer, she proposed to oversee the distribution of the children's money, as it would prevent Mosley from having access to it. Diana had recently begun to bring her two sons, Jonathan and Desmond Guinness, with her to Savehay

Farm. To Irene it was reminiscent of Curzon and Grace, and she feared Mosley planned to spend the children's money on his mistress and her children. She was further troubled by the rumour told to her by the nanny that Mosley had spoken of hiring a governess to care for the Mosley and Guinness children, which would remove Irene from the picture.

During this period Irene accepted an invitation from the German government to attend the 1936 Olympic Games in Berlin. Given her stance on Mosley and the BUF, she initially declined and later wrote in her memoirs, 'I did not want to be the guest of the German Government.' When she learned that many distinguished guests were attending the games, she agreed to go. Baba would also be there, along with Diana, though not together, and Irene observed a different Germany than that of Mosley's two mistresses. Flying alone to Nuremberg she was met by one of Hitler's henchmen and taken to the hall of the National Hotel, where she was overwhelmed by the crowds of Blackshirts (the BUF), Brownshirts (Nazis), and army generals, naval officers, and press. Unlike many of her fellow Britons she could speak German and therefore understood every word of Hitler's menacing speeches. When she met him, after one of his rallies, she felt his cold, dark eyes piercing through her soul and she recoiled when he kissed her hand. She critiqued his appearance, and advised him to wear hair-cream as it would tame an errant strand that fell over his brow. Despite the supposed Nazi hospitality, enjoyed by so many who would later denounce their association with Hitler, the meeting had left her cold. This was confirmed at a dinner given for the head of all sports and physical training in Germany, during which elderly women in white coats distributed packets of sausages. Irene turned to the healthy young SS man next to her and scolded him for not doing the job, and claimed that Nazis only used their womenfolk for breeding and housekeeping. Disgusted by all she had witnessed, she abruptly ended her German trip and went home.

Her political insight into Nazi Germany had further tainted Irene's view of Mosley and his BUF, and more than ever she did her best to keep the children from his political life. It was a decision inspired by the recent decline in his popularity, the result of a series of rallies which had ended in violent brawls, particularly the clash of the Blackshirts and

Communist supporters at the Olympia, and the ill-advised march down Cable Street, after which the wearing of the BUF uniform had become illegal. She was also unaware that Mosley and Diana had leased Wootton Lodge, in Staffordshire, and were co-habiting. There had been rumours of their living together but each time Irene approached Mosley for clarification, he dismissed it as gossip. She remained oblivious when they were secretly married in October 1936, in the presence of Hitler, Unity Mitford, and Joseph and Magda Goebbels, at the Goebbels' Berlin home. Hitler had offered to keep the marriage certificate, a ploy to escape press attention, and the newly-weds returned to England. The news was revealed after the birth of their son, Alexander, two years later.

The news of the marriage had, ironically, brought out the best in Irene, in contrast to Baba who reacted hysterically. She wrote to Mosley and asked to meet with him, and when they spoke she sensed he was embarrassed by the secrecy and how his family had learned of it from a newspaper announcement. Such empathetic feelings were the reason she agreed to his request to meet with Diana. Since learning of Mosley's affair with Diana, Irene was driven by hatred for her, despite having never spoken to her, and only observing her from afar. It was a feeling inspired by her loyalty to Cimmie, as she could not forget the despair the affair had caused her. Therefore it was hardly surprising when Irene failed to understand the affair from Diana's perspective, nor did she look for any redeeming qualities.

When Irene met Diana on Box Day, in 1938, she was struck not by her fabled beauty but her voice, which she thought affected. She privately criticised the setting, and how the windows, which were barely opened, made her feel suffocated. Furthermore she thought the slices of bread and butter and Christmas cake accompanying the afternoon tea were pathetic. She was also offended by a framed photograph of Hitler and longed to 'smash it into atoms'. But the sight of Diana and Mosley's newborn son warmed her heart and she considered him big and advanced for his age. When Diana's mother, Lady Redesdale, joined them, Irene wondered 'how that battered washed-out woman could have produced those six hooligan girls'. It was an observation influenced by the strange, domestic scene playing out before her eyes: Mosley and Diana, the new baby, a nursemaid, and the visiting mother-in-law.

For a brief period, Irene and the children accepted they were no longer part of Mosley's life. The youngest child, Micky, remarked that he was not his father's youngest son and it sent a pang to Irene's heart. During that time Vivien had come out as a debutante, and Irene gave her a ball and observed it from a bath-chair, as she had recently injured herself in a hunting accident. It provoked the usual arguments with Baba, about who would manage the season and, being unmarried, it fell to Baba to present Vivien at Court. The parties during the season of 1939 were a distraction from the threat of war, though Irene, who maintained a friendship with Nevile Henderson, spoke earnestly on the subject and she knew it was a reality. She realised Mosley's latest pacifist campaign was unwise, for his past involvement with Fascism and association with Hitler played a part in leading Britain to war with Germany.

In 1940, a year after the Second World War was declared, Irene bore the consequences of Mosley's actions. He was arrested under Regulation 18B, a law enforced by Winston Churchill permitting those suspected of being a threat to the war effort to be imprisoned without trial. Although Diana frequently visited Germany, Mosley had made his own pre-war visits to secure loans from Hitler for the BUF, and to discuss an idea of collaborating on a radio station to advertise German household products with a percentage of the revenue funding his party. However, war put an end to the idea. Months later Diana, who had recently given birth to their second child, was also arrested, and imprisoned at Holloway. The children were Irene's concern, as was their family home, Savehay Farm, where Mosley and Diana had lived before their imprisonment. She learned that the War Office intended to rent the property and as a precaution she removed Diana's jewellery to her home. Then she approached Mosley with an offer to pay for its upkeep, for the benefit of the children. It was a suggestion that troubled him. Since he was still entitled to a share of the children's inheritance, which paid for the home, he sensed Irene was trying to oust him. He then threatened to remove Micky from her care and entrust him to Baba, a move he predicted would scare her. Instead, Irene, accompanied by her lawyer, visited Mosley at Brixton Prison and asked for guardianship of the children. Declining her proposal at first, he relented and offered her Vivien, but not the two boys. A judge later ruled in her favour and appointed her their legal guardian.

With Mosley and Diana imprisoned and the fate of the children settled, Irene turned her attention to the war effort. She worked at the Cynthia Mosley Day Nursery in Lambeth, and was appalled by the poor appearance of the child evacuees leaving East London. 'What is really shameful is that our system has allowed such creatures to grow up,' she wrote in a letter to *The Times*, and pleaded with the government to prevent their parents from taking them back to their squalid conditions. She passed her days attending committee meetings and giving speeches to the Federal Union Club, the Sisterhood in Lees Hall, and the Canning Town Settlement, where she spoke on behalf of the Responsibility Movement – which was founded to encourage a duty of responsibility within all Britons. The war also brought Irene and Baba together, and they shared a suite at the Dorchester Hotel, said to be the safest building in London due to its concrete and steel infrastructure. During the nightly air raids Irene and her friends established a 'sleeping colony' amongst the Turkish baths in the basement of the hotel. Her own home was being used to shelter victims of the bombings, where they were provided with mattresses, candles and food, and she gave away her clothes to maids at the hotel, a decision she regretted after rationing was introduced.

Although Irene's war work occupied much of her time she felt increasingly lonely and isolated, as Nicky was serving in Italy with the Rifle Brigade and Vivien was working in a factory. A proposal from an old friend, Victor Cazalet, did little to raise her spirits and she rejected him; he continued to propose several times throughout the war but her answer remained the same. She often wondered if she had made a mistake after his death in a plane crash and she fell into a deep depression and turned to alcohol. Baba called her a failure and forced her to address her alcoholism, and in turn she promised to give up drinking for Lent, but this lasted only momentarily. An argument ensued and after a heated exchange Baba slapped Irene across the face, signalling a bitter feud which only ended once she agreed to enter a clinic to treat her addiction. However the sisterly bond was never entirely restored, for as the years advanced Irene became increasingly neurotic and resorted to talking to psychiatrists.

The postwar years saw a change in Irene's private life, and with the children grown up, she turned to sherry. Although she never overcame her alcoholism, she refrained from appearing drunk when in public, and continued to work with her youth clubs and various charities. In 1953 her memoirs *Many Rhythms* were published by Weidenfield & Nicolson, but Mosley sued on the grounds of libel and the book was withdrawn. 'Well done him, a big loss for the publishers,'[14] Diana wrote to her sister. In 1958, Irene was created a life peeress for her work dedicated to youth clubs, and taking her seat as one of four women admitted to the House of Lords, she dedicated her speech to the discrimination against East End prostitutes. Shocking the bemused men, she said, 'They will charge a fiver, your lordships will forgive me for being so sordid and vulgar, for a long spell and £1 for a quick bash.' For the rest of her life, until her death in 1966, Irene remained devoted to public service and spoke on behalf of those whose voices were seldom heard. It was a triumph that she was able to do either, as Curzon had never wanted his daughter to be anything but decorative and subservient. But Irene often rose above such prejudices. Her obituary in *The Times* spoke of her being a 'tower of strength … in everything she did she was passionately involved'.

Rosemary and Mariga, Japan, 1936. (By kind permission of Patrick Guinness)

Rosemary Blackadder, before her marriage to Prince Albrecht von Urach. (By kind permission of Patrick Guinness)

Rose Bryson, Mariga, and Professor Huxley picnicking in the Glens of Antrim. (By kind permission of the Bryson family)

A Georgian cricket match, Furness, 1963. (By kind permission of the Bryson family)

A turf cutting picnic at Sallagh Braes. L–R: Corinna Huxley, Huxley au pair, unknown child, George Huxley, Mariga, Lady Huxley, Harriet Huxley, unknown child, Hugh O'Neill (Lord Rathcavan), unknown adult. (By kind permission of the Huxley family)

A painting of Mariga by Derek Hill, © The Derek Hill Foundation. (By kind permission of Lord Gowrie)

Enid and Valentine Kenmare, Brompton Oratory, 1943.

Sylvia Ashley, around the time of her marriage to Douglas Fairbanks.

The Rajah and Ranee of Sarawak with their daughters, Leonora, Valerie, and Elizabeth.

Sylvia Brooke in traditional Malay dress.

Irene on board the Arabia en route to India, Christmas Day 1898. (British Library: India Office Records and Private Papers. Photo 430/75/18, Qatar Digital Library)

Christmas, Aden, 1898. L–R: Lord Suffolk (Henry Howard, 19th Earl of Suffolk, ADC to the Resident at Aden), Mr Meade, Mr Lawrence, Capt. Marker, Lord Curzon (Resident at Aden), [Charles Alexander Cunningham or Sir Garrett O'Moore Creagh], Mary Curzon. (British Library: India Office Records and Private Papers. Photo 430/75/17, Qatar Digital Library)

Irene with the children from her Highway Club.

Irene in Hollywood with Charlie Chaplin.

Jean Massereene,
c. 1912.

Diana Skeffington, taken shortly before her
death in 1930.

Members of the local Ulster Volunteer Force during Sir Edward Carson's review of the South Antrim UVF in April 1914. On the far right is Lord Massereene, wearing his Boer War decorations, including the DSO.

Ardanaiseig House.

A gathering at Antrim Castle for Sir Edward Carson's visit, Easter 1914.

The Massereenes at the funeral of Diana Skeffington, November 1930.

Lord Massereene on the golf links of Massereene Golf Club, c. 1920s.

The Massereenes inspecting Diana's grave, Antrim Castle Gardens, November 1930.

8

THE GIRL WHO BECAME MUV:
SYDNEY REDESDALE

The legacy of Sydney Redesdale was embedded in her six daughters, who were each unlike the other: Nancy, a novelist; Pamela, a countrywoman; Diana, a fascist sympathiser; Unity, a friend of Adolf Hitler; Jessica, a communist; and Debo, the Duchess of Devonshire. 'The house rests upon the mother,' an old Eastern proverb attests, but Sydney was a woman whose chief interests were housekeeping and poultry, and whose temperament was described as vague. Her daughters' lives encapsulated the great events of the twentieth century and it was through that lens that many historians viewed the interwar period and beyond. But what of Sydney?

Born Sydney Bowles in May 1880, she was named after her paternal aunt, Sydney Milner-Gibson, who, shortly before her namesake's birth, had succumbed to typhoid. Thus a foreboding sense of sadness had already attached itself to her childhood. Her mother, Jessica (*née* Evans-Gordon), had little tolerance for childrearing, and she viewed her children as competitors for her husband, Tap's, love. Like women of her era she dreaded the certain fate of many pregnancies and long periods of confinement, and was often laid aside by illness and exhaustion. Perhaps Jessica's lack of physical strength had contributed to a doctor convincing her that an abortion was necessary to prevent a life-threatening fifth pregnancy, then advancing in its fourth month. The operation proved fatal, for Tap turned the doctor out of the house and Jessica died a few days later, whether from haemorrhaging or an infection remains unclear. Sydney was 7-years-old, and she recalled being sent to see her father, as the presence of his children often cheered him, but on this occasion he dismissed her from the room. Consumed by grief and guilt, it was left to him to raise his four motherless children.

Although sadness was a significant element of Sydney's childhood, her life was also marred by the social stigma of her father's background, as he had begun life as an outcast. Thomas Gibson Bowles, known as Tap, was the illegitimate son of Thomas Milner-Gibson, a Liberal politician and social reformer, and Susannah Bowles, a servant employed in his household. The exact date of his birth was unknown, but he was born some time in 1841 in a crowded house in Whitechapel, which, according to the census, had thirteen residents. When Tap was three he was taken to live with his father, who had a London residence at 48 Eaton Square, and a country manor in Surrey. It remains unclear why Susannah gave up her infant son, except, perhaps, she thought Milner-Gibson in a better position to raise him. There was also the fact that Tap was Milner-Gibson's only surviving son, as two children, a boy and a girl, had died years before his birth, although he had a surviving daughter at the time and five more children would be born throughout the years. Though, as with many prominent men, he could have denied Tap his birthright. Following Susannah's arrangement with him, Milner-Gibson bought her a house in Gravesend and provided her with an annuity of £52 10s. A second annuity was settled on Harriet Allen, who also bore him a child. It was also rumoured that Milner-Gibson and Susannah had two more children: a daughter named Jane, and a son named William. However, Jane's middle-name was Stanley, and, according to Tap's great-grandson, Jonathan Guinness, she was either the daughter of the Earl of Derby or Lord Stanley of Alderley.

It was fortunate for Tap that his stepmother, Arethusa Milner-Gibson (*née* Cullum), was sympathetic to her husband's predicament and was willing to raise him as her own. Due to his illegitimacy he was sent to boarding school in France, as no private school in England would accept a boy of his status. Arethusa's sympathy for the boy, born out of wedlock and burdened as such, might have been influenced by her own indiscretions, as she spent lengthy periods in Paris, and was the mistress of Sir George Wombwell, an officer in the Charge of the Light Brigade. 'This is Tom Bowles,' she told her guests. 'Be civil to him or leave the house.'

Sydney thought her father eccentric, a trait that was passed on to his descendants. It was perhaps a quality he learned at his father's house, for his stepmother dabbled in spiritualism and mesmerism, and held a séance for David Dunglas Home, during which it was rumoured that he levitated. She was also a controversial figure in the radical politics of the day, and having spent her early years in Italy she was sympathetic toward Giuseppe Mazzini, an Italian revolutionary who was instrumental in the unification of Italy, and she courted scandal by wearing the tricolour to the opera in Genoa. The literary side of Tap's character, which his granddaughters inherited, was inspired by Arethusa, for her salon hosted the likes of William Makepeace Thackeray, Victor Hugo and Charles Dickens, the last having written his final novel whilst living at her London home. The most significant idiosyncrasy, however, was Tap's mistrust of the medical profession, hardly surprising given the fate of his wife. He also did not believe in illness and believed 'the Good Body would heal itself'. Sydney inherited this idea, for her views on the medical profession were considered unorthodox and her refusal to have her own children vaccinated has been regarded with criticism. Another staple of her childhood was the presence of chickens in the garden of their home, Cleever Lodge, in Knightsbridge. Tap followed the dietary laws of the Old Testament, and never forced his children to eat anything they disliked. Imitating this with her own children, Sydney forbade them to eat 'the dirty pig' and if they complained they were hungry, she said, 'Eat a chocolate bar, it's a meal in itself.'[1] As indulgent as Tap was with his children, there were to be no birthday or Christmas presents, as he believed they ought to be grateful for being fed, clothed and having a roof over their heads.

At the time of Sydney's birth, her father was a rich man, his fortune entirely self-made, with the exception of Milner-Gibson giving him an annuity of £90. His ambition was the product of his upbringing, for although he was afforded an education befitting the son of a gentleman, he would have to make his own way in the world. An introduction made by Milner-Gibson saw him find employment as a junior clerk in the succession duty office at Somerset House, where he worked for five years. He then pursued a career in journalism, writing for his half-sister's theatrical newspaper, *The Glow Worm*, and a column for the *Morning Post*, covering the Siege of Paris in the Franco-Prussian War by use of balloon and carrier pigeon. In 1868 he borrowed £200 to found *Vanity Fair*, a weekly magazine renowned for its caricatures of prominent men, and sold his stake after the death of his wife. In 1885 he founded *The Lady*, a magazine for gentlewomen, and later hired his mistress and the children's former governess, Miss Henrietta Shell, known as Tello, as its editor. Tello had also borne him three illegitimate sons: Humphrey, Oliver, and Peter.

For Sydney, home had many definitions, on land and at sea. After the sale of Cleever Lodge the children were brought to live in a rented country house in Hampshire, where Sydney and her sister, Weenie, were taught by a governess. Her two brothers, George and Geoffrey, were later sent to boarding school. The children stayed in Hampshire until 1888, after which they lived with Tap aboard his 500-ton yacht, the *Nereid*. They boarded the yacht at Southampton, accompanied by Tello, Miss Griffin (Weenie's nurse), and their terrier, Smiler, with their belongings packed in disposable wooden boxes, as there was little space to store trunks. On their maiden voyage they sailed to Dieppe and back to England, heading north to Portsmouth and Cowes, too late for the annual regatta.

The next sailing was to Gibraltar. However, before their departure one of the twenty crew gave notice and they sailed a man short; Miss Griffin also resigned and was replaced by a crewman's sister, Miss Jenny Cable. It was a rough crossing, with Tello and Miss Cable bed-bound with seasickness, and Sydney and Tello suffering the discomfort of a leaking skylight. But they could not report it to Tap, for he expected his yacht to be watertight and such criticism infuriated him. Aside from the water entering the cabin, the issues with the skylight would not have annoyed Sydney, as Tap ordered the nursery windows to be opened six inches all year round, regardless of the weather. The worst part of the voyage, however, was the death of Smiler, who jumped from the dinghy to which he was tethered and strangled himself with the rope. They also ran out of food, so Tap slaughtered a dolphin to supply them with meat. All her life Sydney recalled the rations she faced at sea and would only fill a glass of water halfway. From Gibraltar they went to Algiers and on to Malta, the crossing now calm and allowing for Sydney to join Tap on the top deck to learn the constellations. A tailor came aboard and measured Sydney and Weenie for sailor suits and caps, which became her childhood uniform.

For Sydney the least favourite parts of the voyage were spent in Alexandria and Jerusalem. In Jerusalem she visited the Wailing Wall and was astonished at the emotion displayed by the tourists, and in Alexandria she was sent to a Turkish bath, which she thought dirty, and subsequently caught lice. Fixated with Turkish baths, Tap had once converted an empty dog kennel into one and demanded his butler stand on the roof of the house and hurl buckets of freezing water over him when he emerged. They were offered a respite to their nomadic existence when Tap became reacquainted with a former mistress, Lady Sykes (*née* Christina Cavendish-Bentinck, known as 'Jessie'), and joined her for a cruise down the Nile. The others remained behind on the *Nereid*, which had been anchored in Alexandria. For the first time Sydney fell in love, with an American admiral who gave her a bracelet and made her promise to never remove it, and Tello had an affair with a naval lieutenant who came aboard and serenaded her with 'Queen of My Heart'. When Tap returned, he discovered Tello's infidelity and in a rage he set sail from Alexandria against the advice of the port authorities and ran into a hurricane, which almost shipwrecked them off the coast of Syria. They soon left their vessel and entrusted it to the crew, and sailed home to England on a P&O ferry. In *The Log of the Nereid*, Tap wrote of their voyage and reported on the current affairs of the countries they visited. 'Mr Bowles writes himself "Master-Mariner", and, we doubt not, can sail a yacht to perfection,' wrote the *Spectator*. 'But this does not imply that he is wise in matters beyond his nautical knowledge.'[2]

Having spent nine months at sea, Sydney's next home was to be Wilbury, a Palladian country house in Wiltshire. It was rented from Sir Henry Malet, whom Tap employed at *Vanity Fair*, on the condition that the owner could visit with his wife, Laura, and their daughter, Vera. The Malets soon moved back in and the two families shared the daily expenses, though Tap continued to pay rent. It was an arrangement that lasted for several years, despite Tap and Sydney disliking Lady Malet, who seldom moved from a sofa in the Blue Room and, unhappy in her marriage, often quarrelled with Sir Henry. She was also a spiritualist, a vocation perhaps inspired by the untimely death of her eldest daughter, Dora, and she channelled spirits to operate her hand with a paintbrush. The results were two portraits of leaves and lilies that hung above the doors of the drawing room, which Sydney thought appalling. Tap also disapproved of such supernatural meddling, and he grew tired of Lady Malet's incompetent running of the household and the quick turnover of servants, whom she mistrusted and mistreated. He particularly loathed their loyal butler, Malpas, who liked to stand on one leg and recount his family's history, boasting of a cousin he had in Australia. Sydney shared her father's sentiment, especially toward Vera Malet, who collected amphibians and stalked the dark passages, recounting ghost stories and playing pranks on her mother.

Shortly after their return to England, Sydney was saddened by the disappearance of Tello, who had left without an explanation and changed her last name to Stewart. She was unaware at the time that Tello had conceived a child with the naval lieutenant in Alexandria and therefore Thomas thought it indecent for her to continue as a governess to his daughters. However, Tap continued his affair with Tello, with whom he later had three sons. He bought her a house and employed her as editor of *The Lady*. They never married, despite his being a widower and her bearing his children, for Tap could not accept her eldest son – a hypocritical stance, given his own dubious beginning. Years later Sydney saw Tello on Sloane Street with her four sons, and recognised the eldest as the product of the affair in Alexandria. The other three, Sydney came to learn, were her half-brothers, all of whom were given Tap's name. In the meantime Sydney was aware of her father's other mistress, Lady Sykes, whom she thought wore too much make-up and drank too much booze. Her appraisal of Lady Sykes was perceptive, for she was an ambitious (some would have said vulgar) woman who had entrapped her husband, Sir Tatton Sykes, thirty years her senior, into marriage after he had discovered her stranded and alone, and delivered her to the train station to join her party. Lady Sykes's mother, Prudence, thought it improper that they were not chaperoned and ordered him to marry her daughter at once, or risk social shame.

Sydney's rejection of flamboyance was often demonstrated by the words, 'What a set', a phrase she used when her own daughters grew older and befriended the Bright Young Things. However this aversion was founded in childhood, perhaps the consequence of Tap's regard for the theatre and his failed career as a playwright. As a young man he submitted several of his plays to theatre companies, and they were rejected, with only one, *Marriage by Command*, being performed by an amateur dramatic company in Bristol. He also attracted controversy, namely for the gossip he printed about the Prince of Wales in *Vanity Fair*, and then trying, but failing, to engage the prince in a correspondence. Through his magazines he met writers who were on the brink of celebrity. One such friend was Lewis Carroll, who existed on the fringes of the Bowles's family life and composed puzzles for *The Lady*. Carroll was charmed by the 11-year-old Sydney, whom he had first met at Wilbury, and sent her a copy of the original manuscript of *Alice's Adventures Under Ground*, later published as *Alice's Adventures in Wonderland*. This copy was bound in white cloth and inscribed, 'To Sydney Bowles from the author, May 25 1891'. 'If only I had known of your existing I would have sent you *heaps of love*,'[3] he wrote to her. 'Please give my love, and a kiss, to Weenie and Vera [Malet] and yourself (don't forget the *kiss* to yourself, please: on the forehead is the best place).'[4]

Throughout Sydney's childhood she had been accustomed to distinguished guests coming and going from her father's house, and she was unmoved by celebrity. It was this practicality that Tap admired most and when the family moved to Lowndes Square, in London, he appointed Sydney as his housekeeper. She was by then 14 and used to being viewed as an adult by Tap, for each day they rode together at Rotten Row, and on those outings he treated her as a confidante. The male servants, however, resented taking their orders from her and she struggled to control their drunkenness and insubordination. All her life she maintained a mistrust of male house servants and when she became chatelaine of her own homes she made it a rule to only employ female servants. The move to London coincided with Tap entering parliament, in 1892, as a Conservative MP for King's Lynn, Norfolk. He made a controversial politician, beginning with running his election campaign from aboard his new yacht, the *Hoyden*, which attracted attention as he delivered speeches in a Norfolk dialect. On polling day Sydney and Weenie joined their father in a landau pulled by the local undertaker's horses. In parliament he became renowned for his rousing speeches, which were typed by Sydney, attacking the Liberal government. His theatrical ways were not foreign to those who knew him, for as a young man his elaborate sense of fashion made him a sartorial star in the gossip columns, and he earned praise for his performance in *Romeo and Juliet*. During parliamentary recess Sydney accompanied Tap on the *Hoyden*, sailing to the south of France and the Orient. It was a passage she knew well and it offered her glimpses of other cultures, though she was never drawn to the exotic.

At the age of 14 Sydney met her future husband, David Mitford, the second-born son of Algernon Bertram Mitford, the 1st Baron Redesdale. Their fathers were close friends and Sydney had accompanied Tap on a visit to Lord Redesdale's family seat, Batsford Park, where she saw David, standing by the fire, wearing a gamekeeper's jacket. He was 17 and soon to leave for Ceylon, where he was expected to earn his fortune in tea-planting. His ambition to become a soldier remained unfulfilled, as he had failed the entrance exam for Sandhurst. In an unpublished memoir, written when Sydney was elderly, she claimed it was love at first sight, though perhaps she was being sentimental. In her early youth, the man she loved most was her ice-skating instructor at the Prince's Club, a Swede named Henning Grenander. It was a one-sided romance, and she wrote in her diary, 'I love being with him. I would do almost anything he asked me. I would let him call me Sydney, I would even let him kiss me.'[5]

The interim between Sydney's meeting David and her coming out as a debutante was largely uneventful. The rhythm of each day followed the last, with the exception of an incident that occurred in 1895, when she was 15. Each day she rode with Tap to the House of Commons, though on this particular occasion her horse slipped on the pavement, and Sydney hit her head and suffered a concussion.[6] She was taken to the home of Jonas Kellgren, at Eaton Square, whom Tap entrusted with his family's medical needs. The Swedish-born Kellgren had gained a following amongst the smart set who took the cure at his sanatorium in the village of Sana, and was reported to have successfully treated epileptics without the use of drugs. In London his use of natural remedies and techniques of massage divided opinion amongst those in the medical field, and many viewed him as a charlatan masquerading as a faith healer. The latter appraisal was attributed to a mantra he instilled in his patients, who called him 'doctor' even though he held no medical degree, that most ailments were a figment of the imagination. Another momentous event which happened around that period was Sydney discarding her sailor suit for grown-up clothes. At the age of 18 she was launched in society and attended her first dance at the Duke and Duchess of Devonshire's house in Piccadilly. There was also talk of her attending Girton College at Cambridge, an opportunity she did not pursue, for she was not particularly fond of academia. It was not an unusual stance, and Sydney refused to let her own daughters go to school. A view popular at the time was that 'young girls have not the physical stamina to endure hard work, vicious excitement, and the competition which form a part of college life'.[7]

By then Sydney was a celebrated beauty and was painted several times by Paul César Helleu, who had befriended Tap during his yachting expeditions to Trouvill. There were also two significant romances in her life: a young man who was killed in the Boer War, and Edward 'Jimmy' Meade. The latter almost led to an engagement but ended when she realised he could not be faithful to her. It was the Boer War that served to bring David Mitford back into her life, for having spent four unsuccessful years in Ceylon he returned home on his first spell of leave. His homecoming, however, coincided with the war and he enlisted in the Royal Northumberland Fusiliers. Five months into battle David was wounded in his leg and hospitalised at Bloemfontein, and a year later he was wounded in his chest and lost a lung. He was nursed in a field hospital for four days and then returned to camp in a bullock cart, his wound infested with maggots. Having survived his initial prognosis, he was declared out of danger and invalided home to England.

Sydney's first meeting with David since returning home in 1902 resulted in a marriage proposal. As his income was £400 per year, many wondered if she could be happy as the wife of a poor man. They were married on 6 February 1904 at St Margaret's, Westminster, and honeymooned aboard the *Hoyden* and in Paris. In London they settled in a small house on Graham Street and later moved to a larger house on Victoria Road, and David took a job as office manager of *The Lady*. The latter might have been Tap's suggestion, for instead of increasing Sydney's allowance he thought it best her new husband earn his living, albeit with his help. David, who was described as possessing a violent temper (he had once threatened to kill his father), was only happy in the countryside, and was therefore ill-suited to managing a gentlewoman's magazine. He spent his days in the basement hunting rats with his mongoose.

Nine months after Sydney's marriage to David their first child was born. It was a disappointment at first, for Sydney had wanted a boy and to name him Paul. Instead she was delivered of a girl with curly black hair and green eyes, so unlike herself and David with their fair colouring and pale blue eyes. Sydney thought her baby, initially called Ruby, resembled a pirate's moll and so she was christened Nancy, after the seafaring shanties. Letters written during that period described David's happiness. Never a social man, he was content to stay at home and eat a supper of bread and milk from his lap in the drawing room. Sydney, however, must have been restless or unhappy, for she considered leaving David for another man. At the eleventh hour she changed her mind and decided to stay, having considered her baby in the nursery and the social shame it would have brought her. 'My mother has always lived in a dream world of her own and no doubt was even dreamier during her many pregnancies,'[8] Nancy wrote of her childhood. In matters relating to childrearing, Sydney was equally dreamy, for she hired the daughter of Tap's captain to look after Nancy despite her having no experience, but she hoped this connection to the sea would be passed on to her child. A few years later this woman was replaced with another known only as Unkind Nanny, who was dismissed for banging Nancy's head off a wooden bedpost. Unable to confront the nanny, Sydney took to her bed and it fell to David to dismiss her. Sydney also followed the advice of her sister-in-law, Frances, who told her no child under the age of 5 should be punished or hear a cross word, and that tantrums were best settled with bromide instead of a slap. Therefore Nancy became a spoilt child, prone to fits of rage, as her father had been, and who had little respect for authority. Three years later a second daughter, Pamela, was born, who was a pleasant child and whose looks resembled her parents. Of her two children it was Pamela who dominated Sydney's attention, as she developed infantile polio and several doctors predicted she would never walk. She was reluctant to trust medical advice and instead engaged Dr Kellgren to administer a regime of exercise and massage, and as a result Pamela was cured and her mobility restored. Two more children followed, Tom in 1909, and Diana less than a year later. They, too, joined Nancy and Pamela in the nursery, and David, on his way home from *The Lady*, bought them a pony which he housed in a small downstairs room.

The detached way in which Sydney treated her children might have been inspired by her own mother, who prized her husband above her children. Both Sydney and Jessica viewed themselves as their husbands' equals, and although Sydney did not encourage David in his financial schemes she did not prevent him from pursuing the latest fad, even if she knew it would founder. Thus David invested heavily in a piece of equipment said to comb the ocean floor in search of treasure, only to realise it had been a con. He had an opportunity to invest in an early patent for ice cubes but rejected the idea as 'damned foolishness'. Instead he and Sydney sailed to Canada every two years to prospect for gold and lived in a wooden shack without servants, though that scheme also proved unsuccessful. For their crossing in 1912 they booked a second-class cabin on the *Titanic* but delayed their sailing and therefore avoided tragedy. To ease their money problems Sydney kept chickens and bees and sold their eggs and honey to London restaurants, using the profits to pay for the children's governess. She also saved on the laundry bill by removing linen napkins from the table; however everything else was sent to be laundered at Harrods. It earned her the nickname 'Penny Pinching Peeress'.

The arrival of the First World War in 1914 saw David resign from *The Lady* and re-enlist with the Northumberland Fusiliers, with whom he went to the Front as a regimental transport officer. It was a dangerous post, as each night he went on horseback to deliver ammunition to his men and was therefore an easy target for snipers. In August Sydney gave birth to their fifth child, a daughter named Unity Valkyrie, and after her confinement she closed up the London house and went with the children to live at Old Mill Cottage, in High Wycombe, Buckinghamshire. They also stayed with Tap at Bournehill, a fishing cottage overlooking the Solent, which caught on fire in the summer of 1915, and Sydney and the children watched from the lawn as Tap hurled valuables from the window. David was in London, on leave, when he learned of the fire and was told there had been no survivors; he was therefore surprised at that moment to see Sydney and the children pull up in a taxi. On another spell of leave Sydney met David in Paris, and returned home with French officers' army coats, which she had altered to fit the children. In 1917 David was invalided home due to extreme exhaustion and when he recovered he accepted the post of Assistant Provost Marshal, and took rooms at Christ Church, where he installed a pianola and put rainbow trout in mercury.

In 1916 David inherited the Barony of Redesdale and Batsford Park from his father, as his elder brother, Clement, was killed in the war. It increased the family's money worries, for David's army pay was too little to keep a growing family and maintain an enormous house with five staircases and over 100 rooms. Sydney's allowance had been reduced by Tap, which he explained was due to rising taxation, and so she let Old Mill Cottage and moved into Batsford with the children, whilst David remained at Christ Church. Her sixth child, a daughter, Jessica (known as Decca), was born there in 1917. She knew the house would have to be sold, and so she covered the antique furniture in dust sheets and opened a few rooms to accommodate the family. There was a fete organised by Sydney to raise money for wounded soldiers and held on the grounds of the estate. Its 50 acres had been landscaped to resemble Japanese gardens, inspired by Bertie Redesdale's time in Japan, where it was rumoured he had fathered children with a Geisha. The children were tasked with putting on a play and selling tickets; however, during the rehearsal Sydney decided it was awful, and said, 'I'm very sorry, children, but I'm afraid you can't do your play.'[9] On her stall she placed Japanese treasures from the house and garden, and David managed to save his father's antique Buddha, which he bought off her for sixpence.

In 1919 the family moved to Asthall Manor, a Jacobean country house in the village of Swinbrook, Oxfordshire. Although there were fewer rooms, the house proved troublesome, for it was haunted by a poltergeist who was said to have hurled cutlery across the dining room and torn off the housemaid's clothes. David and Pamela suffered from the hauntings, but Sydney did not. She did not believe in the supernatural, though she entertained ideas of an afterlife, as it would, she said, be nice to see her girlhood friend, Cicely, again. In matters of religion she identified with the Church of England, only because she wished to support the state. She asked, 'But what happens when people pray? How can they think of enough things to ask for?'[10] It was at Asthall, in 1920, that Sydney's last child, a daughter named Deborah, known as Debo, was born. 'I knew it was a girl by the look on his Lordship's face,' Mabel, the parlourmaid, said. Sydney, who had hoped for a boy, made no mention of her newborn child and instead recorded in her appointments book, 'Chimney swept'.

In 1926 the family moved into Swinbrook House, a property David had designed and built on a piece of land he owned in the village. All except Debo and Pamela hated the house, particularly Sydney, who possessed an eye for interior design: she frequently found treasures in junk shops. The dark wooden interior at Swinbrook contrasted with her preference for chintz, and her children complained about the doors, which were warped and would not close. 'Damned good wood,' David would bellow. Instead Sydney suffered in silence, in the similar way she had quietly accepted his gift of a peach, which he bought with his pay from *The Lady* – he only discovered years later that she loathed the fruit. During that period she founded the Asthall and Swinbrook branches of the Women's Institute and lectured on her three favourite subjects: Queen Victoria, Lord Nelson, and bread.

The family's years at Swinbrook were a focal point for the girls' lives, for it was to be their last family home and a representation of what made them miserable. All of Sydney's daughters, with the exception of Pamela and Debo, longed to run away for a life of excitement: an antidote to country life with a mother whose chief interests were in running a house, and a father whom they described as 'violent, but harmless'. Their lives, however, were anything but ordinary and they were given opportunities of going abroad for a year, which served as a finishing school before coming out as a debutante. Nancy went to Florence, and the others, except for Debo who did not want to miss a season's hunting, were sent to live *en pension* in Paris. There were visits to the homes of grand relatives, particularly weekends spent with their cousin Clementine Churchill at Chartwell, though Sydney often rationed their recreation as she did not think it beneficial to have too much fun. Nancy, Unity and Decca begged to go to school but Sydney refused, thinking it pointless for girls to be highly educated, and David supported her view as he feared playing hockey would give them 'legs like gateposts'. In terms of affection Sydney was drawn to her prettiest child, which during their childhood was Diana, and on her birthday the children made her a daisy crown. Her children recalled the idea of Rat Week, a period when one of the girls would fall out of favour with Sydney and David, and they suffered their parents' scorn. It was mostly taken in jest, but at the dinner table, David was prone to fits of rage if anything spilled on to the table cloth. By contrast Sydney's tactic was not rage but silence, and she ignored her daughters when they were naughty and often gave in to their idiosyncrasies, most notably Unity's diet of mashed potatoes and preference for slipping under the table during mealtimes. The most difficult relationship was with Nancy, as she accused Sydney of not loving her or showing affection to the children when they were young. 'I had the greatest possible respect for her; I liked her company, but I never loved her,'[11] Nancy wrote to Decca.

Sydney was blamed for the choices Nancy, Diana, Unity and Decca later made. Nancy fell for men who did not love her and married a wastrel named Peter Rodd, who spent her money and subjected her to bailiffs. In an attempt to escape the family home, Diana married at 18, to Bryan Guinness, whom her parents liked – though Sydney disapproved of the family's wealth – but she left him for Sir Oswald Mosley. Unity took up with the fascist cause in Britain and later went to Germany and befriended Adolf Hitler. Decca, who at the age of 7 had opened a Running Away savings account, became a communist and eloped to Spain with her second cousin, Esmond Romilly. Pamela, the most similar to Sydney in temperament, was courted by John Betjeman but instead married Derek Jackson, a millionaire scientist and amateur steeplechaser. Debo, who like Pamela caused no trouble for Sydney, married Andrew Cavendish, who unexpectedly inherited the Dukedom of Devonshire after the death of his elder brother and father. The changeable nature of her daughters was unexpected and often controversial, but Sydney took scandal in her stride and remained loyal to them, even though David severed ties with Diana after her affair with Mosley, and also estranged himself from Decca.

The 1930s were a turbulent decade for Sydney, which altered the dynamic of her marriage to David. Politics had become a significant part of their family life, beginning with Diana's involvement with Mosley's British Union of Fascists: she had travelled to Germany to meet with Adolf Hitler in an attempt to forge links between British fascism and Nazism. The introduction to Hitler had been made by Unity, who had moved to Munich in the mid-1930s to study art and pursue Nazism, something she became attracted to after she and Diana visited Berlin years before and attended a Nazi rally at Nuremberg. It was also through Unity that Sydney and David were introduced to Hitler, though Sydney took to him more readily, as they discussed the benefits of wholemeal bread and new potatoes. She thought taking tea with him was harmless, and Nancy accused her of being naïve and entirely manipulated by Diana and Unity. Eventually David turned violently against Hitler and denounced him in the House of Lords, which marked the beginning of the disintegration of his marriage to Sydney.

Before the arrival of the Second World War and its ramifications for Sydney, the most troubling event of this period occurred in 1937 after Decca eloped with Esmond Romilly: he was her girlhood hero, who had fuelled her communist beliefs. A forged letter inviting Decca to join her friends, the Paget twins, in Dieppe had fooled Sydney and she reluctantly agreed, as she had booked a cultural cruise for her younger daughters. Sydney saw Decca to the train station, unaware that Esmond was on board and they were heading to Spain, where he had a job reporting on the Spanish Civil War. For months Decca's whereabouts remained unknown to her parents, and when she was traced to a hotel in Bayonne, south-west France, Sydney crossed the Channel to bring her home. However, Decca refused to leave Esmond, and confided to Sydney that she was pregnant, and so it was agreed she must marry him. Sydney bought Decca a sundress to wear as a wedding gown and afterwards took the newly-weds and Esmond's mother, Nellie Romilly, to lunch at a smart hotel. It was a heavy sacrifice for Sydney, who adored her clever and funny daughter, or 'Little D', as she called her. She knew she had lost her to Esmond, who hated her family. David, who loathed his cousin Esmond and his left-wing views, never forgave Decca and they remained estranged until his death.

Two years later Sydney was faced with a bitter feud between her daughters. It had been brewing for years and imploded in 1939, after war was declared, and Unity attempted suicide by shooting herself in the head. It was an action prompted by Britain entering war with Germany, the two nations Unity loved most. It was months before Sydney could get to Unity: Hitler had sent her to a nursing home in neutral Switzerland, an action that deepened her feelings of fondness and admiration for all he had done. Such feelings were infuriating to Nancy and Decca, though they both agreed Sydney was naïve and easily manipulated. It fell to Sydney to care for Unity, who had become mentally and physically disabled from the bullet that had lodged itself in her skull and was pressing on her brain. David was far less tolerant of Unity's stumbling around the house and her violent reaction to anyone she deemed a threat to her relationship with Sydney. He also abhorred Sydney's tolerance of Hitler and, after forty years of marriage, left her to go live at Redesdale Cottage with their parlourmaid, Margaret Wright, with whom he began a relationship which lasted until his death in 1958.

The war years were a demanding period for Sydney, as her daughters came to rely on her practicality and calm demeanour. When Debo married Andrew Cavendish in 1941, Sydney opened their London home, Rutland Gate, a casualty of the Blitz, and bought rolls of grey and gold wallpaper and hung them like curtains over the broken windows of the ballroom. She also divided her time between Debo and Pamela: in 1941, they each lost their babies. During that time Nancy suffered an ectopic pregnancy and had to have an emergency hysterectomy, prompting Sydney to remark, 'Ovaries. I thought one had 700, like caviar.'[12] And when Nancy complained of her scar, Sydney said, 'But darling, who's ever going to see it?'[13] There was also news from America, where Decca and Esmond were living, that he had been killed whilst serving with the Royal Canadian Air Force. Sydney wanted Decca and her baby daughter to come home to England, but she refused. She remained in America and in 1943 married Robert Treuhaft, a civil rights lawyer. During that time Diana had been imprisoned at Holloway, as Nancy had secretly informed on her to the Home Office, claiming her sister was 'a very dangerous person'.[14] Nancy suggested they examine her passport for evidence of frequent trips to Germany. Sydney often visited Diana in prison and appealed to Winston Churchill for her release, which he denied. Then Sydney approached Clementine Churchill, with whom she was on good terms, and asked that Diana's living conditions in prison be improved. Consequently Sir Oswald Mosley was transferred from Brixton prison to live with her in a parcels house at Holloway. When the bus stopped outside the prison, Sydney suffered the indignity of the driver shouting, 'Lady Mosley's suite.' In March 1945, weeks before the war ended, Sydney learned that Tom, her only son, had been killed by a sniper's bullet whilst serving with his Devonshire Regiment in Burma. She was living with Unity at Inch Kenneth, her private island off the West Coast of Mull, and received the news in a telegram from David. Three years later Unity died from meningitis, the result of the bullet in her brain becoming infected. Due to the bad weather it was days before Sydney could take her to Oban for treatment, and by then it was too late.

As the years progressed, Sydney became immortalised in Nancy's works of literature, the most famous being the character of Aunt Sadie in *The Pursuit of Love* and *Love in a Cold Climate*. Sydney did not elaborate on whether she was flattered by the tribute, though when Nancy's first novel, *Highland Fling*, was published in 1931, she said it was 'killing her by inches'. When Decca was writing her memoirs, *Hons and Rebels*, published in 1960, Sydney requested 'there should be no bitterness in it' and wrote to the publisher, Victor Gollancz, to say she disliked the title. The publicity surrounding *Hons and Rebels* after its release infuriated Diana and Debo, particularly a review from *The Observer*, which wrote, 'If they [David and Sydney] were at the other end of the social scale they might well have been thought unfit to look after their own children.' However, it was Nancy's essay in *The Water Beetle* which vexed Sydney the most, for she was portrayed as an absent parent in her children's lives. 'I wish you would not do any more portraits of me until I am dead,'[15] Sydney remarked.

The later years of Sydney's life were spent at Inch Kenneth, where she kept a herd of goats and two horses. She claimed to like the island due to its lack of tourists, though she spent her days scanning the mainland with her telescope, looking for a tent to appear, and when it did she sent her boatman to bring the tourists to the house, where she served an enormous tea. In old age she became ill with Parkinson's Disease and although she believed 'the Good Body would heal itself', she agreed to take medicine to prevent her hands from shaking. 'She's only taking one pill a day when the doctor said she can have up to three. So she could be three times as well,'[16] Debo wrote to Nancy. As Sydney's health declined she looked forward to death and scolded Nancy for 'dragging her back from the grave'[17] by following the doctor's orders and giving her water. She died at Inch Kenneth, and Nancy wrote of the funeral customs of the Scottish island, finding humour in the macabre. The coffin was delivered two days later, by an undertaker who muttered in Gaelic and drank whisky with James MacGillivray, the boatman and caretaker. In the early evening they sailed with Sydney on the *Puffin*, its flag at half-mast, accompanied by a piper. In the weeks before Sydney's death she was cared for by Nancy, Pamela, Diana and Debo, which made her sentimental for the old days. As with their lives together, at the end there was 'a good deal of hilarity mixed up with the sadness.'[18]

9

THE MUSE:
HAZEL LAVERY

The obsession between Hazel Martyn, as she was then known, and Sir John Lavery began in 1903, at an artists' colony in Beg Meil, a seaside town in Brittany, north-west France. She was to be painted by John Milner-Kite for a portrait commissioned by her mother, Alice, but he struggled to depict his subject and asked his friend, Lavery, for help. Despite Lavery's competence as a portrait painter, especially of women, he also failed to capture Hazel's likeness. This perhaps marked the beginning of Lavery attempting to portray her in still life. He immortalised her in his greatest works; however, these remained in the distant future. 'I am not an ordinary woman,' she wrote, at the time of their meeting, 'and I do not love in an ordinary way.'[1]

A girl like Hazel was not expected to fall in love with a man from Lavery's background. She was born in Chicago, Illinois, on 14 March 1880, and on her birth certificate she remained nameless, as her parents, Edward Jenner Martyn and Alice (*née* Taggart), could not settle on a name. For a brief period she was called Elsa,[2] but it was an uninspired choice, for Elsa, with her enormous brown eyes, was later christened Hazel. A second daughter, Dorothea, was born seven years later and would always remain in Hazel's shadow. It was a privileged childhood, with the Marytn family fortunes changing as Edward's prospects advanced: he began working as a messenger boy for Armour and Co., the largest meat-packing firm in the Midwest, then progressed to chief advisor, and finally to vice-president and director of the Union Stock Yard and Transit Company of Chicago. The Martyns lived at 112 Astor Street, a prestigious address, and were close friends with the Palmers, the Wallers, and the Hodges – leaders of the Chicago social set. The family was listed in the Social Register, and Edward, a devout Episcopalian, co-founded and financed St Chrysostom's, the neighbourhood church. Following the tradition of well brought-up girls, Hazel was educated at home before being sent to Sleboth-Kennedy School, and in her teens she attended Kempner Hall, a boarding school in Wisconsin, and the Misses Masters' finishing school in New York where it was said the girls were taught two things: how to wrap a present and how to make an omelette.[3] In 1899 Hazel came out as a debutante and the local press waxed lyrical about her dark eyes and purple-red hair, calling her 'the most beautiful girl in the Midwest'.

The world from which John Lavery came was Dickensian by comparison. He was born in Belfast in 1857 to Catholic parents and spent the first three years of his life on Queen Street, where his father, Henry, ran a public house. In 1859 Lavery was orphaned, as his father drowned in a shipwreck off the coast of Wexford, and his mother, Mary, died three months later. He was sent along with his brother and sister to live with relatives, first on a farm in County Down, and then to Saltcoats, Ayrshire. It was in Scotland that he began to pursue art, as he was inspired by the local grocer who did pencil portraits, and he painted real-life scenes. When he was 17 he moved to Glasgow and worked as an apprentice for the photographer J.B. MacNair, and the money he earned paid for art classes at the Haldane Academy. He opened a studio with a brass plate on the door, which read 'John Lavery, Artist', but struggled to establish himself as a painter and when his studio burned down he used the insurance money to study painting in London and Paris.

There were parallels between Hazel and Lavery, as she had also lost a parent at an early age. In 1900 her father died, which began a period of uncertainty for the Martyn family, for Alice could no longer afford to maintain their home despite having borrowed money from Armour and

Co. They eventually left their house and moved into the Virginia Hotel, a 400-room establishment with granite interiors and marble statues. Soon after moving into the hotel, Hazel left for Paris to study etching in a dry-point style, and in the summer of 1902 she worked on her portfolio, which she exhibited a year later in Chicago. Critics compared her to Paul César Helleu, a French artist renowned for his portraits of beautiful society women, and the Arts Collectors' Club sponsored the publication of a book containing six of her sketches of women. As much as Hazel's paintings attracted attention, it was her looks which won her admirers, and in 1904 she was photographed for the *American Book of Beauty*, representing Chicago. Produced by Isabella Cameron, daughter of the New York shipping magnate Sir Roderick William Cameron, it was an exclusive tome largely made up of upper-class beauties, and the first edition was limited to twenty-five copies and cost $500.[4]

Lack of family support and patronage marred John Lavery's early years as an artist. An unsuccessful term at the Heatherley School of Fine Art in London during the winter of 1881 inspired him to go to Paris, to study the *avant-garde* style of Parisian art. He enrolled in the Académie Julian, under the mentorship of Tony Robert-Fleury and William Adolphe Bouguereau, famous for their historical and mythological paintings. However Lavery was inspired by scenes depicting modern life, particularly the paintings of Jules Bastien-Lepage. Having spent three years in Paris, he returned to Glasgow and began work on 'The Tennis Party', a study depicting upper-middle-class men and women playing a game of tennis on a lawn at Cartbank, for which he won a bronze medal in the Paris Salon. In 1888 he was commissioned to paint Queen Victoria's state visit to the International Fine Arts Exhibition in Glasgow. It took two years to complete, and he was granted a single sitting at Windsor Castle with the queen, who wore the bonnet from her visit, and chatted to her ladies-in-waiting about flannel underclothes. The portrait was not a critical success, but it launched Lavery as a society painter and attracted commissions from aristocratic women.

The initial attraction between Hazel and Lavery happened from afar, when she glimpsed him from her seat on a hotel veranda as he rushed past with a six-foot easel strapped to his back, and she thought him the epitome of a bohemian. During her portrait sessions with Milner-Kite and Lavery they discussed art, and her regard for the latter as a master painter boosted his ego. On their third meeting Lavery took Hazel to Pont-Aven, and there she confessed her feelings for him. Some time after their encounter, she wrote, 'And you are not to mention the ever (to me) embarrassing fact that it was *I* who was the first to discover. That you wanted me to come into your garden.'[5] However, Alice thought Lavery an unsuitable love interest for Hazel, as he was twice her age, had already been married, and was the father of a teenaged daughter, Eileen. Alice would have preferred Hazel to marry one of her admirers from Paris or Chicago. At her mother's insistence a young man, Pompey Howard, whom Hazel had met in Paris, followed her to Beg-Meil to declare his love, which she rebuffed. There was also Dr Edward 'Ned' Livingston Trudeau Jr, a Yale graduate who had studied at the College of Physicians and Surgeons in New York, whom she had met during her term at the Misses Masters' finishing school. It would have been a respectable marriage, for Ned was the eldest son of Dr Edward Livingston Trudeau Sr, a pioneer in the treatment of tuberculosis, whose studies of infection control, particularly in the fields of germ control and overcrowding, were adopted by medical professionals. It was a one-sided love affair, for despite Ned's overt interest in Hazel, she considered him nothing more than an east coast acquaintance.

The age difference between Hazel and Lavery caused him concern and he wondered if she would soon grow tired of him or they would be happy. He drew on the experience with his first wife, Kathleen MacDermott, whom he had married in 1889, as the feelings he had at the beginning of their relationship were similar to how he felt about Hazel. As with Hazel, his attraction to Kathleen had been instant and they had met by chance, when he saw her selling flowers on Regent Street and asked to paint her portrait. Thereafter Kathleen became his model and muse, and they soon began living together as she had run away from home and had nowhere else to go. After their marriage, Kathleen grew unhappy, due to his cruel treatment of her, and often ignored by him, she went to live in Kilmacolm with her lover, William Patrick Whyte. In 1891 she died at the age of 21 from tuberculosis, shortly after the birth of their daughter, Eileen. However, the death of his wife and the responsibility of a child could not distract Lavery from his work, and thus Eileen was brought up by Whyte, whom she considered her real father. This, Lavery confided to Hazel after her mother had 'been told things'[6] about him. He also confessed to having been cruel to his sister, Jane, as he had forced her to marry the man by whom she became pregnant even though she did not love him. Deeply unhappy and trapped in an abusive marriage, Jane committed suicide by jumping from a bridge, and Lavery later denied his connection to her, thinking the scandal might ruin his career.

These revelations confirmed Alice's opinion of Lavery as an unsuitable match for her daughter, and she thought him a degenerate given the treatment of his family. Hazel, however, was not shocked that he would value his career over marriage and she admired his ambition. It was more than Alice cared to tolerate and she sent Hazel to Paris to continue her studies in etching; soon after her departure, Lavery left for London. Their fascination with one another appeared to be over, for Lavery invited Hazel to come to his studio at 5 Cromwell Place, South Kensington, but she made her excuses and remained in Paris. He then suggested she submit a portrait to the Society of Portrait Painters' gallery in London and recommended her work 'Self Portrait', which she had previously exhibited in Chicago; however it was declined. Then he asked Hazel to marry him, as he thought it would solve the dilemma of their separation. Rightly sensing she would not disobey her mother, he asked her to place her happiness above all else. 'It's not a question of knowing each other – no; it is of knowing ourselves.'[7] It was Alice who responded with a telegram, stating it was impossible for Hazel to go London as they could not travel, though she would have refused to let 'the child' go. Far from a child, Hazel was 23 – she consistently lied about her age, often subtracting five years – and in her own letter to Lavery, she wrote, 'I am only a girl who is afraid to become a woman.'[8]

The fate of Hazel's future was decided by Alice when she cabled Ned Trudeau to 'come quick' or risk losing her to Lavery. Hazel was unaware of her mother's meddling and when Ned arrived in Paris, she wrote to Lavery to inform him of the 'complicated matters'. Lavery then went to Paris and attempted to convince Alice that forcing Hazel to marry Ned was a mistake, but it proved unsuccessful and he returned to London. The Martyns and Ned set sail for New York. During the crossing, Hazel wrote to Lavery and confided how helpless she felt, a feeling which, in her own words, left her breathless. It was then decided that she would marry Ned without delay, though she knew she did not love him – nor did she pretend otherwise. The wedding date was set for 28 December, and on her way to Chicago, Hazel sent Lavery a photograph of herself with the parting sentiment, 'Goodbye John Lavery.'

In the new year of 1904, Hazel and Ned moved to Park Avenue, New York, to live in an apartment furnished by his parents, with a studio built for her. It was a solitary life, for Ned worked long hours as a surgeon at the Vanderbilt Clinic and tended to his patients at his private clinic and at Bellevue Hospital, an establishment founded in the eighteenth century for the poor and destitute. The latter would compromise his health, for in 1904 a pneumonia epidemic swept through the hospital and in the month of March, 300[9] known cases were being treated at Bellevue. 'Pneumonia has attacked persons in all stations of life. The mortality among the poor is almost unprecedented, and the number of deaths among the well-to-do is unusually large,' reported the *Sacred Heart Journal*. Ned contracted pneumonia in April and after spending several weeks in hospital he returned home, whereupon he fell to the floor and died instantly from a pulmonary embolism.

Hazel was unmoved by Ned's death and her lack of grief caused her to become estranged from her parents-in-law, who knew she had never loved their son. She was four months pregnant and returned to Chicago, to await the birth of her baby. Disappointment was on the horizon, for she wanted a son but gave birth to a daughter, and almost died during labour. The baby, whom Hazel thought looked 'ugly and queer',[10] was named Alice, after her grandmother. A telegram was sent to Lavery, informing him of Ned's death and the safe delivery of the baby, though his response was not recorded. It was evident she still loved him, for she wrote to him of her plans to recuperate in the English countryside and hoped he would visit. Nine months later, Hazel and her baby were accompanied by her mother and sister on a trip to Worcestershire, where she took the cure at a health spa. Lavery sent a parasol for the baby and a box for Hazel to carry her canvases, and she completed her first painting in months, a composition of the infant Alice, sun-tanned in her pram, entitled 'The Brown Baby'. Their meetings were to be sporadic, as her mother considered it disrespectful to Ned's memory, and so Lavery used his visits to paint Hazel in her mourning clothes, a portrait called 'Dame en Noir'. Their involvement came to a halt a month later, when Alice and Dorothea decided to sail to France, and Hazel had little choice but to consent to their plans. She and Lavery talked of eloping, an empty threat, for Alice's hold over Hazel was stronger than before; cut-off from her rich in-laws and with a baby to care for, she was at the mercy of her mother. The family took lodgings at the Hotel des Roches Blanches, at Étretat, in Normandy. In August Lavery visited Hazel at the hotel, a watershed moment in their relationship, for she confessed to Alice they were having an affair.

The news shocked Alice, for she knew Hazel's behaviour meant social ruin for herself and her child. Far from having the infant in mind, Hazel had struggled to bond with her baby and throughout the years they would treat one another with a detached interest. It was Alice who made the first move, to invite Lavery to their home, so they could discuss the couple's future. She suggested Hazel and Lavery part for six months, during which time they could not write to one another, and if they were still in love at the end of this period, they could marry without any objection on her behalf. The couple agreed, though Hazel had written to Lavery, before leaving for Paris, to tell him of her whereabouts. He stopped in Paris on his way to Venice, but missed Hazel and sent her a note, written in Italian, to arrange a meeting on his return. The letter did not fool Alice, whose original feelings of anger and mistrust were restored. Sensing this, Lavery also wrote to Alice, asking her to let Hazel marry him, as he believed it would cure her various ailments. Having suffered from nephritis since pregnancy and thereafter, Hazel complained of migraines and fatigue, which supported Alice's argument that she was in no fit state to marry. Lavery thought it a psychological response to her unhappiness, provoked by the conflict she was experiencing with her mother. In turn, Alice blamed Lavery for the ill feeling between herself and Hazel.

In December the Martyns went to Rome, so Hazel could be treated by a doctor, and to place a greater distance between themselves and Lavery. Still, the couple found a way to correspond, and Lavery knew of her latest whereabouts and was updated on her health. She was also suffering from tonsillitis and a chill in her kidney, and she feared she would not live to be reunited with him; however, she made a recovery within a week. With her health restored, Hazel fell in love with Leonard Moorhead Thomas, the second secretary to the United States Embassy in Rome and a rich Philadelphia banker. She wrote to Lavery, telling him that although she knew Thomas was the 'wrong man', she begged him not to come to Rome or write to her, but she told him the family's bankers would know of her future whereabouts.

In the summer of 1906 Hazel returned to Chicago and waited for Thomas to join her. They had agreed to be married, but on the night before their wedding he vanished and Hazel discovered she had been jilted. Four years later he would marry the actress Blanche Oelrichs, who wrote plays and poetry under the nom de plume Michael Strange. After a decade of marriage, Blanche left Thomas for John Barrymore, whom she had met in a jeweller's when she went to exchange a diamond tiara for a string of pearls. However, his comeuppance remained in the distant future and in the meantime Hazel felt humiliated by his disappearance. It was claimed that Thomas had fathered illegitimate children, perhaps the reason for his leaving Hazel, though many believed she had started the rumour out of spite.

In November Hazel wrote to Lavery for the first time in months and he responded with an affectionate letter, telling her that wherever she was 'there is danger'.[11] A telling remark, for a fortune-teller had previously told Hazel that she was 'dangerous to others' and would 'therefore have bad luck'.[12] She planned to go to Europe in 1907 but the departure was thwarted by the declining health of her maternal grandparents and her mother's nervous breakdown, which was followed by her death from appendicitis two years later. In 1909 Hazel finally travelled to London to see Lavery and they were quickly married at Brompton Oratory, in the presence of her sister, Dorothea, and several of his friends. They went on their honeymoon to Southend-on-Sea, where it rained for the duration.

Hazel's early married life was marred by her ill health and, as with her courtship with Lavery, they were to be separated once more. She went to Chicago with her mother's ashes and to settle her estate, valued at $65,000, from which Alice's loan from Armour and Co. and medical bills were to be paid. The remainder of the money was to be held in trust for one year, after which it would be paid as an annuity to Hazel and Dorothea. It therefore fell to Hazel to financially support Dorothea, whose health had been declining for several years due to anorexia nervosa, a condition misunderstood in the early 1900s and one that was attributed to fasting 'for health and comeliness'.[13] Dorothea was sent to convalesce with friends in the countryside and Hazel sold the contents of their mother's home to pay for her medical treatment. Both Hazel and Lavery invited Dorothea to come to London but she refused and went to live with her elderly grandmother; after this relative died in 1909, Dorothea stayed with family friends.

With her family affairs in order, Hazel could reinvent herself as a society hostess, and she opened the doors to 5 Cromwell Place to artists, aristocrats and politicians. Her home was a salon dedicated to her individual taste and was photographed for *Vogue*, which showcased its drawing room covered in crinkled gold cloth, a collection of Moroccan butterflies, and a yellow and black dining room with a cabinet covered in mirrors from King George IV's state carriage. The studio where Lavery received his sitters also became Hazel's domain and she entertained his patrons there, the unfinished portraits hidden by Chinese screens. In America she was a vague presence in the social columns, renowned for her beauty and artistic talent, but in London she became a star. Reville and Rossiter, Queen Mary's couturiers, thought Hazel a good celebrity endorsement and suggested they dress her. She declined their proposal, as she preferred to wear clothing that resembled costumes. This originality set her apart from her fellow American socialites, who wished to conform to the British upper classes and belong to the aristocracy, even if their background and breeding made this impossible. A close friend was the Liberal prime minister, H.H. Asquith, whom Hazel met through Lavery, and they were frequent guests at The Wharf, the Asquiths' country house at Sutton Courtenay, in Berkshire. Margot Asquith, his wife, was renowned for her waspish behaviour and she often played to Hazel's insecurities, asking why she was losing her looks and claiming to see no future for her as a socialite. It was a view echoed by Margot's stepdaughter-in-law, who considered Hazel a bore.

Although Hazel was a sought-after guest, she was not particularly sympathetic toward women, and was at her best when surrounded by men. She often held male-only parties, and it was her self-deprecation which inspired admiration in the opposite sex: 'I don't think that we women can ever do anything as well as the best men, with the possible exception of acting. Take painting for example. No woman has ever been a great painter, for the simple reason that she has not the requisite amount of physical and nervous strength.'[14] Whether her feelings were genuine remains unknown, for it was Hazel who had taught her neighbour and friend, Winston Churchill, how to paint, when, one day, she saw him standing before a canvas, attempting to paint a sky scene. 'Painting!' Hazel said. 'But what are you hesitating about? Let me have a brush – a big one.'[15] It began a series of informal lessons, and Churchill, often dismissive of accomplished women, appreciated Hazel's talent as an artist and mentor.

As with Hazel's courtship with Lavery, the first years of their marriage were beset with problems. Dorothea's illness and inability to work resulted in her becoming a recluse, prompting Hazel and Lavery to go to Chicago to intervene. On this particular homecoming Hazel was feted as a celebrity, and Lavery was given a tour of the Chicago Art Institute. They convinced Dorothea to return to London with them, where Hazel hoped an introduction to various literary connections would revive her interest in writing, but the situation remained hopeless and she left for America. There, Dorothea's health continued to decline and she was hospitalised; when the news reached Hazel and Lavery they booked a transatlantic passage. However, two days into their crossing, Dorothea died from complications brought on by 'fasting', or anorexia nervosa, in St Luke's Hospital and they learned of her death upon their arrival in Chicago. It was a bitter blow for Hazel, a feeling that was intensified by newspaper reports that Dorothea's death was avoidable: 'Miss Dorothea Martyn died of malnutrition recently as the result of using "beauty fats", which she, in common with a number of other young women, took up as a fad a year ago.'[16] There were also reports that Dorothea had been abandoned by Hazel, whose head was turned by fame and money, and doyennes of high society were shocked that a young woman, whose parents had once been in the Social Register, had died in a public hospital.

During this period Hazel also suffered from ill health, the consequence of a head injury from a car crash that killed the driver. The concussion healed but it served as a catalyst for the misfortune she had previously endured – the death of her first husband, her mother, and her sister – and she had a nervous breakdown. She became fixated with the idea that something terrible would happen to Lavery, a fear enforced by the arrival of the First World War and Lavery's desire to go to the Front with the Artists Rifles, despite being too old to enlist. When he was rejected on medical grounds, as he could not complete the rigorous training, he suggested he enlist as a war artist and was commissioned by Charles Masterman, head of the British War Propaganda Bureau. The news was kept from Hazel, as she had become possessive of him and fretted when he was out of her sight – a rarity, for he only left her side when she was sleeping. His plan was to sail to France and telegram her when he arrived, thus avoiding any confrontation. Those plans were abandoned when he realised how fragile her emotional state was. Instead he remained in London and painted scenes on the Home Front, depicting battleships on Southampton Water and the Royal Navy's Grand Fleet anchored off the Orkney Islands, and he painted Hazel watching a Zeppelin raid from his studio window. After Hazel's recovery she helped with the war effort by organising several fundraisers and charity matinee performances, then popular with society women, and she joined E.O. Hoppe's theatrical group, The Plough, which produced plays that were new and original in their concept.[17]

In 1918 Lavery was knighted for his war work and Hazel became Lady Lavery, though to her dismay her new title was often misheard as 'ladies lavatory'. It signalled a new identity for her and inspired her to take an interest in Irish politics, the place of her paternal ancestors (the Martyns from Galway) and a country of which she held a romantic view. Lavery, an Irish Catholic from Belfast whose early years were blighted by poverty and sectarianism, thought her vision of Ireland was unrealistic and he struggled to appreciate her fondness for the countryside and the Georgian architectural landscape of Dublin. He too, however, was charmed by the Earl and Countess of Kenmare who received them at Killarney House in County Kerry. The visit fuelled Hazel's obsession with Ireland, and she began to speak with a slight Irish accent and changed her birthday to St Patrick's Day, three days after her original birthdate of 14 March. Still, in those early days, her admiration was founded on Ireland's Anglo influence, with visits to stately homes and invitations to the Viceregal Lodge, then symbols of the Protestant Ascendency.

At the time of Hazel's first visit to Ireland, in 1913, the third Home Rule Bill, proposing that Ireland free itself from British rule, had been introduced, which led to the Home Rule Crisis. Many aristocratic women took an interest in the crisis, notably Ulster's gentry in the north, the majority of whom wanted to remain part of the Union and therefore opposed Home Rule. Jean, Viscountess Massereene, Lavery's most recent subject ('A Lady in Black', 1917), was an anti-Home Ruler and although friendly with Hazel through their mutual friends, Theresa and Edith Londonderry, the women were at opposing ends of the political spectrum. Lady Massereene shared the view of several high-ranking individuals, particularly men, who thought the economy of Ireland was dependent on trade with England. This was true of Charles Londonderry, who, on one occasion, became enraged by Hazel's pro-Home Rule argument and grabbed her by the arm so forcefully it left a bruise. Unlike Lady Massereene and her fellow peeresses from Ulster, who counted the Unionist politician Sir Edward Carson (founder of the Ulster Volunteer Force) as a close friend and ally, Hazel's Home Rule sympathies were inspired by Lavery's friendship with T.P. O'Connor, a member of the Irish Parliamentary Party, and his support for Home Rule. Such views did not hinder their friendship with H.H. Asquith, who felt the strain of the Irish Question, and was relieved when the First World War postponed further action on the Home Rule issue. Asquith, aware of Lavery's ideology and privy to his reading aloud from the nationalist *Freeman's Journal*, nicknamed Hazel the 'Queen of Ireland'. With her ego boosted from such a compliment, even though it was given in jest, Hazel began to describe herself as 'a simple Irish girl' and came to loathe Irish-Americans (though she was one) and their over-exaggerated sense of culture. She adopted a different stance regarding her love of Ireland and Irish ancestry, and used art as a way of fusing her identity with that of the country. When Lavery was commissioned to paint the Nationalist leader John Redmond and the Unionist leader Sir Edward Carson, in 1916, he agreed on the condition that each portrait hung side by side in a gallery in Dublin. It played to Hazel's belief that such paintings could be part of an Irish art collection, which could help both those proposing and opposing Home Rule to understand one another's ideologies.

Hazel's view of using art to settle the political differences in Ireland remained nothing more than an idealistic dream. She did, however, use art as a way of gaining access to the Irish Republican Brotherhood, a secret organisation which fought in the Easter Rising, on 24 April 1916, cementing Ireland's first steps to becoming a republic. Lavery supported the Rising and those revolutionaries who were arrested by the British government and interned in camps, many of whom were not part of the conflict. He also painted a canvas, to be sold by the National Aid Society with monies benefiting the families of those interned. Three months later, he was commissioned by Mr Justice Darling to paint the trial of Sir Roger Casement, an Irish Nationalist who worked for the British Foreign Office, and who arranged for German arms to be smuggled into Kerry, to aid the Brotherhood. Thus Casement was declared a traitor and was sentenced to death. Lord Birkenhead, appointed Solicitor General by H.H. Asquith, led the prosecution and thought Lavery's composition of the trial 'was in the worst possible taste'.[18] It was a sentiment echoed by many Britons, who were appalled by Casement's Black Diaries, believed to have been forged, which detailed his homosexual affairs. As homosexuality was a crime, it undermined any support for his clemency and he was hanged on 3 August 1916. 'Who was the lady who sat near the painter in the jury-box?' Casement wrote in a letter during his trial, having observed Hazel sitting in the gallery, where Lavery also painted her. 'I thought I knew her face. It was very sad.' She had attended the High Criminal Court several times and was haunted by his fate.

In December 1916, four months after Sir Roger Casement was executed, David Lloyd George replaced H.H. Asquith as prime minister. Hazel asked her friend, Sir Philip Sassoon, to arrange a meeting between herself and Lloyd George, as she hoped to provoke his sympathy for Ireland and its quest for Home Rule. Having charmed Asquith she was dismayed when his successor, at the suggestion of Winston Churchill, then Minister for War, ordered the Royal Irish Constabulary Special Reserve (known as the Black and Tans) to fight the Irish Republican Army (IRA) in their battle for Irish independence. The action did little to endear Lloyd George to her. It also threatened Hazel and Lavery's friendship with Churchill, evident in a letter sent by Lavery in 1920, suggesting that Churchill, in his position as Minister for War, suppress his heavy-handed approach in fighting against Ireland's independence. Further commissions to paint Protestant and Catholic leaders brought Lavery and Hazel to Ireland that year, particularly the north, which Hazel professed to dislike, owing to their loyalism and wish to remain part of the Union. During this time Hazel converted to Catholicism and received religious instruction from Father Joseph Leonard, a decision that baffled her closest friends. Lavery, although a Catholic, was not religious, nor did he adhere to the strict teachings of his faith. Perhaps Hazel's conversion was done to ally herself with Ireland's revolutionary leaders and to be taken seriously as an Irish Republican sympathiser.

In 1920 Hazel was growing increasingly militant, though this was veiled by her outwardly romantic approach to Ireland and its heritage. She became fixated with Michael Collins, a revolutionary leader ten years her junior, and wished to find him so Lavery could paint his portrait. Churchill, still on friendly terms with Hazel and Lavery, thought it controversial and advised against it: 'Be careful, my dear John, our men are not all good shots.' The opportunity arose in 1921, as the Government of Ireland Act was passed the year before, permitting two parliaments to be formed in Ireland: one in Belfast and the other in Dublin. Irish Nationalists refused to acknowledge a British administration in Ireland, therefore on 22 June 1921 Northern Ireland was created, formed from the six counties of Ulster (Donegal would remain part of the Republic of Ireland, despite being located in the north) and its new parliament at Stormont was governed by British rule. Southern Ireland would become a Free State in 1922, though during the partition of Ireland its status remained undecided and Lloyd George invited a delegation to London from the Dáil Èireann, southern Ireland's self-appointed parliament, which had been formed in 1919, to discuss its future as a legitimate government. Hazel suggested her house as a neutral meeting place, where the Republican delegates could also have their portraits painted by Lavery. Her invitation was met with disapproval and suspicion; her peers did not approve of Irish revolutionaries, viewing them as paramilitaries and the natural enemy of the British, and several of the aforementioned thought Hazel a spy for the British government. Michael Collins, however, came to the conclusion that Hazel was his natural ally.

Hazel finally met Collins in October 1921, several months after the delegation visited Lloyd George and returned to Dublin, only to have their proposals of a truce rejected. It was on their second visit to London, in which Collins was included, that he reluctantly accepted Hazel's invitation to Cromwell Place and arrived unannounced to have his portrait painted by Lavery. She thought Collins dramatic, a quality which appealed to her and repelled Lavery, and as the years progressed she thought her husband withdrawn and difficult to live with. In turn, Lavery thought Hazel's behaviour on par with a spoilt child, and he often retreated to his studio to escape her demands for attention. In Collins Hazel had found a kindred spirit, though she competed with many socialites who were also attracted to his sense of danger and reputation as a murderer. Unlike her competitors she had expressed an interest in Irish politics and thought of herself as an Irish heroine. She had been following him for years, and, upon his arrival in London had found the address of his sister, Hannie, in West Kensington. She sent him a letter, but it remained unanswered.

Collins was living at Cadogan Gardens with his bodyguards, as he was a prime target for assassination since the earliest days of his association with the Irish Republican Brotherhood, through which he had become involved in the Easter Rising of 1916 and was amongst the revolutionaries interned as a prisoner of war. After Collins's release from prison in December 1916, he moved through the ranks of the Irish Volunteer Force and became affiliated with Sinn Féin, founded by Arthur Griffith in 1905 as a response to Sir Edward Carson's Ulster Volunteer Force. He was appointed Minister for Finance in the Dáil, upon its formation in 1919; however members continued to meet in private residences at Mountjoy Square, as they were considered traitors to the British government and risked imprisonment or worse. During the Irish War of Independence, Collins was appointed Chief of Intelligence for the IRA and became renowned for his guerrilla strategies and the assassinations of undercover British intelligent agents, known as the Cairo Gang. Speaking of the killings, Collins said:

My one intention was the destruction of the undesirables who continued to make miserable the lives of ordinary decent citizens. I have proof enough to assure myself of the atrocities which this gang of spies and informers have committed. If I had a second motive it was no more than a feeling such as I would have for a dangerous reptile. By their destruction the very air is made sweeter. For myself, my conscience is clear. There is no crime in detecting in wartime the spy and the informer. They have destroyed without trial. I have paid them back in their own coin.[19]

Hazel's enthusiasm was dimmed by Collins's temperament during his visit to London in the winter of 1921. For four years he had been adhering to clandestine practices, talking in code and planning highly secretive operations to undermine the British government's presence in Dublin, and he therefore found it difficult to mix with high society and tolerate its formalities. Contrary to this, Collins formed a lasting friendship with J.M. Barrie, author of *Peter Pan*, who was drawn to his shyness and love of theatre, and the two spent afternoons at London's museums and galleries. Barrie considered Collins an incarnation of Peter Pan, the eternal boy – an interesting observation, for Collins himself was fascinated by the story and felt akin to the character. Another friend was Lord Birkenhead, an unlikely ally given his prosecution of Sir Roger Casement, though their introduction was the cause of a misunderstanding when Hazel's dog jumped at him, for which she apologised. Birkenhead said, 'Oh I am sorry. I thought you were making advances.' The remark did not amuse Collins, and he rose to his feet and accused Birkenhead of insulting her. However, as their friendship developed, Birkenhead showed Collins the alleged Black Diaries, written by Casement, and he confirmed they were authentic as he claimed to recognise his handwriting. It was an interesting remark, for Collins had never met Casement and it was therefore believed he validated the diaries to inspire friendship and trust from the British government.

As the months advanced, Hazel became a confidante to Collins, and Lavery came to accept their relationship, the depth of which remains unknown. It was rumoured that Hazel and Collins had begun an affair during the winter of 1921, a belief encouraged by the compliments he paid to her through his poetry. Of the two poems he composed for her, the first read:

Oh! Hazel, Hazel Lavery,
What is your charm Oh! Say?
Like subtle Scottish Mary,
You take my heart away.
Not by your wit or beauty,
Nor your delicate sad grace,
Nor the golden eyes of wonder,
In the flower that is your face.

They were often alone, as Hazel drove Collins to meetings with Lloyd George at Downing Street, where the conditions for an Anglo-Irish treaty were being negotiated. Such trips in the motorcar confused the newspapers and one mistakenly reported that Collins had 'driven with his sweetheart'. Lavery credited Hazel with being a calming influence on Collins, who began to accept her point of view that Ireland's independence should be gained slowly. It placed him in a difficult position with his comrades, who felt they had fought long enough for a Republic. Collins had found in Hazel a person with whom he could be himself: a young man from Cork, who was drawn to literature and art, and who appreciated her flamboyance and sense of theatre. Hazel's own identity, particularly her youth, was important to her, and now aged forty she had begun to preserve her looks by dyeing her hair a reddish-purple and spending hours applying her make-up, which came to resemble an alabaster mask. Anita Leslie, an Anglo-Irish aristocrat and society biographer, remarked that Hazel and Collins were 'soulmates rather than bedmates'. It was a sweeping remark, for Leslie was a child during the Irish War of Independence and was not close to Hazel, but her father, Shane Leslie (née Sir John Leslie), a Catholic convert and Home Rule supporter, was on friendly terms with Hazel and for years wrote her poems and sent her roses. Years later, Shane Leslie said, 'She merely whistled to men and they obeyed as if it were a whip fashioned of her eyelashes.' Letters from Collins to Hazel were destroyed, which further inflamed rumours of an affair.

Their bond was often undermined by Collins's romantic entanglements elsewhere, as he was engaged to Kitty Kiernan, the daughter of a Longford merchant. Hazel did not view Kitty as competition, perhaps thinking Collins would devote himself to the formation of a new Ireland rather than surrendering himself to marriage; however she thought their mutual friend, Moya Llewelyn Davies (*née* O'Connor), a threat to her happiness with him. Moya, an Irish Republican activist and a friend of Hannie Collins, had known Collins since 1910, and it was through this connection he had been introduced to J.M. Barrie, who had modelled Peter Pan on Moya's nephew, Michael, who had drowned in ambiguous circumstances in 1921. The drowning of Michael Llewelyn Davies came as a profound shock to Collins, who saw it as a sign that his life would also be cut short. It was rumoured that Collins and Moya had continued an affair throughout the years, beginning a decade before when Collins lived in London, and resuming when she moved to Ireland with her two children in 1919 to work as a spy for the women's branch of the IRA. Before her arrest in 1920, Moya's home, Furry Park, a mansion in Clontarf, was a refuge for Collins. Moya was openly militant; Hazel was not as blatant, and the contrast between the two women appealed to the differing facets of Collins's character and his love of Ireland. It would have also pleased Hazel that many debated the closeness of Moya's friendship with Collins, despite her claiming he was the father of her son, Richard, born in 1912, and she was often dismissed as a stalker.

In the new year of 1922, Collins and the delegation returned to Dublin to present the Anglo-Irish Treaty, signalling the end of the Irish War of Independence and introducing the status of Ireland as a free state though it remained part of the Commonwealth. In London Hazel anxiously waited for news from Collins, and had bought a mass candle to pray for his victory. However, in Dublin opinions were divided, as Ireland's separation from Britain remained unresolved, due to members of the Dáil having to swear an oath of fidelity to King George V, and Eamon de Valera accused Collins and the delegation of ignoring his instructions regarding negotiations. De Valera resigned as president, and a new provisional Dáil was formed consisting of eight men – Arthur Griffith (elected as the new president), W.T. Cosgrave, Kevin O'Higgins, Eamon Duggan, Joseph McGrath, Fionán Lynch, Patrick Hogan and Collins, whose new position was chairman of upholding and implementing the Treaty. It seemed as though Collins had followed Hazel's advice, to introduce independence slowly, for he remarked that the treaty gave Ireland the 'freedom, not the ultimate freedom that all nations desire and develop to, but the freedom to achieve it'.[20]

However, those who opposed the Treaty had formed an organisation, known as the Irregulars, which undermined the negotiations with Lloyd George at Downing Street. Collins, who sympathised with the Irregulars, was also working with British cabinet ministers to enforce the Treaty. Once again Hazel attempted to intervene in Irish affairs, and she invited Collins, Duggan and O'Higgins to a dinner party at Cromwell Place, to introduce them to her aristocratic friends, though many continued to think of the revolutionaries as murderers. Charles Londonderry, a member of the newly-established Northern Ireland Senate, was amongst those whom Hazel wished to convert, as he, too, considered Collins an 'assassin'. Eventually Londonderry agreed to meet Collins, as one politician to another, at the conference chamber at the Colonial Office to discuss sectarianism in Northern Ireland. The meeting was a success and Londonderry changed his opinion of Collins, having found him agreeable and 'quite different' from the character he had read about. Likewise, Collins admitted to Hazel that his perception of Londonderry was influenced by his own struggles at being self-educated and self-made and having risen through the ranks of politics without the advantages afforded to the aristocracy. Happy that her meddling had inspired respect, if not friendship, between Collins and Londonderry, she forwarded the letter to the latter. It was believed the letter had been forged by her, as it was unsigned, undated and written in pencil, something Collins never did. As with the rumoured affair between herself and Collins, it was said that she also had a relationship with Londonderry which came to an end when she affiliated herself with Irish revolutionaries.

In the spring of 1922, conflict arose between the Irregulars and Pro-Treatyists, and Collins appointed a bodyguard to protect Hazel, as she became vilified as the woman who had influenced him to betray his friends. The assassination of Sir Henry Wilson, security adviser to Northern Ireland, was committed by two IRA gunmen and it provoked the old suspicions that Hazel was a conspirator and that Collins had ordered the killing. It marked a period of unrest, prompting the British government to order Arthur Griffith, as president of the provisional Irish government, to use force against the Irregulars who occupied the Four Courts and several buildings in Dublin. However as Sinn Féin won a majority in the general election and were Pro-Treatyists, Collins wanted to refrain from fighting, but by late June he was being pressured by Britain to exert his government's authority in Dublin, or they would use troops to attack the Four Courts. Collins relented, and the attack signalled the beginning of the Irish Civil War, which saw him surrender his position in the Dáil and accept the role of commander-in-chief of the Free State Army. Hugh Kennedy, the first Attorney General of the Free State, wrote to Hazel, asking her to keep her distance from Collins, as he felt she was a distraction to the political cause. It was referred to as 'ending the chapter', which Kennedy knew was a period of glamour before Collins assumed his dangerous position in the war. Hazel was furious and she begged Kennedy to let her 'hold the end of the reins … so I may imagine I am guiding the splendid studs that you will control and handle so well'.[21] Her plea went unanswered, and with Dublin in ruins from bombs, she remained isolated in London and implored Lavery to cable Kennedy, to ask if he could paint the scenes of warfare. Lavery was rejected. Perhaps his request was viewed as a frivolous one, as a cable was sent, informing him that the Four Courts were burned out, street fighting was taking place, and civilian lives were at risk. Unbeknownst to his men, Collins sent Hazel a poem, calling her his 'little bird, little love'.

Although the Civil War would last until the following year, Hazel was desperate to visit Ireland and was offered lodgings at the vacant Viceregal Lodge in Phoenix Park. She declined, as she was reluctant to stay at an address steeped in British history and a target for anarchists. The day before her arrival, Arthur Griffith suffered a brain haemorrhage and died, which shocked Collins, particularly when he was warned that his own life was at risk. He stole away to be with Hazel, using his tour of Cork as an excuse to spend time with her, and she later confided they had spent a clandestine weekend together. Years later, Hazel claimed that Collins had begged her to leave Lavery and to run away to America with him, and at the eleventh hour she had a change of heart and decided to remain with her husband. There is no proof of such stories, except for Hazel's remark that she was a Catholic, and Catholics do not believe in divorce – she did not elaborate whether she, as a Catholic, also believed in infidelity. Her daughter, Alice Trudeau, dismissed any notion of an affair or secret weekends spent together whilst the country was caught in a civil war, by suggesting her mother was 'undersexed ... she liked things to be beautiful', and that Hazel had once said, 'Affairs are such shabby things.'[22] Their last encounter occurred on a weekend in August, when Hazel asked Collins to Kiltreagh, Foxrock, the home of her friend, Sir Horace Plunkett. She and Collins travelled in his train carriage, and were greeted by Plunkett's dinner guests, George Bernard Shaw, Daisy Fingall and Charlotte Shaw, but they left early as Collins was going to Cork the following morning.

Throughout Hazel's time in Ireland she feared for Collins's safety and often awoke in the night, pale and screaming, having dreamt he was covered in blood. She had been with him twice before when he had avoided assassination attacks: once at the Royal Marine hotel, where her position blocked a sniper from shooting Collins, and afterwards when a car carrying them both was ambushed by bullets and he grabbed her by the neck and pushed her into the well of the car, thus saving her life. The premonition was not unfounded, for on the evening of 22 August whilst Collins and his convoy were driving through Béal na Bláth, a small village in Cork, his car was ambushed by Irregulars. Ignoring orders to 'drive like hell', Collins got out of the car and attempted to fight his attackers. The fight lasted for forty minutes, before he was fatally shot in the head. Hazel learned of the news the following morning, and said, 'I knew it before I saw the papers. I had seen him in a dream, his face covered with blood.' Consumed by grief, she wanted to wear widow's weeds but was convinced by Daisy Fingall not to, as she thought that right belonged to Kitty Kiernan. Lavery painted Collins lying in state and draped in the flag of the Irish Free State, and entitled it 'Love of Ireland'; at the funeral at the Pro-Cathedral in Dublin, he also painted the Requiem Mass from the gallery. At Collins's graveside, at Glesnevin Cemetery, Hazel waited for the mourners to leave before throwing her rosary beads, made from real pearls, onto the grave, but Lavery retrieved them. She defied Lavery and threw them down again; he, once again, picked them up, with the warning that someone would steal the beads. They were later displayed under glass and placed on the grave.

Returning to London, Hazel remained in deep mourning and to channel her grief she wrote poems in Collins's memory, began a scrapbook of his life and their time together, and copied the letters he had sent to his sister, Hannie. Amongst her collection was a shamrock, given to her by Hannie, from where Collins had fallen in Béal na Bláth. Collins's personal belongings relating to Hazel were sent to her: part of a letter he had written to her on the day he was killed, a lock of her hair, and a ruby brooch. As with Hazel's attachment to Collins when he was alive, Lavery accepted his wife's grief for another man, perhaps knowing all along that he was 'her Sunday husband'.[23] Following political affairs in Ireland and the progress of the country as it endeavoured to sever ties with Britain made Hazel feel close to Collins, and she began to correspond with his friend, Kevin O'Higgins, vice-president of the provisional government.

Through her friendship with Kevin O'Higgins, Hazel had hoped to continue the work that had begun with Collins, in helping Ireland and Britain to find a solution to their ideological differences. In 1923 she resumed her visits to Ireland, firstly for the unveiling of a cenotaph to commemorate Collins, during which she sat in the front row next to Hannie and was mistaken for Kitty Kiernan, and secondly to attend the Dublin Horse Show. On a later visit, accompanied by Lavery, they stayed at the Viceregal Lodge as the guest of the Governor-General Tim Healy, and at the home of O'Higgins. During this period she found herself cast in a new role, as Healy's wife had suffered a stroke and his daughter disliked entertaining, and so Hazel became a temporary vicereine when the occasion called. Her friends thought her visits to Ireland were foolhardy, as they continued to think of it as a dangerous place. Lytton Strachey asked whether Hazel was in Scotland shooting things, or in Ireland being shot at.

Perhaps this new sense of power inspired Hazel's latest view that Ireland should be united, at the cost of Northern Ireland forfeiting its ties to Britain. It was a dangerous stance, and Charles Londonderry accused her of being naïve and short-sighted, and his original feelings of mistrust toward the Free State and those who had formed it were restored. When

Ramsay MacDonald succeeded Lloyd George as Britain's first Labour prime minister in 1924, Hazel seized the opportunity to influence his decision on Ireland. She invited the Colonial Secretary, J.H. Thomas, to meet W.T. Cosgrave, president of the provisional government, but he refused as he thought it would reflect badly on the British government's involvement with Northern Ireland, though he accepted an invitation to dine alone with Hazel and Lavery. It was an unsuccessful evening, for instead of discussing Ireland he spoke only of himself. Months later, when Stanley Baldwin's Conservative government replaced MacDonald's, Hazel also clashed with Churchill, then Chancellor of the Exchequer, over his opinion that the Free State was making a mistake in agreeing to the partition of Ireland. At the Savoy she encountered Lloyd George, who shared Churchill's opinion, and unsuccessfully demanded of him, 'I want to settle this Irish dispute tonight.' She dismissed Churchill and Lloyd George's lack of interest as 'selfish'.

By 1924 Hazel was the recipient of Kevin O'Higgins's admiration and it boosted her fragile ego. Once again she felt at the forefront of Irish politics, and as with her relationship with Collins, O'Higgins, too, began to send her poetry. In a poem composed from the letters of her name, his line on 'L' spoke of her being the love of his life. His personal feelings for Hazel were unabashedly described in his rambling letters, which often lacked any mention of politics, and spoke of her being 'the sweetest, most wonderful influence'[24] in his life. It is interesting that Hazel destroyed the letters from Collins, and now, with O'Higgins's letters, she cut out certain words so their tone could not be misconstrued and placed the cuttings in envelopes, which she dated. What became clear from their correspondence was that he was in love with her, a feeling that was intensified on his trips to London, to discuss politics, though in person his 'poor old stunned brain'[25] was unable to think coherently. His admiration brought Hazel closer to politics than ever before, with an invitation to visit the Dáil to listen to questions put forward by visitors in the gallery. It was a surprising invitation, for O'Higgins was known to exclude women stenographers if he felt certain subjects might corrupt them.

Although Lavery had tolerated Hazel's fixation with Collins, he was less enthusiastic about her growing friendship with O'Higgins and took her to New York for the winter. It had been fourteen years since Hazel last visited America and she did not want to go, but followed Lavery as he had several commissions from rich families on the Eastern Seaboard and he extended their stay by a further two months. Frustrated, Hazel behaved poorly toward his patrons, which did not have the intended effect and they were all the more eager to have Lavery paint them; one patron gifted her a diamond bracelet. The prolonged stay conspired to make her feel homesick, though not for London but Ireland. A brief visit was made to Ireland, when she and Lavery attended the Horse Show, though Hazel sat with O'Higgins and they looked toward Balls Bridge rather than the turf, lost in thought over the fate of their beloved country. Hazel left for America once more, to accompany Lavery to New York and Boston for his commissions, and then on to Palm Beach for his exhibition. She felt as desperate as before and O'Higgins did not conceal his disappointment at her leaving, and waxed lyrical about the 'spring bringing [her] back'. During their time apart, O'Higgins became estranged from his wife, who had given birth ten days before he wrote a particularly revealing letter to Hazel, confiding he was 'lost and broken' without her.

Hazel returned from America in time for Ireland's general election. She had promised to visit O'Higgins in March, a plan thwarted by the illness of her stepdaughter, Eileen, who was suffering from tuberculosis, from which she would die in 1935. Her own daughter, Alice, was living in Kilkenny and had fallen in love with Jack McEnery, a farmer in his mid-thirties whom she married in 1930. It was a bitter disappointment for Hazel, as she wished her only child to marry an aristocrat, and she never accepted McEnery as her son-in-law. Pining for Hazel, O'Higgins wrote of his desire to lose the general election, as it would give him the freedom to see her when he pleased, telling her, 'I want you, want you, want you.'[26] The political situation, although Ireland was no closer to removing itself from British rule, remained positive for O'Higgins, as his competitor, Eamon de Valera, who founded the Fianna Fáil, had gained seats in the Dáil but could not sit, as he refused to take the Oath of Allegiance to King George V. On his way to a conference in Geneva he visited Hazel at Cromwell Place, and she thought him wretched-looking – the consequence of his unhappy marriage and mounting political responsibilities. They were to meet again, on his return from

Geneva, and spent the day together before he left for Dublin. Three days later, O'Higgins was to suffer the same fate as Collins, when, walking to mass, he was fatally shot.

Hazel grieved for O'Higgins with the intensity that she had for Collins. She blamed herself, thinking that she was a bad omen to the men who loved her to the point of obsession, and refused to attend the funeral, as she did not wish to go to Ireland ever again. She now called it 'that most lovely and cruel country'.[27] Without O'Higgins's influence, Irish politicians ignored her invitations to visit Cromwell Place, as like Lord Londonderry, a decade before, they dismissed her political opinions as romantic and unrealistic. Deeply offended by the snubs that befell her, she exclaimed that she was 'tired of fighting Irish battles on English soil'.[28] Further intensifying Hazel's feelings toward Ireland was the suggestion, by O'Higgins before his death, to propose Lavery as the new Viceregent, thinking that Hazel's empathy toward the Free State and her connections with the British government would settle their treacherous political landscape. This proposal was not accepted, as Hazel rightly sensed that a Belfast-born peer and an American woman would bring farcical undertones to the post. Though, despite her misgivings, she dreamt of becoming, in her words, the 'Queen of Ireland'.

However, Hazel was to have a prominent place in Irish history, when the director of the National Gallery of Ireland advised the Currency Commission to use her portrait on the Free State's new bank notes. Lavery was engaged as the portrait artist and the identity of his model was to be concealed, though the ruse did not fool anyone, as Hazel had been the subject of several of his paintings and her likeness was immediately recognised. She denied any connection to the portrait, and sent a photograph of herself to friends claiming there was no comparison. Perhaps it was done to appease her vanity, for the photograph was sent to the *Irish Times*, who published it next to the portrait from the banknotes. It was to serve as her final influence over a country that had become increasingly foreign to her. Eventually Ireland gained its independence from Britain and the Commonwealth in 1949, although she did not live to see it.

In the 1930s Hazel turned her attention to Ramsay MacDonald, who for the second time, was serving as prime minister. The friendship filled a void left empty by her abandonment of Irish politics, and it appealed to her ego to be on first name terms with the prime minister. A widower whose wife had died in 1911, MacDonald was renowned for his intimate friendships with society women, whose company he enjoyed even if he found them indiscreet. Thus, he refrained from sharing political secrets, though at times he broke his silence with Hazel, who confirmed his suspicions when she repeated their private conversations at dinner parties. She had always boasted of her political liaisons and had shared her letters from Collins and O'Higgins, as though to prove their closeness, even if, after their deaths, she was obsessed with destroying the letters she had sent to them. During their friendship Hazel confessed to being in love with MacDonald and he laughed off her sentiment, but in time responded with poems to her infatuation, calling her presence 'the raptures of paradise'. By then Hazel had quelled her feelings for him, as she had discovered that he distributed similar romantic tokens to his other women friends. The glow of their friendship dimmed when MacDonald became preoccupied with greater political responsibilities, namely the economic depression and the rise of unemployment in the early 1930s.

As Hazel grew older and less secure in her looks, she befriended young men who craved her celebrity and welcomed her society connections. Evelyn Waugh was one such admirer and their friendship was formed as he gathered material for his novel, *Vile Bodies*, which made him a literary star. However as his celebrity grew and his ego was being satisfied elsewhere with the Bright Young Things, he found Hazel too possessive and moved further away from her. She replaced him with Cecil Beaton, then on the brink of fame, who twice photographed her for *Vogue* and featured her in his 1930 *Book of Beauty*. In many ways it was her last hurrah.

As the years advanced, Hazel grew increasingly depressed, provoked by the death of her friends and the loss of her looks, and although she did not retreat from society, she symbolically bowed out of Lavery's paintings by having her likeness painted from behind, or her face concealed from view. A macabre portrait was composed by Lavery, of Hazel reclining in the dentist's chair, having a wisdom tooth extracted. It marked an ongoing period of ill-health for Hazel, for although her health was often fragile, the onset of myocarditis, a life-threatening condition, saw her become bedridden and unable to talk on the telephone or receive guests, as Lavery worried the excitement would kill her. From her sickbed she became the subject of Lavery's penultimate portrait of her, her gaunt frame contrasted by an enormous canopy bed. She died in her sleep, on 3 January 1935. Days later, a final portrait was painted of Hazel encased in her coffin, concluding an end to her time as his muse.

10

SOCIETY STAR:
JEAN MASSEREENE

Jean Massereene was never going to play by the rules, despite her high birth and place as a woman in society. 'The worst of being a woman is the pre-conceived idea of her that is held by the average man,' she said. 'He has formed a mould into which he would fit all womankind. If she does not take kindly to this mould he tries to force her into it.'[1] She was born Jean Barbara Ainsworth, on 3 December 1883, in Kensington,[2] London, the second-born and thus far only surviving child of John Stirling Ainsworth and Margaret Catherine (*née* Macredie), an Australian[3] of Scots parentage. Her father, whose maternal family were Scots, was a wealthy industrialist and headed iron ore mines and flax mills; he was also a merchant banker, the chairman of the Cleator and Workington Junction Railway, and the Liberal Member of Parliament for Argyllshire. As such, he voted in favour of the Women's Enfranchisement Bill of 1908, and in 1917 he was created a baronet for his public services. Three more children were to follow Jean: Thomas and John Stirling, and Margaret Louise. The Ainsworths divided their time between several properties: Ardanaiseig House, in Argyll and Bute, on the edge of Lough Awe, Harecroft Hall in Cumberland (from where John's paternal family hailed), 20 Queen's Gate, London, and later 55 Eaton Place.

With no shortage of money and nine[4] servants, including a governess, a nurse, and a French lady's maid, Jean's upbringing was that of privilege. As with many upper-class girls, she and her younger sister, to whom she was particularly close, were taught by a governess at home whilst her two brothers attended Eton. With a sharp mind, a quality encouraged by her father, and mostly self-educated – she was well-read and followed the latest literary stars – she 'realised more and more what a blessing it was to have a good education when one was young'. She said there was 'nothing that so fitted men and women to take part in the battle of life as a really sound education in childhood'.[5] As clever and single-minded as Jean was, she did what was expected of her: she was presented at court at the age of 18, and at 21 she was engaged to be married, to Algernon William John Clotworthy Whyte-Melville Skeffington, the second son of the 11th Viscount Massereene and 4th Viscount Ferrard, of Antrim Castle, in the Irish province of Ulster.

The marriage to Alergnon, or 'Algie' as Jean called him, was not an ambitious one on her behalf, for he was ten years her senior and not expected to inherit his father's titles or money. Founded in 1660, in the Peerage of Ireland, the Viscountcy of Massereene permitted female descendants to inherit the title; however when it was elevated to an earldom (1756-1818) the latter title became extinct owing to it being passed to a female, before returning to a male heir with the 10th Viscount Massereene. The Viscountcy of Ferrard, also in the Peerage of Ireland, was merged with Massereene through the marriage of Harriet Skeffington, a viscountess in her own right, and Thomas Henry Skeffington (born Foster), the 2nd Viscount Ferrard. There were the additional titles of Baron Loughneagh (1660) and Baron Oriel (1821), the latter belonging to the Peerage of the United Kingdom and under which title the Viscounts Massereene and Ferrard sat in the House of Lords. As with the unconventional passing of the titles, their fortune had also passed through many hands. It was largely squandered by the eccentric John Clotworthy, the 1st Viscount Massereene, who was imprisoned for betraying the Parliamentarian cause and for embezzlement, and who died in 1665; although his son-in-law succeeded him, he bequeathed his estate to his mistress. His brothers challenged the will and successfully retrieved the money and properties, but had to pay her off with a large sum and an annual allowance thereafter. Despite Clotworthy's spendthrift ways, the Massereene fortune increased as his descendants intermarried with the landed gentry, but as land and tax laws were reformed their money reduced. Therefore Algie was expected to find a career and upon leaving the Royal Military Academy Sandhurst he was commissioned as a 2nd lieutenant in the 17th Lancers, moving through the ranks to 1st lieutenant and captain. From 1900–02 he served as adjutant to his regiment in the Boer War, during which he was wounded in the shoulder by a shell splinter, and was twice mentioned in despatches. For his bravery he was awarded a Distinguished Service Order and given the rank of brevet major.

On 16 February 1905 Jean and Algie were married at St Margaret's Church, Westminster. The bride wore a gown of white chiffon velours, trimmed with Limerick lace, and an uncommon wreath[6] on her head made of silver wheatears mixed with orange blossoms and shamrock. The eight bridesmaids were dressed in Elizabethan-style costumes of white satin with the upper part of the bodice and sleeves a lattice-work of satin and pearls, with coils of blue velvet from which hung a tulle veil. They were given sapphire shamrock brooches, a gift from Algie. It can be assumed that Jean's father gave her the use of 55 Eaton Place as a wedding present, for the address is listed in various diaries from the period, all crediting her with throwing parties at the residence. They honeymooned at Algie's parents' home, Oriel Temple, in Co. Louth, and in the years before tensions surrounding Irish Home Rule were to arise, Jean and Algie were prominent figures of Dublin society.

Three months after Jean's marriage to Algie, their fortunes changed under tragic circumstances when his elder brother, Oriel Skeffington, died at the age of 33 at a health resort in Scotland. As Oriel was unmarried and without an heir, his titles were to pass on to Algie following their father's death. This happened three months later, on 26 June, when Lord Massereene died from an illness brought on by alcoholism, and Algie succeeded him as the 12th Viscount Massereene and the 5th Viscount Ferrard. At the of age of 21 Jean found herself the chatelaine of the family's Irish Seat, Antrim Castle, a seventeenth-century castle in the province of Ulster, rebuilt in 1813 as a Georgian-Gothic mansion, as well as the nearby Skeffington Lodge, a hunting residence overlooking Lough

Neagh. There was also Oriel Temple, their preferred Irish residence for its close proximity to Dublin, and a London townhouse at 108 Lancaster Gate. She made a striking viscountess and photographs taken of her during that period show an exotic creature, as her black hair, dark eyes and pale skin set her apart from the typical English roses who were revered for their fair beauty. Said to be self-conscious of her tall, slight figure,[7] she was credited with starting the trend for wearing ropes of pearls down to her waist, elaborate headbands, and long, shapeless dresses, which contradicted the exaggerated forms of the early Edwardian era. It had also become clear not only to Algie but to her contemporaries that she was an eccentric young woman who was far from conventional. Her husband found this charming; however as the years passed, her peers dismissed her as being a peculiar individual, and that was not always a welcomed trait within her circle. In the meantime, she courted celebrity as a fashion icon, and was said to be 'socially ambitious',[8] which coming from her fellow peeresses was viewed as an insult.

In 1909 Jean's celebrity was established with her appearance in the book *England's Beautiful Ladies*, which had an introduction written by Queen Alexandra. She was photographed wearing her viscountess's coronet and an evening dress with a netted shawl, under which a caption read that she was 'an ardent follower of hounds'.[9] Although in the photograph her face was devoid of make-up, she often emphasised her dark looks with cosmetics and sometimes painted a beauty spot on her cheekbone. This undoubtedly attracted criticism, for painted faces were considered common and the mark of an immoral woman, and as the years progressed her fashion was thought inappropriate; she favoured strapless and backless dresses, long opera coats and furs, and earrings that reached her shoulders. Far more scandalous to her contemporaries was the certainty that she was not wearing a corset underneath her flimsy clothes. In doing this, she adhered to Helen Gilbert Ecob's book, *The Well-Dressed Woman*:

The corset curse among women is more insidious than the drink curse among men. Total abstinence from both sins is the only safe ground. A woman can no more be trusted with a corset, than a drunkard with a glass of whisky.

The diary of Lillian Spender made clear her views on Jean, for she wrote, 'I wondered who Lady Massereene was. She looks like a Gaiety Girl. She came to breakfast one bitterly cold, grey morning in a lilac cotton frock and a sunbonnet! Why a sunbonnet? She looked more picturesque, so I suppose that was why.' On another occasion Lillian wrote in her diary that Jean looked 'very actressy, but certainly pretty'.[10] However, Jean dismissed those who thought her vain, and said:

What we need is to think less about appearances and more about doing things. It is better to win races surely, and pit our muscles and brains against our fellows in friendly rivalry than to emulate the peacock. The peacock is a brainless bird, and despised by the sparrow, and those who think only of clothes resemble him.[11]

During the early months of Jean and Algie's marriage they endured long separations due to his military career; though in December 1905 she joined him on his military tour of India and remained there until the following spring. She was expecting a baby and returned to England for her confinement; however, she contracted a virus and gave birth to a stillborn son. In an open letter to her, the *Tatler* wrote, 'I may say that you once had a small son who, however, did not survive and that you have at present no children. Hence the title and estates may pass to a distant relative.'[12] Aside from childbearing she also understood that her role bore social responsibilities, and with Algie's transfer in 1907 to the North Irish Horse where he commanded A Squadron, she settled permanently at Antrim Castle. From there she carried out her philanthropic work and accepted several patronages. She led the Antrim branch of the Women's National Health Association (WNHA), founded in 1907 by Lady Aberdeen and dedicated to eliminating the 'white scourge'[13] (tuberculosis) and reducing high rates of infant mortality in Ireland. Matters relating to health and social conditions would remain a prominent interest, and amongst the WNHA's greatest achievements was providing children with free dental and health checks. She organised the 'Tooth and Nail'[14] drive, which encouraged children to care for their teeth and hands, as she believed in educating children in matters relating to their own health. Each year she hosted a party for 500 children on the grounds of Antrim Castle, and prizes were given to those who demonstrated the best care. She also served as patroness to the Antrim Philharmonic Society, and to the local infant schools.

In February 1909, Jean gave birth to a daughter named Diana Elizabeth Margaret Skeffington. It was evident from letters and newspaper articles that she was an indulgent mother, and from an early age Diana was her constant companion and often accompanied her to social gatherings and charity outings to visit the poor and infirm.[15] She also called Jean by her first name, a demonstration of how close they were. Years later in the 1920s she attended a fete at Mount Stewart, the Ulster seat of the Marquess of Londonderry, and a guest remarked to Lady Londonderry that a certain 'tall, good looking girl' in the refreshments marquee was 'working harder than any waitress'. In years to come Jean granted Diana an amount of freedom that was unheard of for an aristocratic child, for she was a member of the Antrim Girl Guides and the local hockey club. More startling to those who worked on the estate was Diana's friendship with the head gardener's daughter, for when she visited their home she entered through the back door and therefore had to pass through the scullery. But the idiosyncrasies of her upbringing were apparent and when Diana wanted to return to the castle she merely stood up, a signal for her nanny to put on her coat. It was not done out of haughtiness; she had simply known no different.

Fourteen months after Diana's birth, Jean was delivered of a son who lived for a day. She had been manning a stall at an exhibition of Irish goods in Dublin the month before, and a few days prior to his birth she had attended a party at Dublin Castle. She convalesced for a month at Oriel Temple, and then spent a week at her father's house in London. Returning to Antrim Castle in August, Jean opened a bazaar in aid of a Masonic lodge in Randalstown, and she appeared in good humour, as her speech joked about the secret society and its rituals. In November she offered the use of the castle's Oak Room to hold a meeting for those in favour of forming an Antrim committee for the National Society for the Prevention of Cruelty to Children. Addressing the large numbers who answered Jean's call, Algie spoke of his personal views on the charity and how he hoped no child would suffer needlessly. It was agreed by the charity's representative for Ireland that a branch of the NSPCC would be founded in Antrim, and that a ladies' committee would also be formed. Jean was appointed secretary of the new committee, and she said it was 'a sincere pleasure to her to help forward the work of the society in any way'.[16]

In 1912 Jean and Algie embarked on a lengthy period of travelling, beginning with a three-month 'pleasure tour' of Australia. In Canberra they stayed at Government House with the Governor-General and Lady Denman, and a ball was given in Jean's honour by the Young Women's Christian Association. At the Tablelands, in Queensland, they were the guests of Mr and Mrs W.F. Ogilvie, and before leaving the region they stayed with Mrs W. Collins at Beaudesert. 'I loved all the outdoor life, the polo, the shooting,' Algie said of their visit. 'It was wonderful to be up at 4 a.m., and, in Queensland, essential, too, for I found the heat a bit too much.' There was a weekend spent with the opera singer Dame Nellie Melba, at Coombe Cottage, Coldstream, with its pergolas of roses, brilliantly coloured birds, and swimming pool. Jean, a collector of antique china, undoubtedly admired Dame Nellie's priceless objects of art. At a race meeting Jean surprised onlookers when she debuted her newest style of dressing: a long skirt, which she left purposefully unbuttoned twelve inches above the hem to display her petticoat. It was reminiscent of an Assyrian dress she had worn to Lady Desborough's ball at Taplow Court, with a sheer bodice, a skirt with carefully placed panels, and a shawl tied around her hips. 'At first glance it looks rather odd, not pretty or graceful by any means,'[17] a newspaper reported of her race outfit. Three months later, Jean and Algie left Australia for New Zealand, where they stayed for several weeks, before sailing through the Pacific Islands to begin a tour of America.

During this time Jean had taken an interest in Irish politics, particularly the issue of Home Rule, which she opposed. It marked a period of ill-feeling between herself and her father, who sided with the Home Rulers and thought his daughter was being influenced by Algie, a member of the Orange Order and head of the Skeffington Loyal Orange Lodge. Regardless of her father's disapproval and their differing political ideologies, she allied herself with Ulster Unionists and believed Ireland should remain part of the United Kingdom and under British rule. With a large Protestant stronghold in Antrim she appealed to Unionist locals and spoke at the local Protestant Hall about remaining loyal to the king:

'The people of Antrim had always been noted for their loyalty to their King and Empire.'[18] On one occasion she drew on the Williamite War in Ireland to give a rousing speech on the 1688–89 Siege of Derry, and afterwards she unveiled a banner which displayed a painting of Algie in his North Irish Horse uniform. She also wrote an article asserting the fiscal reasons for remaining under British rule:

> Assuming, for example, that an Irish Parliament were to impose a duty on foreign corn for the purpose of benefiting the Irish farmer, what effect would this measure have on the artisans and mill hands in Belfast? Are the workers in the shipbuilding yards of Belfast and in the linen mills in the North of Ireland to pay more for their daily bread in order that the farmer in the South of Ireland may obtain a higher price for his corn? … Great Britain is the best market for Irish produce in the world, and might conceivably, though improbably enter upon a policy of retaliation.[19]

This interest in politics saw Jean becoming increasingly militant, and she and Algie sympathised with Sir Edward Carson, a Unionist politician, and his appeal to Ulster to reject a Home Rule Bill. Further wounding her father was Jean's involvement with Carson's Ulster Volunteer Force, founded in 1913 to resist Home Rule, and Algie was appointed officer in command over the 3rd South Antrim Battalion. It was largely a secretive operation, with the Massereenes, the Londonderrys, and Lord O'Neill, of the neighbouring Shane's Castle, opening their homes and grounds as meeting points for local men to enlist in the UVF, and to hold fundraisers. The Massereenes land became a parade ground for the UVF, where, after marches and various displays of pageantry, Jean inspected the men and passed out cigarettes, known as 'smokes',[20] and gave rousing speeches to the local supporters. As her father had predicted, it placed both Jean and Algie in a dangerous position and they became the target of Irish Nationalists, particularly when he removed his great-great-grandfather, John Foster's, chair and mace from the National Museum of Ireland. Foster, or Lord Oriel, had been the last Speaker in the Irish House of Commons, and Algie had gifted the items five years prior to removing them to Antrim Castle.

He feared Nationalists would claim the items for themselves, and his actions caused outrage, with the *Dublin Telegraph* accusing him of 'raping' the museum of its rightful heritage.

A rumour had spread through Antrim that Algie had been arrested and that Carson was hiding at the castle. In a letter to her friend Theresa, Lady Londonderry, Jean described how the rumour had provoked an 'angry' and 'over-zealous' crowd to follow their housekeeper, who was manhandled in an attempt to retrieve information. 'The servants have bolted,' she added, and she was left with a butler, footman, housekeeper and cook. Owing to the discord, she missed the London season and opted to remain at Antrim Castle with Algie. She wrote:

> I'm afraid I will not be in town this season, unless I come with Algie when the [Home Rule] Bill comes up in the Lords as I don't like leaving him here as they [Irish Nationalists] have threatened to shoot him when they get the chance. Of course I would probably feel anxious all the time if I was living without him.[21]

Jean's fears for Algie were not unfounded, for he had been privy to secret information regarding the UVF and on an April morning in 1914 he watched from a safe distance in his chauffeur-driven car as 25,000 guns and several million rounds of ammunition were smuggled into Larne Harbour. Known as the Larne Gun Run, it was organised by Major Frederick H. Crawford and Captain Wilfrid Spender, and Algie kept 150 rifles at Antrim Castle, inspiring his nickname the 'Machine Gun Lord'. However, Captain Wilfrid and his wife, Lillian Spender, held a dim view of Jean, whom they thought vain and self-serving, a feeling provoked when she appointed herself in charge of various fundraisers that were supposed to be presided over by Lillian. As she had done in an earlier diary entry, Lillian attacked Jean's appearance, and wrote to Captain Wilfrid that her nemesis was 'looking quite impossible as she always does'.[22]

Far from defeated by the heightened tensions from Nationalists and the disapproval from the Spenders, Jean founded the Volunteer Aid Attachment Corps of nurses. The training consisted of five weeks with the Red Cross or St John Ambulance to ensure the women were equipped to care for the UVF if they went into battle with the Nationalists. She said:

'We don't want to fight, but by jingo if we do!' sums up the feeling in the North of Ireland today pretty accurately, and should furnish an answer to the question whether Ulster will fight if the Government succeed in passing a Home Rule bill.[23]

A dressing station was established in Randalstown, five miles from the Massereene seat, whilst Antrim Castle and Shane's Castle were on standby to be transformed into clearing hospitals.

On Easter Monday of 1914 Carson came to Antrim Castle to review almost 3,000 volunteers from the three south Antrim battalions. A luncheon was given at the castle in his honour, and amongst the UVF hierarchy were the Marquess of Londonderry, the Duchess of Abercorn, and various lords and ladies from the Peerage of Ireland. Afterwards Carson inspected the nursing corps, led by Jean, on a swarm facing the castle; it was comprised of eighty members from Antrim and its surrounding towns of Randalstown, Lisburn, Glenavy and Crumlin. Prayers were followed by the formal dedication of the UVF's colours, made by the Lord Bishop. After this, Jean presented Carson with the King's colour and the regimental colour of the battalion, a personal gift from her. She wrote to Theresa Londonderry, 'I must say I felt extremely proud of my Algie as he rode past at the head of his men.'[24]

As there were no women in local government, Jean was a rare female voice in a field dominated by men. Her views on women's roles in society were made clear when, opening a bazaar in the village of Dunadry in aid of Muckamore New Schools, she referred to the topical Suffragette movement. The school's colours of purple, white and green were Suffragette colours, and she joked that if any such ladies were present they should not begin 'operations by destroying the New Schools'. She added:

I believe in the higher education of women – the reason was that education makes them much better wives and mothers. The future of the empire depended to a very large extent, if not altogether, upon the mental training of mothers, and the way in which they brought up their children.[25]

The speech was an example of her chameleon-like tendencies to appeal to whichever crowd she was addressing. However ten years later, in 1925, in a column for the *Daily Express*, Jean championed a woman's right to work for a living: 'A right to work should be the privilege of every woman, whether she marries or not, even if she is a rich man's daughter.'[26] She also wrote an article for the *Girl's Own Paper* on the importance of young women learning a vocation. On the subject of her involvement in politics, she said, 'Men would give [women] a higher place if she demanded it, and it would be well for her if she did.'[27]

The arrival of the First World War saw Jean move out of her husband's shadow and into a role that was entirely her own. On 20 August 1914 Algie left for the Front with the North Irish Horse, and on his departure from Antrim Castle there had been scenes of gratitude as he travelled the short distance to the railway station. He was accompanied by Jean and their 5-year-old daughter, Diana, and the Massereene Brass and Reed Band, founded by Algie's father, played a number of patriotic tunes on the platform as the train departed. It was an era in which Jean's charity work came to the forefront and divided locals seemed to forget about, or at least forgive, her alliance with Sir Edward Carson. In Algie's absence she joined a distress committee aimed at helping dependents of soldiers and sailors who had gone to war. She also stepped into the role of welcoming visiting royal representatives and servicemen who came to Antrim, either to speak on behalf of the Empire or to convalesce at Shane's Castle. Along with members of the local branch of the Red Cross she collected money for wounded soldiers, thousands of which were being cared for in the town. And she performed with her 'bird like voice' at a Protestant Hall concert to raise funds for St John Ambulance and the Dental Clinic for local schools. The National Institutes of Health presented Jean with a silver salver in 1916, in appreciation for her fundraising work. She was a trained soprano and perhaps would have preferred a career on the stage than a conventional life, though such a vocation would have been frowned upon. Interestingly, Algie's sister, Norah Johnston, was a professional soprano and ballad singer, and having married a penniless clergyman, Rev. Charles J. Johnston, she scandalised society when she adopted the nom de plume, Mme Esperance, and performed at the Belfast Hippodrome.

On 22 October 1914 Jean's war work was temporarily interrupted by the birth of her son, whilst Algie was in France with the North Irish Horse.* Born a week after the death of Jean's younger brother, John, who was the first of the 11th Hussars to be killed in action, she named the child after him. He was christened John Clotworthy Talbot Foster Whyte-Melville Skeffington, and was known by his nickname 'Jock'. His godparents were the Marchioness of Londonderry, his grandmother Florence the Dowager Viscountess Massereene and Ferrard, Mr George Spencer-Churchill and Sir Edward Carson.[28] In her typical way she shunned tradition by not only refusing to adhere to a suitable mourning period, as her sister's husband was also killed a month later, but by shirking her confinement after Jock's birth. Her baby was less than a month old when she began collecting money for a motor ambulance service, which she planned to send out to France,[29] and she arranged for a fancy dress party to be held in Antrim in aid of the North Irish Horse Ambulance Fund, and donated plants from the castle's garden for the occasion. In 1915 she was appointed Commandant of Women's Legion Canteens, founded by Edith Londonderry, which over the period of the war had enlisted 40,000 female volunteers. Dressed in her usual flamboyant style, a group of soldiers mistook Jean for a prostitute and asked if she had had much luck at Piccadilly the night before.[30] With her usual good humour she laughed it off and repeated the anecdote for years to come. She trained as a Red Cross nurse and volunteered at London hospitals, tending to the wounded. In 1918, Jean, along with other aristocratic nurses, appeared in uniform in a Hollywood silent film, *The Great Love*, starring Lilian Gish.

★ Algie led his squadron through the retreat from Mons advancing to the Aisne, and in the subsequent fighting around Ypres. He was twice mentioned in despatches: in October 1914 and February 1915. In May 1915 he was appointed deputy assistant adjutant and quartermaster general in the adjutant general and quartermaster general's staff in Egypt. Later that year he was appointed assistant quartermaster general with the temporary rank of lieutenant-colonel. He served in similar General Staff roles throughout the war. He relinquished his commission in the North Irish Horse on 5 July 1924.

The post-war years saw Jean resume her hedonistic social life and with spiritualism on the rise she began to speak openly about her psychic experiences. She befriended the society spiritualist Violet Tweedale and contributed to her book *Ghosts I have Seen*, and became renowned for her parties at Lancaster Gate, in which her friends partook in séances. The fascination with spiritualism was always there, for at a garden party in 1918, which Jean hosted in aid of the Women's National Health Association, she hired a palm reader[31] to tell fortunes. That year her mother had died, and this might have prompted her to take a more serious interest than before. In the mid-1920s Jean began to write a column, 'in a most interesting and forceful style',[32] for the *Daily Express*. Her articles ran the gamut of how to entertain a large number of guests, to her sightings of ghosts. The candour in which she wrote was reminiscent of her personality, and although after the war the occult had become a fashionable topic, she still ran the risk of appearing foolish. Of her ghostly encounters, she wrote:

If you say nowadays you have seen a ghost you are no longer greeted with superior derisive smiles. Scientific research has established beyond a doubt that certain phenomena exist, which, commonly called ghosts, are held by many to be the souls of the departed, and which come back for some reason or other to the earth they once inhabited in human form ... I was driving back after a long day with the hounds, with two friends, Lady J, with whom I was staying, and a Mr X, who had an estate a few miles away. We were going along a narrow road when I saw just in front of us a man in a pink coat riding on a grey horse. I turned to Mr X and asked if he knew the man in front, as I had not noticed him during the day ... 'There is no man there,' said Mr X. I appealed to Lady J, but she could see nothing. Finally, however, they both became convinced that I saw something ... Two days later Lady J and I received an invitation to lunch at Mr X's place. When we arrived, Mr X took us straight to the dining-room and pointed to an oil painting over the fireplace. I gasped. It was a picture of the man I had seen riding on the grey horse before.[33]

Before the 1920s Jean had not only spoken of her supernatural encounters but also of her abilities as a psychic. The first of her many confessions was in 1912, and it was prompted by her tiara going missing. She believed it had been stolen by a 'respectable, although rather seedy looking man',[34] whom she had seen on the grounds of the estate. The tiara itself had been brought from the strongroom at Antrim castle, with the purpose of showing it to a relative. Afterwards, she placed it in its tin box and left it in her bedroom, without returning it to the strongroom. It was only when she sent for the tiara, and a servant brought the empty box, that she realised it had been stolen. Speaking in a personal statement, Jean recalled going to her bedroom later that evening, which was above several empty rooms, and she remembered her terrier barking and thought it was at the wind and draughty sounds throughout the old castle. Furthermore she had a dream on three different occasions in which she saw the tiara lying on the bed of the Six Mile Water, on the banks of which the castle had been built. Following her intuition, she told the police of her dream. Under constabulary supervision, Lough Neagh fishermen were ordered to comb the riverbed in the hope they would find the tiara, but they did not.[35] The tiara, worth £2,000 and set with white diamonds, was believed to have been stolen by a network of jewel thieves, as their loot had been discovered in London and several accomplices were arrested. Jean, however, was not reunited with her tiara and she claimed it would have been broken into pieces[36] in order to smuggle it from the castle.

During this period, when the supernatural dominated Jean's interests, she found a kindred spirit in Evan Morgan, the son and heir of Courtenay Morgan, the 1st Viscount Tredegar. The family seat, Tredegar Park, in Wales, was a hub for unique individuals, with the family's interest in the occult well-documented amongst their contemporaries. Viscountess Tredegar, formerly Lady Katharine Carnegie, was a close friend of Jean's and a renowned eccentric; it was rumoured she sat in an enormous bird's nest and that the family practised 'Monarch Mind Control'. It is easy to gauge Jean's attraction to the Tredegars, for despite Evan being a dedicated occultist (perhaps Jean regaled him with her ghost stories), the parties thrown at Tredegar Park were unique, unpredictable, and a world away from the formality of the 'smart set' in London. A homosexual,

Evan, in years to come, took a fancy to Jock, but his infatuation was one-sided, for Jock preferred the opposite sex. An interesting point relating to Jean's personality and her open-mindedness in an age when homosexuality was illegal, was her close friendships with men of that persuasion. Many were married to women, for the sake of appearances, but were privately conducting their own affairs. Harold Nicolson was one such individual whom Jean revered, as one may infer by consulting Sir Robert Bruce Lockhart's diary. Reading between the lines of his entries it was clear that she had something of an unrequited crush on him, '[Pam Chichester] told Max [Lord Beaverbrook] that she could never get on to me for Harold being rung up by Jean Massereene.'[37]

However, with much of Jean's social life being spent in the company of men whose taste ventured to the flamboyant, she felt at home at Tredegar Park. The household was run by handsome menservants, and Evan lived there surrounded by Great Danes and a boxing kangaroo, which visitors had to fend off with a stick. It was common for Evan to tell his guests' fortunes, and an incident recorded in John Bedford's memoirs recounts a familiar evening, with Evan undertaking this in his bedroom, accompanied by a few guests, with the flames from the fire illuminating the four-poster bed. An owl flew around the room, and Evan wore clothing which had belonged to a witch from the past; he also held up the skeleton of a witch's hand. Despite the theatrics, his guests took his 'terrifying interest in black magic' seriously, and there were altars throughout the house. He would become a close friend to Aleister Crowley, and perhaps Jean had met the infamous occultist during her many visits to Tredegar Park, but there is no record detailing this. Recalling a typical house party there, something which Jean would have experienced, John Bedford wrote:

[Evan's] notions of hospitality were pretty bizarre. One of the evenings we were there he settled in his house-party of twenty or thirty people down to dinner and then went off to some regimental or local do, abandoning his guests to carry on as best they could. He had asked some Welsh singers to entertain us during dinner. They stood outside the dining-room windows, which we had to keep open. In the end freezing to death in the icy draught, we got up and shut them, leaving the Welsh singers barbling on happily outside. Folk-songs are not exactly the ideal accompaniment to a meal. Lady Cunard was the only one of us who was civil enough to go out and thank them. Lord Tredegar then came back from what had obviously been a liquid occasion, and flew into a terrible rage when he discovered we had shut the windows on his favourite choir.[38]

Such associations fostered the general belief that Jean was, to quote Alice de Rougement, 'quite mad', but it did not deter her. She took exception to Patrick Balfour, an author and columnist, whom she had invited to Ardanaiseig House to report on a party she was giving. 'Of course write anything you like while you are here,'[39] she wrote to him ahead of his visit. She did not understand how her evening of 'more than three people being in or adjacent to a church yard at the full moon'[40] on Inishail, an island on Loch Awe, could have been misconstrued as a witches' sabbath.

> I can't tell you how it has distressed and upset me. I am quite sure you have no understanding of the meaning of a witches Sabbath or you would never have made a bitchy fictitious statement, which must do me infinite harm. A witches Sabbath is a terrible thing … You have written what you did in pure ignorance and done it as a joke, but having done it, it is up to you to undo the harm you have done.[41]

Although Jean believed in the supernatural and claimed to be psychic, she had 'a horror of anything to do with black magic and witchcraft'.[42] It did not help when Balfour's article went into circulation, and another wrote of Jean leading a coven of witches to 'Loch Awe's haunted island':

> Visitors to the country houses in the district around Loch Awe are all keenly interested in the haunted island in the middle of the loch. Once Count Esterhazy, who was staying with Lord and Lady Massereene at Ardanaiseig, rowed over to this island after dark. On the island is an old cemetery. When he entered the cemetery Count Esterhazy suddenly noticed strange beams of light, like searchlights, rising from the tombs. Whenever these lights are seen it is a sign that someone in the neighbourhood is about to die. Next day the party heard that one

of the crofters by the loch side was dead. Last week Lady Massereene's party went over to the island by moonlight, and held a witches Sabbath among the tombstones. But they saw no searchlights.[43]

The rumour that Jean was a witch and practised the dark arts left her with no alternative but to sue the *Weekly Dispatch*, unless they sent 'deepest and sincerest apologies for such a libellous misstatement'.[44] She warned Balfour that unless he retracted his report she 'shall not be able to prevent Algie writing to the solicitor'.[45] She wrote to Balfour:

> I can't tell you how sorry I am to have to write this letter ... I blame myself for not insisting on seeing what you had written before you left but I never thought or dreamt of your writing anything I could take exception at.[46]

The 1920s were a tumultuous decade for the Massereenes, perhaps foretold in Sir John Lavery's macabre painting of Jean. Years had passed since their association with Sir Edward Carson and the UVF, and during the war Jean had redeemed herself with locals from both Protestant and Catholic backgrounds. But Nationalists did not forget and Antrim Castle became a target for their militant attacks, beginning with the torching of the nearby Galgorm Castle and Shane's Castle. During the latter incident, Lord and Lady O'Neill were taken hostage inside their home whilst it was doused with petrol. In light of the arson attacks, a policeman was sent to guard Antrim Castle; however around October 1922 he was removed and Algie lost his appeal to have him reinstated.

On 28 October 1922, Jean and Algie hosted a party for six guests and after a game of bridge in the library they retired to their bedrooms around midnight. In recent days Algie had been vigilant in ensuring all fires were extinguished and all points of entry were locked, and on the night of the party he carried out this familiar routine. However, at three o'clock in the morning his agent, Colonel Richardson, was awakened by smoke billowing into his bedroom and he immediately raised the alarm. Algie was the next to rise, and he rushed down the passage to Jean's bedroom and found it covered in smoke. Unable to continue he went to the other side of the castle and discovered another fire had started close to the billiard room, and there were also independent fires burning in the Oak Room and dining room. When he tried to activate the cistern, which held almost 2,000 gallons of water, he realised it had been drained and that the windows of the boot room and larder had also been tampered with. He then channelled his efforts into saving the guests and servants: the latter's rooms were 50ft above the ground. An American guest, who was storing her furniture at the castle ahead of her sailing to New York, ran down a burning staircase and suffered injuries to her legs and feet, and Grace d'Arcy, daughter of the Protestant Primate of Ireland, jumped from an upstairs window onto the lawn. A larder boy was hauled from his room and thrown onto the damp grass, which gave him a shock and he ran off in his nightshirt and was later found 10 miles away. There was one fatality, a maid, Ethel Gillingham, who succumbed to smoke inhalation and later died in hospital.

Meanwhile Jean had left her bedroom upon hearing the voice of Colonel Richardson yelling, 'Wake up, Algie, they're in below,' and, like Algie, had rushed out, taking a revolver with her. She went first to Diana's bedroom and pulled her under the staircase and into the night nursery, then she managed to get Jock's nurse out of the room and to safety. However, Jean and the children became trapped on a burning stairwell, and they looked on as the nursery cat's fur caught on fire. 'You must be very good and do as you are told and you will be all right,' she said to the children. As the smoke surrounded them and their chance of escaping grew less likely, she warned the children they might die. They managed to climb out of the nursery window, which led to the chapel roof several feet below, and Colonel Richardson tied sheets together and lowered Jean to safety, and then sent Diana and Jock, one by one, down to her. They became trapped once more and, calling for help, Algie used the gardener's tall ladders for pruning trees to bring them safely to the ground.

Locals surrounded the castle and concentrated their efforts on saving its contents. They threw silver and china out of the windows, and managed to retrieve a billiards table, thinking it of great importance to the family. Paintings and antique furniture were lost, as were historical papers from Oriel Temple, which had been sold recently. The most significant artefact was Speaker's Chair, an ironic casualty, for Algie had believed he was protecting his family's history from the Nationalists of southern Ireland.

In the wake of the fire the Massereenes moved into Skeffington Lodge, a short distance from the remains of Antrim Castle. A few months later, Algie went to the West Indies to recuperate, and Jean left for Paris. In 1923 an insurance claim of £90,000 was made, for malicious damage, and was eventually rejected, for there was no proof as to who or what had started the fire. The evidence presented before the High Court in Belfast, which included a paraffin barrel that had been full before the fire and afterwards was found to be empty, failed to reach a verdict. It was also said that windows in the basement had been forced open, thus enabling the flames to spread at a quicker pace throughout the castle. Perhaps Colonel Richardson had been correct in his statement, that they were being attacked from below. It was suggested that a servant might have acted as an accomplice to the IRA, as not only were the cisterns drained before the fire, but several items of furniture were covered in mineral oil. Regardless of the IRA's arson attacks on stately homes and properties representative of British rule, it was questioned why the Massereenes thought themselves targets of such individuals.

In the weeks leading up to the fire, Jean had received anonymous letters, warning that she would soon 'meet her maker', which she had shown to Algie but not the police. Such letters were sent in retaliation to her pro-Unionist speeches, particularly one she had given in 1920, with the message: 'Let's arm ourselves that Ulster will never surrender an inch of her soil or title of right to the insidious bloody foe.' The investigation seemed to overlook this, and instead questioned Jean about the repairs which had been carried out on the fireplaces, for there was a theory that a chimney had caught on fire. She replied that she had had a dream that a fire had broken out in her bedroom and therefore decided to have the grate in that particular room replaced. Her response prompted much laughter from the jury. It was concluded that Antrim Castle had burnt down as a result of several independent fires, rather than a single blaze. 'I have lost everything in the world,' Algie had reputedly said on the night of the fire, and, following the rejected insurance claim, his words rang true.

After the First World War the Massereenes finances had begun to decline, a common theme amongst the aristocracy, as the government's new social reforms saw the landed classes paying property and income tax, as well as rates, on their country estates. It marked an uncertain period, for Jean's allowance from her father could no longer sustain the lifestyle she had known before the war and she amassed debts with the Ulster Bank.[47] Algie had also sold cottages belonging to the estate and used the money to renovate Clotworthy House, a large stable block which he converted into apartments. He also bought Knock House, an eighteenth-century country house, on the Scottish Isle of Mull, an estate surrounded by 40,000 acres which had once belonged to the Dukes of Argyll. Throughout the years Algie leased it to friends, one being the Duchess of Leinster, who rented it for a summer season and extended her stay until October, but declined his offer of taking a longer lease.[48] He was seldom there, for he lived permanently at Clotworthy House due to his appointment as H.M. Lieutenant for County Antrim and his serving in the Northern Ireland Senate – Northern Ireland had been created in 1921, formed by the six counties of Ulster, and would remain under British rule. In time, Jean became attached to the house and began to frequent it more often as the years progressed, eventually making it her permanent residence.

In 1922, the year their misfortune began, Jean was named by society photographer E.O. Hoppe as one of the most beautiful women in the world, and she represented Scotland in his comprehensive study of 'the loveliest living specimens of their sex'.[49] She continued to attract controversy, whether it was intentional or not. A significant incident occurred in 1924, when she failed to produce her driver's licence after being stopped by the police in Warwick. She was summoned to Kineton Court and pleaded not guilty, and the case was dismissed with her ordered to pay certain costs. It was a petty issue as far as she was concerned, for she was an enthusiastic and competent motorist, and drove herself whenever possible. Two years later she moved at the centre of the General Strike when she drove a lorry transporting vegetables.[50] In 1926 Jean entered into a partnership with Elspeth Fox-Pitt, a famous costume designer and high society dressmaker. Together they opened a shop in central London. For years she had been designing her own clothes, and the merging of her artistic talent with the skills of Fox-Pitt seemed a natural business venture for her. Their premises attracted attention because, instead of a large showroom, there were a series of small rooms for the individual client. Further cementing the shop's success was their part in dressing the Duchess of York for her royal tour of Australia in 1927.

The youth of the 1920s caused concern for Jean, and although she gave Diana permission to attend parties and to live an independent life since coming out as a debutante in 1926, she disapproved of the 'speed age' of fast motorcars and aeroplanes, and felt society was moving and changing at a rapid pace. She joined in with the Bright Young Things and their parties, partly due to her friendship with Patrick Balfour, who, despite their ominous first meeting at Ardanaiseig, became a loyal friend. She wrote to him from Scotland, asking him to run errands for her in London and to relay messages to her housekeeper before her arrival, as she disliked letter writing and preferred to use the telephone. 'My dear Patrick,' as she called him, had begun writing as 'Mr Chatterbox' for *The Sketch*, and in her letters to him she was blatant in her desire to see her name and photograph in print, and was dismayed when he left her out of his book, *Society Racket*, a parody of their social set. 'From an age point-of-view I can aspire to be a Bright Young Thing as this end. I am an Edwardian Dowager at the other!'[51] she wrote to Balfour. She liked publicity and attention, and in 1927 she played a live game of bridge for a London radio broadcast alongside Algie, the Countess of Ossory, and the famous gossip columnist, Viscount Castlerosse. In 1928 she was a notable guest at a debutante ball in Mayfair, given by Mrs Bower Ismay for Miss Del Ismay, which warranted press attention for a fire that broke out in a marquee. There was also an invitation to Diana and Bryan Guinness's tropical-themed party aboard the *Friendship*, a riverboat moored on the Thames, which inspired Evelyn Waugh to write his novel *Vile Bodies*. Following the trend for themed parties, Jean threw a party for Diana in the garden of her London home, which was lit by Chinese lanterns, and engaged a group of Italian singing troubadours to entertain her guests. She was a trusted confidante to her young friends, particularly Daphne Vivian who called on Jean for an alibi during her romance with Henry Thynne (then Viscount Weymouth and heir to the Marquess of Bath), when she wanted to spend three secret days with him before their marriage. A 'romantically minded woman who delighted in helping frustrated lovers',[52] Jean provided Daphne with an alibi and said she was staying with her in London.

In the spring of 1930, and having come of age, Diana had become something of a rising society star in both London and Scotland, and amongst her chief interests were horse racing, hunt balls, singing and performing in plays for charity. She was best friends with Lady Georgiana Curzon and existed on the fringes of Lois Sturt's[53] circle. It was a daring friendship, for Lois was a society 'wild child' and actress, with a fondness for booze and men, and in 1928 she married Evan Morgan. Her parents, Humphrey Napier 'Nap' Sturt and Lady Feo (*née* Yorke), were friends of Jean's, and during the war she had acted as one of the sultanas alongside Lady Diana Cooper in Nap's Persian sketch.[54] Diana had also been friendly with Gwyneth Morgan, the daughter of Courtenay and Katharine Tredegar, but the latter had become entangled with drug dealers and her body was discovered washed up on a riverbank of the Thames. There were rumours that Diana had caught the eye of Edward, the Prince of Wales, but he preferred the company of older, married women, and the romance had been nothing but a tall tale. Diana had been close to relatives of the British royal family, namely her mother's friends, Princess Maud of Wales and the Prince and Princess of Connaught, who attended her debutante ball given by Jean at Lancaster Gate in 1926. Her lack of scandal (surprising, given her 'fast' company) and gentle disposition made her a catch amongst upper-class men. However, aside from her companion Hubert Duggan, son of Grace, the Marchioness of Curzon, there were no serious boyfriends and, like Jean, she had many close male friends who were homosexual. As a testament to Diana's popularity, she was asked by her friend Lady Dorothea Murray to be the godmother of her son, the future Earl of Mansfield. With a bright future on the horizon, nobody predicted the storm clouds which lay ahead for Diana, and in November 1930, the light in Jean's life would be extinguished forever.

In October 1930, Diana went to Scotland to stay with Lord and Lady Mansfield at Scone Palace. During that same month, she served as a bridesmaid at the wedding of her friend Miss Susan Roberts to the Hon. Somerset Maxwell Farnham. The visits to Scotland, and then

London, followed her usual round of countryside pursuits and society balls. However, during the last week of the month she developed a fever and complained of having a sore throat, which nobody, including Diana herself, felt concerned about. A week later she collapsed at Knock House, and Jean sent for a doctor. Diana was diagnosed with typhoid fever, which was believed to have been brought on by drinking contaminated water at a social event. Jean and Algie took Diana to their home at 63 Rutland Gate,[55] where the family had moved after selling Lancaster Gate in 1928, and a specialist from Harley Street was summoned. It appeared her health was improving, for on Trafalgar Day – she was a member of the Club of the Veterans' Association – she went out with a group of friends to sell flags in aid of servicemen. The weather was cold, and friends expressed their concern for Diana's health, but she joked, 'If I go to bed now, it will be weeks before I shall be up again.'[56] She developed pneumonia and her condition was deemed serious enough for newspapers to print daily updates regarding her health.

Jean continued to believe that the specialist from Harley Street could cure Diana, and her spirits were momentarily lifted when her daughter appeared to be growing stronger. On the evening of 5 November, Diana's health declined and she died the following afternoon with her parents by her side. Jean and Algie brought Diana's remains to Antrim, where her funeral commenced, and as a mark of respect all businesses suspended trading that afternoon and the flags at Antrim Castle flew half-mast. Wreaths from her parents, in the shape of a cross and dedicated 'to our darling', decorated the coffin, and Jean carried a bouquet of white roses which she placed inside the grave. The hearse carrying the coffin broke down[57] as it reached the barbican gates of Antrim Castle, and led by the town's troop of Girl Guides, the final journey was made by foot. Jean asked for Diana's grave on the grounds of their estate to be re-dug, as she wanted it to face her home in Scotland. Days before Diana had been diagnosed with typhoid fever, Jean wrote a newspaper article, expressing her thoughts on reincarnation:

Would you live your life again if you had the chance? How many of us would answer 'yes', if we had the opportunity?

Very few I believe.

It would be a weary business going over the same ground, and human-beings are ever on the outlook for something new.

Living again, having to go through the same troubles, the same sufferings, even the same joys, would not be a really entrancing prospect. Childhood, adolescence, maturity; illness, mistakes, failures, good times and bad. What is past is past, for good or ill.

I believe it is only the very young who would be willing to start their present existence again. They have not had enough of the world to realise the futility of reliving their former years. If they were cut off abruptly before their prime, reliving to them would be a new life which next time they might continue to its natural end.

People have been known to remember places and persons that they have certainly never come across before in their lives. If reincarnation were a fact it would be quite understandable.

Now that science is investigating many mysteries perhaps we may one day discover whether reincarnation is a fact or not.

It would certainly add to the attractiveness of existence if it were true. 'What shall I be next time?' would be an interesting speculation.[58]

The death of her daughter proved too much for Jean, and in 1932 she suffered a nervous breakdown.[59] She had previously written in a newspaper article that 'troubles crumble if you laugh at them and lose half their sting. The man who looks on the bright side, come what will, is the one who gets the best out of life. As for the rest, it is on the knees of the gods'.[60] But Jean, despite her strong belief in the spirit world, could not seek comfort from this, and after Diana's death she did not wish to live. In many ways it marked the beginning of the end for her. She was admitted to a nursing home for several months, during which time she missed the London season. On her doctor's orders she spent the remainder of her convalescence at Knock House, where she was forbidden to do any entertaining. But she was feeling better by September, and planned to greet the Argyll gathering the following month.[61] This marked a period of ongoing ill-health for her, and newspaper reports often wrote about her bouts of sickness, and how she had collapsed in Hyde Park from a 'mystery illness'.[62] Such illnesses were said to have taken weeks to recover from.

After Diana's death Jean seldom went to Antrim unless it was for an official engagement, and she did not stay for any length of time, perhaps finding the memories of their happy lives together too much to bear. Her short visits were undertaken to carry out duties, such as giving speeches at charity fundraisers and handing out prizes at schools, and she went over to welcome visiting royals, and for the annual garden party at Stormont Estate, the seat of Northern Ireland's parliament. In November 1936 she went to Clotworthy House, the occasion was to acknowledge her son's coming of age and repay the kindness the locals had shown him upon reaching that milestone. She was warmly received and spent her brief visit becoming reacquainted with her friends in the town. It would mark her last visit to Northern Ireland.

Politics continued to hold Jean's fascination and it was rumoured she had considered a career as a politician. With Nancy, Viscountess Astor, taking her seat in the House of Commons in 1919 – the first woman to do so, as Countess Markievicz refused to take her elected seat in 1918 – Jean's ambition would have been challenging but plausible. In 1935 she was enrolled as Justice of the Peace for Argyll, in the Sheriff Court at Oban. She continued to influence public opinion and in 1936, following the Munich Agreement, she along with various noble ladies, wrote an open letter to the *Belfast Newsletter*, claiming they were 'prepared to defend that quarter of the world which we call the British Empire'. During one of her many speeches, she advised young women at Glasgow University to act as 'recruiting agents' for their boyfriends. 'I believe that no young man in this country should be asked to risk his life for a quarrel which is no concern of his,' she said, 'But I do think every young man ought to join the Territorials or the regular Army; and I appeal to you girls to persuade your boyfriends and your brothers to at least join the Territorials.'[63] At women's meetings she asked the crowd to influence their menfolk in the defence against Adolf Hitler:

I cannot understand the mentality of any able-bodied young man who does not, at any rate, join the Territorials because it is a monstrous thing that people who have the advantage of being citizens of the greatest country in the world should take all the advantages and then do nothing in return.[64]

She was determined to spread the message of securing the country at all costs. Before a meeting she boarded a ferryboat and in the process lost her footing and fell to the bottom deck, and despite hurting both of her legs and suffering cuts and bruises, she bore the pain to fulfil a speaking engagement. As she had done in the 1920s, she expressed her fears for modern life, especially those who sought adventure with little regard to human safety. An article written in 1933 was relevant to her speeches on protecting Britain against attack, and she thought of the fast motorcar as a risk toward those wishing to live in peace. She wrote:

Petrol has changed the face of the world. In less than another half century it will have taken complete possession of the air. Will humanity survive? Probably not, if the accidents increase in ratio to the amount of planes and cars. We had as many casualties on the road last year as would occur in a fair-sized war. On the other hand, it is true that the cautious man rarely rises to great heights. He is apt to be so careful that opportunity passes him by.

There is, however, a very great difference between taking a risk and being foolhardy.

We do not yet seem to have got rid of the war-time idea of the cheapness of human life. Human life is not a commodity to be risked at the throw of a dice. It is always the best lives that are lost thus, those we can ill spare.[65]

Although Jean bypassed a professional career in politics, another occupation presented itself in the form of modelling. In her early fifties she loaned her celebrity and fabled beauty to advertisements for Pond's cold cream and setting powder. It was a period when many society beauties were paid to endorse the product, and Jean, photographed in a wistful pose with short, shingled hair whose brunette colour she maintained with dye, praised the cream for preserving her good looks. 'I practically live out-of-doors. Mine is not a hot-house life at all ... I'd be as weather-beaten as a gillie, if it weren't for my skin care.' She also continued a lively correspondence with her young friends in London, though she preferred to talk on the telephone when possible. 'You look on me, tho' you don't write of me, as a member of that now dwindling minority of our aristocracy which has sold its London house so that its roots may not be torn from the countryside!' she wrote to Patrick Balfour. 'Really if I don't get some money soon I shall very soon begin to look just like a boot of leather! I've one evening dress, one day dress and two hats so can meet you anywhere and in any place and still look if no longer actually chic at least not noticeably provincial.'[66]

Toward the end of 1937 Jean's health began to decline. In November she suffered a stroke and was confined to her bed. Her absence was felt on the social scene, and she was notably missing from the annual meeting[67] of the League of Mercy, of which she was honorary secretary for the Scotland branch. Newspapers wrote of a 'mysterious' illness, which they explained had plagued her for some time. The truth was, the stroke had caused her considerable brain damage and she had been left with aphasia, hemiplegia, and bulbar paralysis.[69] For someone as lively and active, both mentally and physically, as Jean, this must have been a cruel blow. She died five weeks later, on 11 December 1937, at the age of 54.

Speaking of her death, the Rev. Collis of All Saints Parish Church in Antrim said, 'Lady Massereene had friends in all positions in life ... and I am sure there will be widespread and sincere regret at the unexpected death of one who was so kind-hearted and friendly to all around her and so noticeably charitable in her judgment of others.'[70] One can only hope that, with her belief in the afterlife, she is languishing on a spiritual plane.

NOTES

Author's Note
1. Wilson, John Howard, *Evelyn Waugh: 1924-66* (New Jersey: Fairleigh Dickinson University Press, 1996), p.92.
2. Ibid.
3. Ibid.
4. Ibid.

1 Princess, Preservationist: Mariga Guinness
1. *The Sunday Star*, 30 March 1930.
2. Smith, Anne (ed.), *Women Remember: An Oral History* (London: Routledge, 2013), p.60.
3. Patrick Guinness to author.
4. Mariga Guinness to Derek Hill, 8/5/1980. D/4400/C/5/59/79. Derek Hill Papers, Public Record Office of Northern Ireland (hereafter PRONI).
5. Courtesy of Patrick Guinness.
6. Ibid.
7. Smith (ed.) *Women Remember*, p.57.
8. *Cambridge Independent Press*, 5 November 1920.
9. Patrick Guinness to author.
10. Albrecht von Urach to Hermione Ramsden, 27 April 1938. Courtesy of Patrick Guinness.
11. Ibid.

12. Shipping register for the *Scharnhorst*, dated 21 April 1938, lists Hermione Ramsden's address: Marley House, Surrey.
13. Patrick Guinness to author.
14. Dr Harrowes to Hermione Ramsden, 27 April 1938. Courtesy of Patrick Guinness.
15. Ibid.
16. Hermione Ramsden to M. Bircher, 28 August 1944. Courtesy of Patrick Guinness.
17. Patrick Guinness to author.
18. *The Independent*, 1996.
19. Her cousins on both sides of her family: on her German side she had a smattering of royal cousins spread across Europe, and on her mother's Scots-Norwegian side her non-royal cousins were living in grander circumstances – her uncle Ian Blackadder's daughter, Barbara (half-sister of Lili St Cyr), for instance, had a brief Hollywood career before marrying Louis Marx, an American toy-maker and millionaire.
20. Albrecht von Urach to Hermione Ramsden, 27 April 1938. Courtesy of Patrick Guinness.
21. After six months of wiretapping and monitoring Albrecht's bank account the Swiss were satisfied he was not a Nazi. See E2001D/1000/1553/1079; E2001E/1967/113/9065; E4320B/1973/17/671. Swiss Federal Archives.
22. In October 1945 Albrecht was interviewed by the US Army and was also declared innocent. See CI-IIR/27 and CI-FR/38. National Archives and Records Administration. References courtesy of Patrick Guinness.
23. Hermione Ramsden to Mr M. Bircher, 28 August 1944. Courtesy of Patrick Guinness.
24. Rosemary von Urach to Hermione Ramsden, 15 January 1944. Courtesy of Patrick Guinness.
25. Ibid.
26. Courtesy of Patrick Guinness.
27. Ibid.
28. Ibid.
29. Ibid.
30. Ibid.
31. Ibid.
32. Ibid.
33. Beaton, Cecil, *Beaton in the Sixties: More Expurgated Diaries*, ed. by Hugo Vickers (London: Phoenix, 2004), p. 110.
34. Patrick Guinness to author.
35. Around 1944 the style of her illustrations had changed. In a letter she drew the heads of pretty girls with their eyes blacked out. Until then the eyes of her drawings were large and visible. Patrick Guinness to author.
36. Rosemary von Urach to Hermione Ramsden, 15 January 1944. Courtesy of Patrick Guinness.

37. Patrick Guinness to author.

38. Ibid.

39. Diana Mosley recalled, 'Mariga was one of those girls who go to Oxford, not as undergraduates but to learn something or other.' Quoted in Peck, Carola, *Mariga and her Friends* (Meath: The Hannon Press, 1997), p.61.

40. Lawford, Valentine, *Vogue's Book of Houses, Gardens, People* (New York: Viking Press, 1968).

41. Patrick Guinness to author.

42. Mariga and Desmond's love of neoclassical buildings began in Oxford. Patrick Guinness to author.

43. Desmond Guinness's letter to the *Irish Times*, 22 July 1957.

44. Mariga Guinness to Derek Hill. D/4400/C/5/59/3. Derek Hill Papers, PRONI.

45. See www.carolinephillips.net.

46. Mariga Guinness to Derek Hill, 1958. D/4400/C/5/59/6. Derek Hill Papers, PRONI.

47. Mariga Guinness to Derek Hill, 4/2/1960. D/4400/C/5/59/9. Derek Hill Papers, PRONI.

48. Petkanas, Christopher, *Loulou and Yves: The Untold Story of Loulou de la Falaise and the House of Saint Laurent* (New York: St Martin's Press, 2018).

49. Lord Gowrie to author.

50. Ibid.

51. Ibid.

52. 'You could be sitting next to Mick Jagger at dinner one day and a plumber the next.' Jasmine Guinness, *The Daily Telegraph*, 17 July 2009.

53. Lord Gowrie to author.

54. Norris, David, A *Kick Against The Pricks* (London: Random House, 2013), p.133.

55. Patrick Guinness to author.

56. Girouard, Mark, *Friendships* (London: Wilmington Square Books, 2017), p.125.

57. Peck, *Mariga and her Friends*, p.126.

58. *Illustrated London News*, 30 May 1970.

59. Ibid.

60. Ibid.

61. Mariga Guinness to Derek Hill, 9/10/1965. D/4400/C/5/59/17. Derek Hill Papers, PRONI.

62. Mariga Guinness to Derek Hill, 11/1/1960. D/4400/C/5/59/8. Derek Hill Papers, PRONI.

63. Mariga Guinness to Derek Hill, 9/1960. D/4400/C/5/59/4. Derek Hill Papers, PRONI.

64. Ibid.

65. Mariga Guinness to Derek Hill, 8/7/1968. D/4400/C/5/59/25. Derek Hill Papers, PRONI.

66. Mariga Guinness to Derek Hill, 4/9/1968. D/4400/C/5/59/26. Derek Hill Papers, PRONI.
67. Ibid.
68. Mariga Guinness to Derek Hill, 8/5/1980. D/4400/C/5/59/79. Derek Hill Papers, PRONI.
69. Patrick Guinness to author.
70. Girouard, *Friendships*, p.129.
71. Patrick Guinness to author.
72. 'So sad not to have been able to ask …' Mariga Guinness to Derek Hill, 8/5/80. D/4400/C/5/59/79. Derek Hill Papers, PRONI.
73. Julia Shirley to author.
74. Patrick Guinness to author.
75. Marina Guinness to author.
76. Doris Morrow to author.
77. Julia Shirley to author.
78. Doris Morrow to author.
79. Ibid.
80. Doris Morrow and Isabel Boyle to author.
81. Doris Morrow to author.
82. Julia Shirley to author.
83. Patrick Guinness to author: 'Mariga carried a basket that included her handbag, a book or two, secateurs to take a cutting or three with, a large hairbrush, a Canon camera (always loaded with black and white film), spare films in yellow tubes, maybe an alarm clock (if the time was needed), a black-pepper mill (when nobody had one), a newspaper or *Cosmo*, napkins, Tampax, aspirins, hat-pins, spectacles for reading, black biros, a sheaf of aide-memoires and letters. Actually very practical, but it probably looked bohemian to many.'
84. Isabel Boyle and Doris Morrow to author.
85. Patrick Guinness to author.
86. Courtesy of Patrick Guinness.
87. Ibid.
88. Mariga Guinness to Derek Hill, 31/3/1982. D/4400/C/5/59/31. Derek Hill Papers, PRONI.
89. Ibid.
90. Ibid.
91. Mariga Guinness to Derek Hill, 2/12/1983. D/4400/C/5/59/33. Derek Hill Papers, PRONI.
92. Mariga Guinness to Derek Hill, 22/11/1983. D/4400/C/5/59/36. Derek Hill Papers, PRONI.
93. *Image*, September 1984.
94. Lord Gowrie to author.
95. Girouard, *Friendships*, p.127.

96. Mariga Guinness to Derek Hill, 9/10/1983. D/4400/C/5/59/34. Derek Hill Papers, PRONI.

2 The Stucco Venus: Enid Lindeman

1. *National Advocate*, 28 February 1913.
2. Dunne, Dominick, *Fatal Charms and the Mansions of Limbo* (New York: Crown, 1987), p.305.
3. Cavendish O'Neill, Pat, *A Lion in the Bedroom* (Sydney: Park Street Press, 2004), p.241.
4. Ibid., p.236.
5. Ibid., p.42.
6. Dunne, *Fatal Charms and the Mansions of Limbo,* p.316.
7. *Truth*, 28 June 1942.
8. Whistler, Laurence, *The Laughter and the Urn: The Life of Rex Whistler* (London: Weidenfeld & Nicolson, 1985), p.221.
9. Cavendish O'Neill, *A Lion in the Bedroom,* p.113.
10. Ibid., p.119.
11. *Truth*, 28 June 1942.
12. Enid Kenmare to Lord Beaverbrook, 2 October 1943. BBK_C_19 Castlerosse Letters. Parliamentary Archives.
13. Ibid.
14. Cavendish O'Neill, *A Lion in the Bedroom*, p.159.
15. Dunne, *Fatal Charms and the Mansions of Limbo,* p.312.
16. Ibid.
17. Ibid., p.313.
18. Ibid.
19. Ibid.
20. Ibid p.314.
21. Lovell, Mary S., *Straight on Till Morning: The Life of Beryl Markham* (London: Abacus, 2009), p.319.
22. Cavendish O'Neill, *A Lion in the Bedroom*, p.418.
23. Lovell, *Straight on Till Morning: The Life of Beryl Markham*, p.322.
24. Ibid., p.233.

3 The Serial Bride: Sylvia Ashley

1. Whitfield, Eileen, *Pickford: The Woman Who Built Hollywood* (Lexington: University Press of Kentucky, 1997), p.275.
2. Baddeley, Hermione, *The Unsinkable Hermione Baddeley* (London: Collins, 1984), p.71.
3. *Boston American*, 8 February 1934.
4. Ibid.

5. Beauchamp, Cari, *Without Lying Down: Frances Marion and the Powerful Women of Early Hollywood* (Berkeley: University of California Press, 1995), p. 295.

6. Powell, Anthony, *Faces in My Time* (London: Holt, Rhinehart and Winston, 1981), p.52.

7. 'For each article which you write, and which secures the approval of the star concerned ...' Mary Pickford Company to Roger Lewis, c/o the Writers Club, outlining the terms and conditions of their agreement, 20 July 1923.

8. Spicer, Chrystopher J., *Clark Gable: Biography, Filmography, Bibliography* (Jefferson: McFarland, 2002), p.244.

9. *The Sun*, 1 January 1950.

10. Brett, David, *Clark Gable: Tormented Star* (Boston: Da Capo Press, 2007), p.208.

11. *The Age*, 11 April 1951.

12. *The Daily Telegraph*, 31 October 1954.

13. *Desert Sun*, 7 December 1955.

14. Ibid.

4 The Ingénue: Joan Wyndham

1. Wyndham, Joan, *Dawn Chorus* (London: Virago, 2004), p.59.

2. Ibid., p.84.

3. Ibid., p.94.

4. Ibid., p.107.

5. Wyndham, Joan, *Love Lessons* (London: Virago, 1985), p.3.

6. Ibid.

7. Ibid., p.1.

8. Ibid., p.14.

9. Ibid., p.24.

10. Ibid., p.35.

11. Ibid.

12. Wyndham, *Dawn Chorus*, p.90.

13. Wyndham, *Love Lessons*, p.86.

14. Ibid., p.93.

15. Ibid., p.95.

16. Ibid., p.96.

17. Ibid., p.123.

18. Ibid., p.128.

19. Ibid., p.129.

20. Ibid., p.147.

21. *The Telegraph*, 14 April 2007.

22. Wyndham, *Love Lessons*, p.174.

23. Ibid., p.156.

24. Ibid., p.183.

25. Wyndham, Joan, *Love is Blue* (London: Flamingo, 1986), p.20.

26. *The Telegraph*, 14 April 2007.

27. Wyndham, *Love Lessons,* p.261.

5 A Dangerous Devotion: Venetia Stanley

1. De Courcy, Anne, *Margot at War* (London: Weidenfeld & Nicolson, 2015), p.86.

2. Brock, Michael (ed.), *Letters to Venetia Stanley* (Oxford: Oxford University Press, 1985), p.547.

3. Popplewell, Sir Oliver, *The Prime Minister and his Mistress* (Morrisville, N.C.: Lulu Publishing Services, 2014), p.126.

4. Asquith, Margot, *Margot Asquith: An Autobiography* (New York: George H. Doran, 1920), p.213.

5. H.H. Asquith to Venetia Stanley, 6 January 1913. MSS. Eng. c. 7091–8. Bodleian Library, University of Oxford.

6. De Courcy, *Margot at War*, p.88.

7. *Daily Mail,* 10 June 2016.

8. Purnell, Sonia, *First Lady: The Life and Wars of Clementine Churchill* (London: Aurum Press, 2015), p.35.

9. Soames, Mary, *Clementine Churchill* (London: Random House, 2011).

10. De Courcy, *Margot at War*, p.21.

11. H.H. Asquith to Venetia Stanley, 22 January 1913. MSS. Eng. c. 7091–8. Bodleian Library, University of Oxford.

12. Asquith, Margot, *Margot Asquith's Great War Diary 1914–1918* (Oxford: Oxford University Press, 2014), p.cvii.

13. H.H. Asquith to Venetia Stanley, 1 April 1912. MSS. Eng. c. 7091–8. Bodleian Library, University of Oxford.

14. Ibid.

15. Popplewell, *The Prime Minister and his Mistress*, p.3.

16. Ibid.

17. H.H. Asquith to Venetia Stanley, 14 August 1912. MSS. Eng. c. 7091–8. Bodleian Library, University of Oxford.

18. See spartacus-educational.com/Venetia_Stanley.htm.

19. Popplewell, *The Prime Minister and his Mistress*, p.66.

20. Ibid.

21. H.H. Asquith to Venetia Stanley, 14 May 1915. MSS. Eng. c. 7091–8. Bodleian Library, University of Oxford.

22. Ibid.

23. Ibid.

24. Cohen, Richard I, *Visualising and Exhibiting Jewish Space and History* (Oxford: Oxford University Press, 2012), p.268.

25. Ibid.

26. Brock (ed.), *Letters to Venetia Stanley*, p.547.

27. H.H. Asquith to Venetia Stanley, April 1913. MSS. Eng. c. 7091–8. Bodleian Library, University of Oxford.
28. H.H. Asquith to Venetia Stanley, 21 August 1913. MSS. Eng. c. 7091–8. Bodleian Library, University of Oxford.
29. H.H. Asquith to Venetia Stanley, 1 January 1915. MSS. Eng. c. 7091–8. Bodleian Library, University of Oxford.
30. Neate, Bobbie, *Conspiracy of Secrets* (London: John Blake, 2012).
31. Popplewell, *The Prime Minister and his Mistress*, p.41.
32. H.H. Asquith to Venetia Stanley, 17 April 1914. MSS. Eng. c. 7091–8. Bodleian Library, University of Oxford.
33. 'I must have a glimpse of you in it, sooner or later.' H.H. Asquith to Venetia Stanley, 22 February 1915. MSS. Eng. c. 7091–8. Bodleian Library, University of Oxford.
34. Brock (ed.), *Letters to Venetia Stanley*, p.605.
35. Venetia Stanley to Edwin Montagu, 6 June 1915. MSS. Eng. c. 7091–8. Bodleian Library, University of Oxford.
36. Levine, Naomi, *Politics, Religion and Love: The Story of H.H. Asquith and Venetia Stanley* (New York: New York University Press, 1991), p.326.
37. Ibid., p.653.
38. Brock (ed.), *Letters to Venetia Stanley*, p.607.
39. Venetia Montagu to H.H. Asquith, 1925. MSS. Eng. c. 7091–8. Bodleian Library, University of Oxford.
40. Ibid.

6 *The Machiavellian Queen: Sylvia Brooke*

1. *Sunday Times*, 2 April 1911.
2. Brooke, Sylvia, *Queen of the Headhunters* (Oxford: Oxford University Press, 1970), p.159.
3. Eade, Philip, *Sylvia: Queen of the Headhunters* (London: Orion, 2007), p.20.
4. *Sheffield Daily Telegraph*, 1 December 1909.
5. Brooke, *Queen of the Headhunters*, p.29.
6. Pybus, Cassandra, *White Rajah: A Dynastic Intrigue* (St Lucia: University of Queensland Press, 1996), p.179.
7. Lees-Milne, James, *The Enigmatic Edwardian: The Life of Reginald, 2nd Viscount Esher* (London: Sidgwick and Jackson, 1988), p.149.
8. Brooke, *Queen of the Headhunters*, p.29.
9. Ibid.
10. Ibid.
11. Eade, *Sylvia: Queen of the Headhunters*, p.86.
12. Brooke, *Queen of the Headhunters*, p.135.
13. Ibid., p.98.
14. *The Telegraph*, 16 October 1941.
15. *Western Mail*, 18 April 1946.

7 The Baroness: Irene Curzon

1. *The Age*, 19 October 1906.
2. Ibid.
3. Ibid.
4. Nicolson, Nigel, *Mary Curzon* (London: Phoenix, 1998), p.99.
5. *The Times Dispatch*, 1 November 1914.
6. De Courcy, Anne, *The Viceroy's Daughters* (London: Weidenfeld & Nicolson, 2001), p.18.
7. *The Times Dispatch*, 1 November 1914.
8. Belien, Paul, *A Throne in Brussels: Britain, the Saxe-Coburgs and the Belgianisation of Europe* (Exeter: Imprint Academic, 2006).
9. The letters from Irene Curzon, Baroness Ravensdale (1916–1931). OMN/A/1/2/10. University of Birmingham, Cadbury Research Library Special Collections.
10. De Courcy, *The Viceroy's Daughters*, p.134.
11. Ibid., p.224.
12. *The Sun*, 19 Dec 1937.
13. De Courcy, *The Viceroy's Daughters*, p.216.
14. Diana Mosley to Deborah Devonshire, 14 May 1959. See Mosley, Charlotte (ed.), *The Mitfords: Letters Between Six Sisters* (London: Harper Perennial, 2008), p.312.

8 The Girl Who Became Muv: Sydney Redesdale

1. Jessica Mitford to Sydney Redesdale, 4 June 1958. See Sussman, Peter Y. (ed.), *Decca: The Letters of Jessica Mitford* (London: Orion, 2007), p.175.
2. *The Spectator*, 21 June 1890.
3. Green, Roger Lancelyn (ed.), *The Selected Letters of Lewis Carroll* (New York: Springer, 1989), p.206.
4. Wakeling, Edward, *Lewis Carroll: The Man and his Circle* (London: I.B. Tauris, 2014), p.359.
5. Guinness, Jonathan and Guinness, Catherine, *House of Mitford* (London: Orion, 1984), p.221.
6. *Yorkshire Gazette*, 27 April 1895.
7. Ecob, Helen Gilbert, *The Well-Dressed Woman* (New York: Fowler and Wells, 1893), p.22.
8. Mitford, Nancy, *The Water Beetle* (London: Hamish Hamilton, 1962), p.18.
9. Mosley, Diana, *A Life of Contrasts* (London: Gibson Square, 2009), p.30.
10. Mitford, *The Water Beetle*, p.21.
11. Mosley, Charlotte (ed.), *Love From Nancy: The Letters of Nancy Mitford* (London: Hodder & Stoughton, 1994), p.589.
12. Nancy Mitford to Diana Mosley, 22 November 1941. Mosley, Charlotte (ed.) *The Mitfords: Letters Between Six Sisters* (London: Harper Perennial, 2008), p.184.

13. Ibid.
14. Nancy Mitford to Violet Hammersley, 20 June 1940. Mosley, *Love From Nancy*, p.132.
15. Jessica Mitford to Virginia Durr, 30 September 1962. Sussman (ed.), *Decca: The Letters of Jessica Mitford*, p.298.
16. Deborah Devonshire to Nancy Mitford, 23 September 1960. Mosley (ed.), *The Mitfords: Letters Between Six Sisters*, p.341.
17. Nancy Mitford to Jessica Mitford, 19 May 1963. Ibid., p.393.
18. Nancy Mitford to Hamish Hamilton. Quoted in Smith, John Saumarez, *The Bookshop at 10 Curzon Street* (London: Frances Lincoln, 2004), p.90.

9 The Muse: Hazel Lavery

1. Hazel Martyn to John Lavery, 28 December 1903. Tate Archive, Lavery Papers presented by Lady Sempill 1972 TGA/ 7245.
2. Census, June 1880.
3. Lourie, Peter, *River of Mountains: A Canoe Journey Down the Hudson* (Syracuse: Syracuse University Press, 1998), p.71.
4. *The Minneapolis Journal*, 14 May 1904.
5. Hazel Martyn to John Lavery, 29 October 1903. Tate Archive Lavery Papers presented by Lady Sempill 1972 TGA/ 7245.
6. Alice Martyn to John Lavery, 23 October 1903. Tate Archive Lavery Papers presented by Lady Sempill 1972 TGA/ 7245.
7. John Lavery to Hazel Martyn, October 1903. Tate Archive Lavery Papers presented by Lady Sempill 1972 TGA/ 7245.
8. Alice Martyn to John Lavery, 11 October 1903. Tate Archive Lavery Papers presented by Lady Sempill 1972 TGA/ 7245.
9. *Sacred Heart Review*, 11 March 1904.
10. McCoole, Sinead, *Hazel: A Life of Lady Lavery* (Dublin: Lilliput Press, 1996), p.22.
11. John Lavery to Hazel Trudeau, 2 February 1907. Tate Archive Lavery Papers presented by Lady Sempill 1972 TGA/ 7245.
12. McCoole, *Hazel: A Life of Lady Lavery*, p.21.
13. *The Evening World*, 14 October 1911.
14. *Northern Whig*, 23 April 1930.
15. Severance, John B., *Winston Churchill: Soldier, Statesman, Artist* (New York: Clarion Books, 1996), p.51.
16. *The Virginia Enterprise*, 24 November 1911.
17. *Studies in Visual Communication* (Los Angeles: Annenberg School Press, 1985), p.9.
18. Cullen, Fintan, *The Irish Face: Redefining the Irish Portrait* (London: National Portrait Gallery, 2004), p.223.
19. See www.generalmichaelcollins.com.

20. McCoole, *Hazel: A Life of Lady Lavery*, p.84.
21. Hazel Lavery to Hugh Kennedy, 24 June 1922. Kennedy Papers, UCDA p4/1430.
22. McCoole, *Hazel: A Life of Lady Lavery*, p.96.
23. Term credited to George Bernard Shaw, who referred to Collins as such.
24. Kevin O'Higgins to Hazel Lavery, 4 November 1924. Tate Archive Lavery Papers presented by Lady Sempill 1972 TGA/ 7245.
25. Ibid., 17 December 1924.
26. Kevin O'Higgins to Hazel Lavery, 6 May 1927. Tate Archive Lavery Papers presented by Lady Sempill 1972 TGA/ 7245.
27. Hazel Lavery to Thomas Bodkin, 31 August 1927. Thomas Bodkin Papers.
28. Ibid., 1 July 1928.

10 Society Star: Jean Massereene

1. *Lancashire Evening Post*, 25 May 1931.
2. Jean's birthplace has often been listed as Scotland. Although of Scottish heritage, she was born in London. Source: 1893 census.
3. Ibid.
4. Ibid.
5. *Ballymena Observer*, 8 August 1918.
6. *The Graphic*, 25 February 1905.
7. *Truth*, vol. 63, 1908, p.63.
8. Vickers, Hugo, *Elizabeth: The Queen Mother* (London: Arrow, 2006), p.76.
9. Roberts, Pam, *PhotoHistorica, Landmarks in Photography: Rare Images from the Royal Photographic Society* (London: Workman Publishing, 2000) p.125
10. Lillian Spender's diary, February 1914. D1633/2/19. PRONI.
11. *The Advertiser*, 18 July 1925.
12. *The Tatler*, 28 October 1908.
13. *Larne Times*, 28 October 1911.
14. *Belfast Newsletter*, 7 August 1913.
15. *Ballymena Observer*, 11 November 1930.
16. *Belfast Newsletter*, 19 November 1910.
17. *Weekly Times*, 16 March 1912.
18. *Ballymena Observer*, 27 January 1911.
19. Ibid.
20. Information given to author by Alvin McCaig.
21. Jean Massereene to Theresa, Marchioness of Londonderry, 15 April 1914. D1507/A/26/8. PRONI.
22. Baguley, Margaret (ed.), *WWI and the Question of Ulster: The Correspondence of Lillian and Wilfrid Spender* (Dublin: Irish Manuscripts Commissions, 2009), p. 220.
23. Information given to author by Alvin McCaig.
24. Jean Massereene to Theresa Marchioness of Londonderry, 15 April 1914. D1507/A/26/8. PRONI.

25. *Ballymena Observer,* 8 August 1915.
26. *Daily Express*, 26 March 1925.
27. *North West Champion*, 11 March 1926.
28. *Daily Express*, 3 December 1914.
29. *The Witness*, 6 November 1914.
30. Vickers, *Elizabeth: The Queen Mother*, p.76.
31. *Belfast Newsletter*, 6 August 1918.
32. Ibid., 31 May 1928.
33. *The Advertiser*, 19 June 1925
34. *Ballymena Observer*, 24 November 1911.
35. *Geelong Advertiser*, 11 January 1912.
36. *Ballymena Observer*, 24 November 1911.
37. Young, Kenneth (ed.), *The Diaries of Sir Bruce Lockhart* (London: Macmillan, 1973), p.66.
38. Bedford, John, *A Silver-Plated Spoon* (London: Cassell, 1959), pp.66–7.
39. Jean Massereene to Patrick Kinross, 1 September 1927. KIN 3977–3982. Patrick Balfour, Baron Kinross Papers 1922–1976. The Huntington Library.
40. Jean Massereene to Patrick Kinross, 20 September 1927. KIN 3977–3982. Patrick Balfour, Baron Kinross Papers 1922–1976. The Huntington Library.
41. Ibid.
42. Ibid.
43. *The Courier and Advertiser*, 9 September 1927.
44. Jean Massereene to Patrick Kinross, 20 September 1927. KIN 3977–3982. Patrick Balfour, Baron Kinross Papers 1922–1976. The Huntington Library.
45. Ibid.
46. Ibid.
47. Ainsworth family of the Flosh, Cleator and Harecroft Hall, Gosforth, iron ore mine and mill owners – 1819–*c.* 1940. YAIN/4/11. Whitehaven – Cumbria Archive and Local Studies Centre.
48. Extracts from the Duchess of Leinster's memoirs, *So Brief a Dream*, provided by William Cross.
49. *Sacramento Union*, 5 November 1922.
50. Courtney, Nicholas, *In Society: The Brideshead Years* (London: Pavilion, 1986), p.135.
51. Jean Massereene to Patrick Balfour, 29 June 1933. KIN 3977–3982. Patrick Balfour, Baron Kinross Papers 1922–1976. The Huntington Library.
52. Fielding, Daphne, *Mercury Presides* (London: Eyre & Spottiswoode, 1954), p.119.
53. Told to author by William Cross, Lois Sturt's biographer.
54. Ibid.
55. The Massereenes also rented Harrington House at Kensington Palace Gardens, 1929.
56. *The Argus*, 20 December 1930.

57. Told to author by the son of Lord and Lady Massereene's chauffeur.
58. *Lincolnshire Echo*, 25 October 1930.
59. *Belfast Newsletter*, 6 February 1932.
60. *Lincolnshire Echo*, 25 October 1930.
61. *Dundee Courier*, 24 October 1932.
62. *Western Daily Press*, 9 May 1931.
63. *Northern Whig*, 17 October 1935.
64. *The Scotsman*, 13 December 1937.
65. *Ballymena Observer*, 22 October 1937.
66. *Northern Whig*, 15 April 1933.
67. *The Scotsman*, 26 November 1937.
68. Jean Massereene to Patrick Balfour, 29 June 1933. KIN 3977–3982. Patrick Balfour, Baron Kinross Papers 1922–1976. The Huntington Library.
69. Death certificate, with thanks to William Cross for providing this for me.
70. *Belfast Newsletter*, 13 December 1937.

BIBLIOGRAPHY

Asquith, Margot, *Margot Asquith: An Autobiography*, 2 vols (New York: George H. Doran, 1920).

Asquith, Margot, *Margot Asquith's Great War Diary* (Oxford: Oxford University Press, 2014).

Baddeley, Hermione, *The Unsinkable Hermione Baddeley* (London: Collins, 1984).

Bedford, John A., *A Silver-Plated Spoon* (London: Cassell, 1959).

Belien, Paul, *A Throne in Brussels: Britain, the Saxe-Coburgs and the Belgianisation of Europe* (Exeter: Imprint Academic, 2006).

Brett, David, *Clark Gable: Tormented Star* (Boston: Da Capo Press, 2007).

Brock, Michael (ed.), *Letters to Venetia Stanley* (Oxford: Oxford University Press, 1982).

Brooke, Sylvia, *Queen of the Headhunters* (Oxford: Oxford University Press, 1970).

Courtney, Nicholas, *In Society: The Brideshead Years* (London: Pavilion, 1986).

De Courcy, Anne, *Margot at War* (London: Weidenfeld & Nicolson, 2015).

De Courcy, Anne, *The Viceroy's Daughters* (London: Weidenfeld & Nicolson, 2001).

Dunne, Dominick, *Fatal Charms and the Mansions of Limbo* (New York: Crown, 1987).

Eade, Philip, *Sylvia: Queen of the Headhunters* (London: Orion, 2007).

Fielding, Daphne, *Mercury Presides* (London: Eyre & Spottiswoode, 1954).

Fintan, Cullen, *The Irish Face: Redefining the Irish Portrait* (London: National Portrait Gallery, 2004).

Green, Roger Lancelyn (ed.), *The Selected Letters of Lewis Carroll* (New York: Springer, 1989).

Guinness, Jonathan and Guinness, Catherine, *House of Mitford* (London: Orion, 1984).

Leinster, Rafaelle FitzGerald, *So Brief a Dream* (Worthing: Littlehampton Book Services, 1971).

Levine, Naomi, *Politics, Religion and Love: The Story of H.H. Asquith and Venetia Stanley* (New York: New York University Press, 1991).

Lourie, Peter, *River of Mountains: A Canoe Journey Down the Hudson* (Syracuse: Syracuse University Press, 1998).

Lovell, Mary S., *Straight on Till Morning: The Life of Beryl Markham* (London: Abacus, 2009).

McCoole, Sinead, *Hazel: A Life of Lady Lavery* (Dublin: Lilliput Press, 1996).

Mitford, Nancy, *The Water Beetle* (London: Hamish Hamilton, 1962).

Mosley, Charlotte (ed.), *Love From Nancy: The Letters of Nancy Mitford* (London: Hodder & Stoughton, 1994).

Mosley, Charlotte (ed.), *The Mitfords: Letters Between Six Sisters* (London: Harper Perennial, 2008).

Mosley, Diana, *A Life of Contrasts* (London: Gibson Square, 1977).

Neate, Bobbie, *Conspiracy of Secrets* (London: John Blake, 2012).

Nicolson, Nigel, *Mary Curzon* (London: Phoenix, 1998).

Cavendish O'Neill, Pat, *A Lion in the Bedroom* (Sydney: Park Street Press, 2004).

Peck, Carola, *Mariga and her Friends* (Meath: The Hannon Press, 1997).

Popplewell, Sir Oliver, *The Prime Minister and his Mistress* (Morrisville, N.C.: Lulu Publishing Services, 2014).

Powell, Anthony, *Faces in My Time* (London: Holt, Rhinehart and Winston, 1981).

Purnell, Sonia, *First Lady: The Life and Wars of Clementine Churchill* (London: Aurum Press, 2015).

Roberts, Pam, *PhotoHistorica, Landmarks in Photography: Rare Images from the Royal Photographic Society* (London: Workman Publishing, 2000).

Smith, John Saumarez, *The Bookshop at 10 Curzon Street* (London: Frances Lincoln, 2004).

Soames, Mary, *Clementine Churchill* (London: Random House, 2011).

Spicer, Christopher J., *Clark Gable: Biography, Filmography, Bibliography* (Jefferson: McFarland, 2002).

Sussman, Peter Y. (ed.), *Decca: The Letters of Jessica Mitford* (London: Orion, 2007).

Vickers, Hugo, *Elizabeth The Queen Mother* (London: Arrow, 2006).

Wakeling, Edward, *Lewis Carroll: The Man and his Circle* (London: I.B. Tauris, 2014).

Whistler, Laurence, *The Laughter and the Urn: The Life of Rex Whistler* (London: Weidenfeld & Nicolson, 1985).

Whitfield, Eileen, *Pickford: The Woman Who Built Hollywood* (Lexington: University Press of Kentucky, 1997).

Wyndham, Joan, *Dawn Chorus* (London: Virago, 2004).

Wyndham, Joan, *Love Lessons* (London: Virago, 1985).

Young, Kenneth (ed.), *The Diaries of Sir Bruce Lockhart* (London: Macmillan, 1973).

INDEX

The History Press
The destination for history
www.thehistorypress.co.uk

Printed in Great Britain
by Amazon